"In this ground-breaking study, Lowenthal lucidly analyzes what Californians have at stake internationally and how we can identify and advance our worldwide interests. *Global California* provides keen insights on trade, investment, immigration, education, and infrastructure, and on relations with Mexico, China, and other nations that will shape our state's future. It charts a way forward for cooperation between state and local officials, business and civic leaders, Congress and the new Administration. A timely and important book."
>—*Howard Berman*
>   *Chair, Committee on Foreign Affairs, U.S. House of Representatives*

"Carefully researched, well-written, and compelling, *Global California* is a must-read for policymakers nationwide. There are lessons here for every state in the union."
>—*Carla A. Hills*
>   *Chair and CEO, Hills and Company, Former U.S. Trade Representative*

"An eye opener. . . . Should embolden Californians, and other centers of economic and political power like Texas, to be more active players."
>—*Richard W. Fisher*
>   *President and CEO, Federal Reserve Bank, Dallas*

"*Global California* is a ground-breaking book, a key resource for policymakers and for all who want to understand global trends and how to address them proactively."
>—*Jon M. Huntsman, Jr.*
>   *Governor of Utah*

"This original and fascinating book shows how to strengthen California's capacity to think globally and act locally."
>—*Joseph S. Nye*
>   *University Distinguished Service Professor, Harvard University*

"Policymakers, scholars, and engaged citizens throughout the United States and around the world should read this book to understand how the United States can chart its way into an uncertain global future. The forces that will most shape that future—climate change, migration, trade, and outsourcing, the rise of India and China, interdependence with Mexico—uniquely affect California, and California has exceptional influence on them as well. An invaluable work."

 —*Mira Kamdar*
  Senior Fellow, World Policy Institute, and author of 'Planet India'

GLOBAL CALIFORNIA

Published in cooperation with the
Pacific Council on International Policy

The Pacific Council on International Policy is a non-partisan organization
headquartered in Los Angeles with members throughout the West Coast of
the United States, across the country and around the globe. The mission
of the organization is to galvanize the distinct voice of the American West
on contemporary foreign policy issues, while providing a window into the
region for the rest of the world. The Pacific Council is governed by a Board
of Directors co-chaired by John E. Bryson, Senior Advisor at Kohlberg Kravis
Roberts & Co., and Warren Christopher, former U.S. Secretary of State. Jerrold
D. Green is the President and CEO of the Pacific Council. Founded in 1995 in
partnership with the University of Southern California and the Council on
Foreign Relations, the Pacific Council is a 501c(3) non-profit organization whose
work is made possible by financial contributions and in-kind support from
individuals, corporations, foundations and other organizations.

GLOBAL CALIFORNIA

Rising to the Cosmopolitan Challenge

Abraham F. Lowenthal

With a Foreword by Kevin Starr

Stanford University Press
Stanford, California

Stanford University Press
Stanford, California

Printed in the United States of America on acid-free, archival-quality paper

Library of Congress Cataloging-in-Publication Data

Lowenthal, Abraham F.
  Global California : rising to the cosmopolitan challenge / Abraham F. Lowenthal ; with a foreword by Kevin Starr.
    p. cm.
  Includes bibliographical references and index.
  ISBN 978-0-8047-6226-7 (cloth : alk. paper)—ISBN 978-0-8047-6227-4 (pbk.)
    1. Globalization—California.   2. Political planning—California.   3. California—Commerce—History—21st century.   4. California—Economic policy—21st century.   5. California—Politics and government—21st century.   I. Title.

HC107.C2L68 2009
337.794—dc22
                                                                            2008040785

Typeset by Westchester Book Group in 11/14 Minion

Contents

Foreword

I N MY CAREER, I have read many books relating to California. *Global California* is among the best. In fact, from the perspective of its usefulness as a clarion call to California, it is perhaps the best book I have read in three decades.

In *Global California*, Abe Lowenthal, with clarity, precision, enormous erudition and a certain kind of effective modesty—a refusal, that is, to claim too much—deals with the fundamental nature and functioning of California as a twenty-first century nation-state. Lowenthal has produced an impressive work of scholarship that is openly a manifesto, a program and a call to action.

Global California could not come at a better time. It does not take rocket science to ascertain that California as a public entity is having difficulty these days envisioning its future. The current budget crisis, in which the state is experiencing a shortfall of $20 billion, is the result of a chronic inability on the part of state government, via the political process, to set the size of government at an acceptable level, to set revenues at a level sufficient to fund these services and—as Governor Schwarzenegger is urging—to set aside excess revenues to be used in future years when revenues may fall short.

This is common sense. Yet the fact that California's state government cannot embrace such a commonsensical solution suggests an underlying crisis, for which *Global California* establishes a partial solution: partial only because its focus is on the international scene.

California has trouble thinking itself through. By this, I do not mean California as a society, as private life and culture, as business, finance, investment and other modes of entrepreneurship. I am not referring to literature, the arts or motion pictures. In realm after realm, in fact, California bespeaks the vitality with which Abe Lowenthal opens his narrative.

The problem is, rather, public policy perspective and suggested programs as a prelude to political action.

Over the past few years, the political science departments of many California universities, the Public Policy Institute of California, the California Research Bureau, numerous foundations and a number of prescient individuals have come to the fore to assist California in this very necessary endeavor of re-thinking itself through. Stanford University, for example, has established the Bill Lane Center for the Study of the North American West, under the direction of Professors David Kennedy and Richard White, specifically to play a role in this developing field of California-oriented futurist studies. Professor Steve Erie of UC San Diego and former *Los Angeles Times* columnist James Flanigan, among others, have published and continue to publish influential works in this field.

Global California, then, emerges from an academic and intellectual environment in which it is becoming increasingly obvious to Californians that they must join in this effort to assist their state in thinking through its challenges, options and destiny.

No one has done this better in one single volume, in my opinion, than Abe Lowenthal. Anchoring himself in an exhaustive command of relevant sources, statistics and commentary, Professor Lowenthal examines from numerous perspectives the fundamental nature of California as an international enterprise; past, present and future.

Yet this is not a history book, although it contains history. It is not a political science or international relations study, although it is rich in such themes. It is not a work of contemporary journalistic investigation, although it is solidly in touch with the present.

It is, rather, all these things combined and moved forward into the future as platform and matrix for the proposals with which Lowenthal concludes this volume. In the beginning of the book, he notes that California is not an independent nation; it is a state with the dimensions but not the sovereignty of a nation, and is hence prohibited by law—and some recent court decisions, which he cites—from conducting foreign affairs.

The proposals that Professor Lowenthal makes, therefore, are animated by this limitation but are by no means weakened by it; for there is plenty that California can do—in trade, commerce and culture; in immigration policy and academic life (I love his call for a California-Mexico Rhodes scholarship); in chambers of commerce and related private and/or foundation sectors—to position, to orient California toward what Lowenthal thoroughly documents as a process already under way: the globalization of the California economy.

Global California is a manifesto, a call for action as well as an academic treatise. As such, it should be reviewed and discussed—not only in the public policy seminar that Professor Lowenthal advocates for Sacramento—but also in the popular press, in business and labor circles and in community organizations and educational centers, for it deals with an issue that is crucial for California's future.

Kevin Starr
University of Southern California
September 2008

Preface

THIS BOOK GREW out of the interaction between my two careers: as analyst, teacher and advisor on international relations and U.S. foreign policy with a strong emphasis on Latin America and the Caribbean, and as the founding entrepreneur and director of three successive organizations at the nexus between the worlds of scholarship and public policy decision-making.

After committing my energies to working with others to build the Pacific Council on International Policy, a forum on global issues for thought and action leaders in California and along the whole West Coast, I began to think about how and why international issues differ in California from those on the Atlantic Coast. In time, I began to consider how much Californians would gain if we were to think more strategically and act more effectively to define and promote our international interests, and about how much we could and should contribute to national policymaking on such issues as trade, investment, immigration, the environment and intellectual property. These big questions have been remarkably under-discussed, perhaps because the mindset of Californians has been to think of foreign policy as a matter for Washington, and because national foreign policymakers tend to think of California as remote and exotic, if not irrelevant.

My aim in writing this book is to challenge these mindsets, to frame important questions and to stimulate discussion and decisions about Global California's international agenda. I do not aspire to provide the last word on this topic but to contribute to opening up a debate in which others will have much more to say.

My career has been shaped by my heritage. My late father, Rabbi Eric I. Lowenthal, taught me about a debate reported in the Talmud. The issue in question was which is more important: the commanded study of the Scripture (Torah) or action according to the Scripture's precepts. Of the various positions taken by the different rabbinic sages, my favorite was that "study is greater than action, for it leads to action." My hope is to contribute concepts, data and analysis to those, in both the public and private sectors, who can act.

I want to express my appreciation to all those who have helped me prepare this book. The University of Southern California (USC) and its School of International Relations have provided a very supportive home, welcoming my work at the boundary of global and local concerns. USC's Southern California Studies Center, directed by Professor Michael Dear, encouraged my initial forays into this terrain and funded my first research on this topic. The College of Letters, Arts and Sciences made available sabbatical support, and the Center for International Studies provided student research assistance. An April 2007 seminar at the Center for International Studies afforded me the opportunity to receive feedback on a draft of Chapter II.

The Public Policy Institute of California, and its former president, David Lyon, also importantly supported my initial research, and the John Randolph Haynes and Dora Haynes Foundation later provided a summer Faculty Fellowship.

The Board, membership, staff and funders of the Pacific Council on International Policy provided an extraordinary vantage point from which to assess California's international ties. In particular, I express my debt to those who participated in the Council's projects on "Enhancing Southern California's Global Engagement," and on "Mapping the Local Implications of Globalization for the North American West"; to Gregory F. Treverton and Michael Parks, project leaders; and to the Haynes Foundation, the San Diego Foundation and the Ford Foundation for their generous support of these projects. Jerry Green, the Pacific Council's current president, has taken a strong interest in assuring that the book reaches state and local officials and broader audiences.

I am especially grateful for the help of several capable research assistants. Most of all, I salute Mark Frame, whose research was initially supported by the Public Policy Institute of California, and who has remained committed to the project long beyond the expiration of his assistantship. Mark has been an assiduous researcher, meticulous about chasing down elusive data and avoiding error or sloppy argument; he is not responsible for any remaining errors or misjudgments.

I also appreciate the research assistance of Elizabeth Blanco, Amanda Botelho, Wendy Cahn, Marisa Cox, Susan Craney, Christopher Darnton, Aubrey Elson, Evans Hanson, Cristina Hernandez, Peter Hillakas, Jennifer James, Melissa Lockhart, Andrew Tyler and Courtney Yoder.

I am much indebted to various colleagues who commented on drafts. Greyson Bryan, Steven Erie, Jane Jaquette, Van Gordon Sauter, Howard Shatz and Kevin Starr were kind enough to read the full manuscript in nearly final form and to make valuable suggestions for final polishing. Helpful comments on individual chapters were made by Harold Brackman, Warren Christopher, Robert Collier, Michael Dear, William Deverell, Philip Ethington, Carlos Gonzalez Gutierrez, Kip Hagopian, Robert Hertzberg, Irwin Jacobs, Jesse Knight, Edward Leamer, Linda Lowenthal, Michael Lowenthal, Doris Meissner, Gustavo Mohar, Dowell Myers, Michael Parks, Bruce Ramer, Sean Randolph, Paul Rhode, Jefferey Sellers, David Shirk, David St. Clair, Peter Trubowitz, Laurence Whitehead, Pete Wilson and Julie Meier Wright. I have tried to take all this feedback into account. None of the mentioned individuals or institutions is responsible for this volume's limits, of course.

I am grateful to the late Professor Susan McGowan of California State University-Sacramento, for sharing some of her unpublished early drafts on California's economic history, and to Professor Steven Erie of the University of California, San Diego, for allowing me to review in manuscript his excellent book, *Globalizing L.A.: Trade, Infrastructure and Regional Development*, which helped guide some of my early work.

Several people, including a few of those who provided research assistance, also helped translate my cramped scrawl into word-processed product; Aubrey Elson skillfully turned out the penultimate version, and Mary Fiske prepared an earlier draft. Melissa Lockhart made the final changes, chased down the remaining references, and kept the momentum toward publication going with unfailing good cheer. Tommy McCall imaginatively produced the graphic displays in the Appendix.

I also express my appreciation to the number of California officials, consular representatives, business executives, journalists, analysts and other observers who granted interviews to me or to my research assistants, answered various questions, and provided data and insights; I hope that they and their colleagues will find this book useful.

Stacy Wagner and her colleagues at Stanford University Press moved this project quickly and skillfully from manuscript to publication.

A special word of thanks goes to my wife, Jane S. Jaquette, who has contributed so much to this project as to every aspect of my life, while continuing her own writing and teaching as well.

1 Global California: Dimensions, Ties and Stakes

C ALIFORNIA HAS THE POWER as well as the global links and interests of a nation. It lacks the legal attributes and policy instruments of a sovereign country, of course, for the American constitution expressly reserves the conduct of foreign affairs to the federal government. Yet to shape a better future, Californians must understand our state's international connections, stakes and impact. We must focus on how Californians are affected by world trends, and consider what we can do to identify and advance our own international interests. This book discusses why and explores how to do so. It begins by highlighting the dimensions and worldwide ties of California and suggesting how they matter.

This chapter includes a narrative drumbeat of relevant data; readers who prefer to absorb data in graphic form might first peek ahead to Appendix for an initial overview.

The Dimensions of California

California is larger in area than Japan, Germany or the United Kingdom. With some thirty-eight million inhabitants, California has more residents than Canada, Chile or Peru; Australia and New Zealand combined; or all of Scandinavia.[1] Four of the twelve most populous cities in the United States—Los Angeles, San Diego, San Jose and San Francisco—are in California. Projections differ, but most suggest that California's population will continue to grow, though more slowly than in the past century, and will likely be nearly 15 percent of the United States total by the year 2025.[2] By 2050, California will likely have some 59.5 million inhabitants.[3]

California's economy is by itself greater than all but six to eight nations of the world: the United States as a whole, Japan, Germany, China, the United Kingdom and sometimes France and Italy, depending on the year and exchange rate. Its estimated gross domestic product of $1.813 trillion in 2007 was greater than all of Africa; more than twice that of Mexico; and larger than that of Canada, Brazil, Russia, India or Korea.[4]

California's economy is more complex and diversified than that of any other American state and of most independent nations. Were California an independent country, it would rank among the largest exporters of goods and services in the world, with at least $13.4 billion in goods alone in 2007.[5] In 2006, California produced 13 percent of the total U.S. gross domestic product and accounted for 12.3 percent of U.S. goods exports.[6] The 2006–2008 Fortune 500 lists of largest U.S. companies include fifty-two from California, more than in any other state but Texas and New York, and California outranked Texas in 2005 and both New York and Texas in 2004.[7] Four of the country's twelve largest mutual fund management companies are based in California.[8]

California's agricultural sector is immense, in recent years producing nearly 70 percent more in value than the second-largest American farming state and almost as much as the next two combined. California's exports abroad of agricultural, food and kindred products amounted to some $9.8 billion in 2006, more than that of many developing countries mainly dependent on primary exports. In the same year, California produced more than 90 percent of U.S. exports of a wide variety of products, ranging from almonds, apricots and artichokes to walnuts, and more than 89 percent of the nation's exports of avocados and wine.[9]

California has been especially prominent in the high-technology sectors. Silicon Valley in northern California has been the world pioneer and leader in semiconductor, computer and Internet technologies, with profound impacts on economic productivity and on worldwide patterns of production and exchange. San Diego is a leader in cellular phone technology and is home to the largest supplier of integrated circuits for the industry. Seventeen of the thirty high-tech companies listed on the Amex Computer Tech Index are based in California's Silicon Valley.[10] About 23 percent of U.S. exports in computer and electronic products in 2007 came from California, almost as much as the combined total of the next two states, Texas and Florida, although California's prominence in the sector has declined somewhat since 2000.[11] Many of the nation's top multimedia firms are based in California, as are three of the five main Internet search engines—Google, Yahoo! Search and Ask—and some of the prime drivers of "Web 2.0," including Wikipedia, Facebook, Google-owned YouTube and Linked-In.[12] Nearly 40 percent of all U.S. biomedical and biogenetic technology research and manufacturing firms in the early twenty-first century are in California.[13] California is also the major center for nanotechnology initiatives and for "clean technology" ventures.[14]

California overwhelmingly dominates the entertainment industry, including cinema, television, music and multimedia. All the major U.S.-based motion picture studios are headquartered in Los Angeles: Disney, Sony Pictures, Metro Goldwyn-Mayer (MGM), Paramount Pictures, Dreamworks SKG, Twentieth Century Fox, Warner Bros. and Universal Studios. Los Angeles is also headquarters for the Fox and Warner-UPN television networks as well as Univision, the largest radio and television company serving a growing Hispanic audience. Many of the operations of ABC, NBC and CBS television are based in Los Angeles, and National Public Radio has opened a major West Coast operation there. Digitization, which has transformed many aspects of the media industry, has taken place mainly in California. California's own media markets are huge, with a decisive impact on national ratings and popular culture. Even with the flight of some production to Canada and other countries and American states, Hollywood still produces over 80 percent of the world market of films.[15] The entertainment industry is a large source of foreign exchange earnings for the U.S. economy.[16]

California leads the United States in the knowledge-based economic sectors, in large part because of its outstanding educational and research institutions. Seven California universities rank consistently among the nation's top thirty in research funding; five are often in the top nine (UCLA, UC San Diego, UC Berkeley, Stanford and UC San Francisco), with the University of Southern California and California Institute of Technology not very far behind.[17] Ten of California's universities are listed among the world's fifty best universities in a widely cited international ranking.[18]

California also has several of the country's most important research laboratories: Lawrence Livermore, Lawrence Berkeley, Sandia, the Stanford Linear Accelerator, the Salk Institute and the Jet Propulsion Laboratory. More than 22,000 U.S. patents were granted to Californians in 2007, more than three times the number granted to the residents of second-place Texas or third-place New York.[19] Institutions in California spend more on research and development than any nation of the world except the United States as a whole, Japan and Germany.[20] The state hosts more Nobel laureates than any country besides the United States.[21] California's creativity is not limited to business, science and engineering; it is equally evident in music, the arts and letters.

California's economic growth has generated enormous personal wealth and fostered increasingly significant philanthropy. Eighty-eight of the four hundred wealthiest Americans in 2007 resided in California (New York was second with seventy-three); in 1982, by contrast, eighty-four on this list were from New York and sixty-one from California.[22] Ten of the nation's fifty largest foundations (by assets) are based in California, including four of the top ten; New York also has ten but it has only two in the top ten.[23] California is the prime source of funding for many political candidates from around the country and also for a variety of national organizations dealing with issues ranging from the environment to the rights of gays and lesbians.[24]

To be sure, California also hosts extensive and troubling poverty, with yawning income gaps between the rich and poor worsening since 1970, and with higher rates of poverty than in the rest of the United States.[25] Homelessness is particularly acute, with recent estimates ranging from 170,000 to 361,000; even the more recent lower figure is greater in absolute terms than that of any other state.[26] California is also plagued by crime, including urban youth gangs; illicit traffic in narcotics, weapons and people; environmental pollution; urban sprawl; and almost unmanageable traffic. The state has been particularly hard hit by the major downturn of the national and international economy since late 2008. California is certainly not paradise. But it is big, in both positive and negative respects, and it is an arena where broader national issues must be confronted, often before they are faced elsewhere in the country.

California's Global Connections

California is not only very large, it is very connected internationally. A national study of the most globally linked cities in the United States, using a variety of measures, listed six cities in California among the top forty in the United States, with Los Angeles third and San Francisco fourth.[27] Three of the five busiest container seaports in the United States are in California. Long Beach and Los Angeles are the only U.S. seaports ranking among the top fifteen in the world in numbers of twenty-foot shipping container equivalents (TEUs) of goods handled.[28] About 34 percent of the total value of U.S. waterborne trade in 2006 passed through California seaports, as did 43 percent of the country's container trade.[29] Los Angeles International Airport (LAX) ranks among the world's top ten or eleven in terms of metric tons of air cargo processed; it also ranks consistently among the world's five busiest passenger airports.[30] San Francisco Airport is likewise a very important export gateway, particularly for the information technology sector.

California's exports of goods rose from $58.4 billion in 1990 to $119.6 billion in 2000. The subsequent drops to $106.8 billion in 2001, $92.2 billion in 2002, and $93.9 billion in 2003 were mainly a result of the bursting of the technology bubble and subsequent softness in the computer and electronics sector, as well as the abrupt but temporary decline in world trade immediately after the events of September 11, 2001; goods exports were back up to $110 billion in 2004, $116.8 billion in 2005, $117.7 billion in 2006 and $134 billion in 2007.[31]

California is also ever more important as the country's main gateway for imports, particularly from Asia. Two-way trade through California's three customs districts reached $342 billion in the year 2000, declined a bit in 2001 and 2002, but rose to more than $400 billion in 2004, then soared to $491 billion in 2006 and $515 billion in 2007 and was forecast to surpass $546 billion in 2008.[32]

California is a huge exporter of services as well. Two of the three largest "design-build" engineering service firms in the United States—Bechtel and Jacobs Engineering—are based in California, as is eleventh-ranked Parsons, and all three have extensive international operations.[33] California is a leading exporter of architectural, design, financial, insurance and legal services, as well as services associated with travel and tourism, energy and the environment, higher education, software and IT, and research and development. California's institutions of higher learning enroll more than 70,000 international students a year, more than in any other state, and these students contribute some $2 billion annually to the California economy.[34]

California's entertainment, high-tech and biotech sectors depend both on international demand and on foreign protection of intellectual property, and have drawn significantly on foreign investment and on immigrant talent. Most of the top revenue producers among Hollywood-made movies in the past few years have earned as much or more abroad as in the United States.[35] More than half of the revenues of many major Silicon Valley firms, in some cases more than two-thirds, also come from overseas sales.[36]

Demographically, California is the most internationally diverse American state.[37] Latinos, Asians, African Americans, Native Americans and Pacific Islanders and their descendants make up 57 percent of California's population, and more than a fifth of the nonwhite population of the entire United States.[38] About 29 percent of authorized immigrants in the United States reside in California.[39] California's share of the country's unauthorized* (or undocumented and thus illegal) immigrants was estimated in 2006 at about 24.5 percent, down considerably from an estimated 45 percent in 1990 but still significantly higher than that for any other state.[40] Six California cities are among the top ten in the nation with the highest percentage of foreign-born residents: Daly City, El Monte, Fremont, Garden Grove, Glendale and Santa Ana. Anaheim, Hayward, Los Angeles, Oxnard, Pomona, San Jose, Santa Clara and Sunnyvale are also among the top twenty.[41] In six cities in California with populations over 60,000, a majority of the residents are foreign-born, and immigrants constitute at least 10 percent of the population in thirty-six of the state's fifty-eight counties.[42] Some 30 percent of California's residents in 2030 will likely be foreign-born, even though a dispersion of Mexican, Central American and other immigrant flows to other regions of the United States is certainly occurring.[43]

More than one out of every four California residents today (27 percent in fact) were born abroad, in nearly eighty different countries: Mexico, the Philippines, China (including Taiwan and Hong Kong), India, Vietnam, El Salvador, Russia, Armenia, Ukraine and other countries in the former Soviet Union, Guatemala, Korea, Canada, Germany, the United Kingdom, Iran and Israel, as well as a number of other countries in East, South and Southeast Asia; Central and South America; the Caribbean; Europe; the Middle East; and Africa.[44] California has the largest concentrations of Mexicans, Iranians, Salvadorans, Guatemalans, Vietnamese and Filipinos anywhere outside their home countries, as well as the largest concentrations in the United States of immigrants from China, India, Japan, Korea, Thailand and Vietnam.[45] More people from the Mexican state of Zacatecas live in Los Angeles than in that state's capital

---

* The choice of a term to describe residents who have not completed and/or abided by the provisions of immigration regulations is itself a political choice in a contentious atmosphere. This book primarily uses "unauthorized migrant," the term used by the U.S. Census Bureau. Other terms used to describe the same population include undocumented migrants, undocumented immigrants, illegal immigrants, illegal aliens and undocumented aliens. See Michael Fix, Doris Meissner and Demetrious Papedemetriou, "Independent Task Force on Immigration and America's Future: The Road Map," Policy Brief 1 (Washington, DC: Migration Policy Institute, July 2005).

city.[46] No fewer than fifty-seven countries—plus Hong Kong and Taiwan—have diaspora populations in California of more than 10,000 persons each.[47]

The state's two largest public school districts, Los Angeles Unified and San Diego Unified, both have "minority" enrollments of more than 75 percent, mainly the result of recent immigration, stretching the very concept of "minority" beyond utility.[48] Forty-three percent of the students in the Los Angeles Unified School District are classified as English Language Learners (meaning they come from homes where the primary language is not English); the total of such students in the Los Angeles County schools is about three times higher than in any other school district in the United States. Statewide, about 43 percent of the population of California above the age of four speaks a language other than English at home.[49]

Immigrant groups have played and continue to play a major role in the expanding California economy, as sources of unskilled and semiskilled labor and, increasingly, as professionals and entrepreneurs. A large and growing share of the state's scientists, engineers, doctors, dentists, pharmacists and nurses are foreign-born, as are many of California's business executives. Of all U.S. universities, only Harvard has more foreign-born professors than UC Berkeley, UCLA and UC San Diego. Los Angeles County has the largest number of minority-owned enterprises in the United States, with more than the second- and third-ranked counties combined. Orange County ranks seventh, San Diego County tenth and Santa Clara, San Bernardino and Alameda counties are all among the top fifteen.[50]

Some of the most successful Silicon Valley companies—Intel, Google and Sun Microsystems, for example—were founded or cofounded by immigrants. Indeed, as of the middle of the first decade of the twenty-first century, 39 percent of start-up technology companies in California were founded by immigrants, the highest percentage in the nation, and more than half of Silicon Valley start-up companies had at least one immigrant as a major founder.[51] According to one study, nearly one-fourth of all Silicon Valley firms in 1998 were led by Chinese or South Asian immigrants.[52] More generally, California's economy today and for the foreseeable future depends on importing highly skilled and well-educated professionals, especially scientists and engineers.[53]

But immigration of poorly educated persons from lower-income strata in less-developed countries also contributes to worsening poverty and increasing social concerns in California. It is partly responsible for declining average educational achievement, gross and widening income disparities and overwhelmed and inadequate public services. Massive immigration, much of it unauthorized, also tends to foster the harmful side of identity politics and fuels ethnic and racial tensions, particularly during recurrent periods of economic downturn. Gaining from what immigrants can contribute while mitigating and compensating for the adverse impacts of immigration is one of California's most pressing challenges.

California's Global Impact and Stakes

California's size; scope; agricultural and industrial output; technological prowess; educational, research and philanthropic institutions; media power; trade-related infrastructure; and extensive international connections make possible a significant potential influence on many global issues. California's advanced telecommunications, computer equipment and software, multimedia, biomedical and environmental technology industries have enormous clout around the world, and affect national and international trends. Cinema, television, music and fashion from California shape values, worldviews and popular culture in a growing number of countries.

Not all of California's impact on the world is positive, of course. Despite California's adoption and rigorous implementation of strict environmental protection measures, the state recently has ranked second among the fifty American states and sixteenth worldwide in total greenhouse gas emissions, even as per capita emissions in the state are among the country's lowest.[54] The use of narcotics by Californians ranks the state high on that unfortunate measure. Crime in California—narcotics production and trafficking, prostitution, child-smuggling, money-laundering, small-arms trafficking, cyber crime, identity theft and auto theft—has serious international dimensions. Subprime mortgage failures and home foreclosures in California, more than in any other state, have severely hurt national and global credit markets and contributed to the national economic downturn.[55] California's sometimes harsh and discriminatory treatment of immigrants has presented recurrent international problems over many decades. California's very success at projecting images around the world no doubt contributes to the resentment directed at the United States by those abroad who reject what they regard as the corrosive effects of violence and prurience on their own culture and values, or who perceive declining opportunity for their own cultural expression amid an inundation of cultural products from the United States.[56] But even when its influence is problematic, California remains undeniably influential.

By the same token, California has more at stake in the international realm than any other American state. Californians and California-based firms have enormous assets abroad. Such California-based corporations as Hewlett Packard, Intel, Cisco Systems, Applied Materials, Advanced Micro Devices, Silicon Graphics, Oracle, Apple Computer, Qualcomm, Sempra, Chevron Texaco, Occidental Petroleum, Northrop Grumman, Hilton Hotels, Warner Bros. and Walt Disney have huge international operations, markets and investments. CalPERS, the mammoth pension fund of California's public employees, has a large fraction of its portfolio invested overseas, and the huge California Teachers Retirement Fund also has major international investments.[57] California-based money management firms, including the Capital Group (the country's largest), Trust Company of the West, Pacific Mutual, Wells Capital Management, Charles Schwab, Franklin Templeton and others have international holdings amounting to many hundreds of billions, indeed trillions, of dollars.[58]

California is, in turn, the largest arena for foreign direct investment in the United States, with much more such investment than second-ranked Texas and twice as much as third-ranked New York. Foreign affiliates own more property, plants and equipment in California than in any other state, totaling $93.7 billion in 2005, with some 542,600 Californians employed in foreign-owned firms.[59] California is the U.S. headquarters for many important foreign companies, including Nestle, Honda, Nissan, Hyundai and Toyota Motor Sales, and for a number of foreign banks, mainly from East Asia.

California is also a very large market for international travel and tourism, with travel spending estimated at $16.7 billion in 2007, and continuing to rise. In recent years, more than 20 percent of all overseas tourism to the United States and some 25 percent of all international tourists (including those coming over land from Canada and Mexico) have come to California.[60] Following a drop after 9/11/2001, international tourism to the state has been climbing again in the past several years; it was back to high levels by 2004 and has continued to rise since then. Further major expansion is projected, especially as international tourism by the Chinese explodes.[61] Cruise ship tourism is growing very rapidly in Los Angeles, Long Beach and San Diego.[62]

The Impact of Global Connections on California

More than any other state's, California's economy is broadly and deeply affected by international trends that influence markets, investments, costs, prices and labor. When the Mexican or major Asian economies do well, California's economy grows in direct consequence, as a result of trade, investment and tourism. California exports of goods grew at about 9.4 percent per year from 1990 through 1997 (at that time considerably faster than the average of the other forty-nine states), slowed in the late 1990s and the early twenty-first century, and more recently have begun to expand again.[63] Given California's preeminence in the export of services—including travel, tourism, education, international freight, intellectual property and research and development—the state is almost certainly the U.S. leader in total exports.

The impact of globalization on California is by no means entirely favorable, of course. When the peso collapses in Mexico or currencies fail in East Asia, California suffers—although it also often benefits, ironically, from the capital flight that these problems stimulate.[64] When international terrorism strikes anywhere in the United States, tourism in California plummets. When East Asia was hit by severe acute respiratory syndrome (SARS), California was affected more than any other American state because of the disruption of trade, tourism, flows of students and the immigration of skilled technicians.

Even when trade and investment are expanding, many Californians are disadvantaged and displaced by the restructuring and relocation of production, the loss of jobs associated with that restructuring, pressure on wages and competition for access to services, overcrowded schools, highways and hospitals. California's status as a major focal point for international trade is by no means an unmixed blessing, as congestion, pollution and high infrastructure costs are direct consequences of the flow of goods.[65] Understanding the various costs and risks of its global links—and learning how to anticipate, reduce, compensate for and manage them—is crucial for California.

California's demographic changes in recent decades have been driven by international developments. Fifty years ago, most Californians were from the other continental American states; only 8 percent of California's population in 1960 was foreign-born, compared with today's 27 percent.[66] California, perhaps together with Florida, is today what New York was early in the twentieth century: the main international frontier of the United States.[67]

In the economy, as in demography, California has been for the past thirty years at the cutting edge of a national trend toward growing international engagement. Foreign trade has expanded faster in California than in the nation as a whole, both with regard to goods and services produced in the state (more than doubling since the 1970s as a share of the total economy) and with respect to total shipments through California's sea- and airports, which have risen by more than 400 percent since 1980. Trade with Asia, the world's fastest growing region economically, has exploded, as has commerce with Mexico, especially since the establishment of the North American Free Trade Area in 1994. Some of the fastest-growing export sectors—especially computer and electronic products, agriculture, biomedical technology, environmental technology, tourism and entertainment—are those in which California leads the nation. California firms have therefore gained more than those in any other state from trade liberalization initiatives.[68]

Californians are or can be powerfully affected not only by immigration and the world economy but by many other international forces: the import of tuberculosis, hepatitis, HIV/AIDS, various flu strains and other contagious diseases; of lead-containing candies and toys that poison children; of narcotics and other dangerous substances; and of harmful agricultural diseases or pests.[69] Californians are also hurt by ozone depletion, global warming and other atmospheric changes; and by pollution along the Mexican border and in the waters offshore, as well as growing trans-Pacific atmospheric pollution.[70] Recent research suggests that Asian industrial pollution is having an intercontinental cloud-seeding effect, making California notably cloudier and stormier.[71]

California is potentially endangered by traditional and nontraditional security threats, as well. When the United States goes to war, as in Iraq in 2003, California suffers considerably more than its share of casualties because of high enlistment rates among immigrants. California would probably be the main U.S. target if North Korea were to acquire ballistic missiles with intercontinental range. Los Angeles and San Francisco are both considered prime targets for international terrorism.

Global California: Thinking Strategically

Yet even with such abundant evidence of California's expanding global ties and stakes, and of the benefits and costs of international engagement, little systematic policymaking or even policy analysis has been done over the years about the issues posed for California by world trends, threats and opportunities. There is no book, and very few articles or papers, on the international policy issues affecting California. International questions never ranked high on the agenda of California's main public policy research institutes and programs until the Global California initiative of the Public Policy Institute of California

(PPIC), which originally commissioned this study—and PPIC has recently dropped this line of research.[72] California-based research and university education programs on world affairs have rarely focused on the state's particular international interests and perspectives. Very little work has been done on how global trends and their domestic consequences are linked. What analysis has been done, focusing sharply on trade and immigration, usually reflects strictly limited conceptions of what Californians can do to affect policy.

In part, the absence of significant California-focused consideration of international issues, relationships and policy choices owes to the traditional tendency to think of "foreign policy" and external relations as exclusively managed by the federal government in Washington. A priestly tribe of experts from the law firms, corporations, universities and think tanks of the Atlantic Coast—residing from Boston to Washington—go in and out of government to take care of those questions.[73] Those who are eager to participate in the making of American foreign policy make their careers, for the most part, along the Boston/New York/Washington corridor.

California does not have the instruments of foreign policy in its control, to be sure. The federal government's near monopoly on foreign policy has recently been reinforced by court rulings. In a series of cases at the federal, appellate and Supreme Court levels, the judiciary has struck down as unconstitutional various state laws and municipal measures impinging on foreign affairs, on the grounds that they interfere with the president's conduct of foreign policy and are therefore preempted by federal supremacy.[74]

In today's world, however, it is wrong for Californians to think that international issues are not our concern, or that we cannot or should not effectively promote and advance our global interests. When private actors have such large roles in production, finance, investment, communications, culture and trade, it is misleading to think of "policy" on international questions as uniquely made by the federal government in Washington. California-based actors—corporations, banks, industry associations, trade unions, entertainment and other media, foundations, environmental protection and human rights groups, nongovernmental organizations of many other kinds, as well as state, regional and municipal government entities and public-private partnerships—routinely make decisions and take actions that directly affect international issues. They invest or withhold investment; trade or decline to do so; develop trade-related infrastructure or thwart it; integrate immigrants or reject them; exert pressure to develop international environmental and labor standards; export America's images and icons; and shape public understanding, in this country and abroad, of a world in flux. They fashion transnational coalitions to promote human rights, protect public health, preserve the environment and foster international exchange. Californians are often making international policy, though like M. Jourdain, the Molière character who did not realize that he was speaking prose, they may not always recognize that they are doing so.

Too much is at stake for Californians to leave our responses to international challenges up to the U.S. government in Washington, to Atlantic Coast think tanks and to ad hoc and episodic local and citizen initiatives. Californians need to think more strategically about international policy. We need to organize ourselves both to understand better and to respond more effectively to global problems and opportunities.[75]

This book suggests how to begin. It does not offer a full-blown foreign policy for California, a notion that makes no sense in the U.S. federal system. Rather, it suggests what Californians can do, within constitutional constraints, to identify and advance our international interests.[76] Chapter 2 reviews how and when Global California emerged, from its original international DNA, through an inward orientation in the mid-twentieth century, and then back to strong cosmopolitan connections. Chapter 3 discusses how California's diverse regions relate today to the world beyond America's borders, emphasizing that all have substantial (if different) interests and relations. Chapter 4 outlines, by way of illustration, three of the main issues Californians need to address to take better advantage of the state's global links and to cushion ourselves, to the extent possible, from the adverse effects of California's international insertion—and it sets forth illustrative recommendations for doing so. The fifth and final chapter highlights institutions and processes that California needs to strengthen in order to identify and advance the global interests of its citizens. And it suggests some of the major questions on which further research and analysis are required, and on which policy formulation and implementation are needed.

2 The Making of Global California

INTERNATIONAL FORCES have played an important role in all the major stages of California's development: the Spanish and Mexican colonization of the coastal region in the seventeenth and eighteenth centuries; the coastal missions and maritime trade from the late eighteenth through the nineteenth century, the mining boom of the late 1840s–1860s; the predominantly ranching era of the mid to late nineteenth century; the rise of California agriculture and horticulture in the late nineteenth and early twentieth centuries; the increasing industrialization from the turn of the twentieth century to the 1940s; the technological explosion after World War II; and today's age of pervasive globalization.

The three factors Gerald Nash identified as crucial in shaping California's economy—environment, population and technology—must be complemented by a fourth: global influences, especially the evolution of the world economy.[1] At various stages in California's history, its demography, society, economy, politics and culture have been transformed by international migration of people, goods, capital and ideas. Without global engagement, California today would be very different. Its accomplishments, challenges and potential derive in large part from its international character and links.[2]

California's Early Growth: International from the Start

California's global connections go all the way back to its colonization by Spain, the forays of Russian fur traders and the arrival of the Yankee clippers fostering commerce with East Asia. The formation of the Golden State as an independent territory and then as a state of the Union resulted from the nineteenth-century conflict of the United States with Mexico; today's California was part of Mexico before the U.S. military campaign of 1846–1848. Mexicans, mainly of Spanish descent, governed California from 1769 until statehood in 1850, established its cities, ran its economy and forged its culture.[3] The historic impact of Spain and Mexico is reflected in California's architectural forms, demographic ties and cultural resonance—and in the names of the state's main cities, principally on the coast: Los Angeles, San Francisco, San Jose, San Diego and Sacramento. Northern California still shows signs of the Russian presence in the early nineteenth century. Chinatowns in San Francisco and Los Angeles recall the East Asian influence from the mid-nineteenth century, of unique dimensions, nature and importance in California. The gold rush and the completion of the transcontinental railroad, events that reconfigured northern California and affected the whole state, had strong international aspects.

From its earliest years in the Union, California was seen by government authorities in Washington and financial circles in New York as a gateway to the Pacific and as a key to expanded contact with China, Japan and the rest of Asia.[4] These concepts, embraced by civic leaders in San Francisco and then in Los Angeles, influenced both regions in the late nineteenth and early twentieth centuries, particularly in response to the Spanish-American War of 1898 and then the building of the Panama Canal.[5] The contemporary notion of California as a bridge to the west and to the south is by no means new.[6]

California's sudden and rapid growth after the Treaty of Guadalupe Hidalgo in 1848, and especially after the discovery of gold at Sutter's Mill that same year, was to a considerable degree due to migration from Asia, Europe and Latin America. It was facilitated by foreign investment, especially from Europe, and responded in part to international economic opportunity.

The Gold Rush coincided with a revolution in communications and transportation that made possible mass migration from all points on the compass, as well as greatly expanded commerce. As one study of California quicksilver argues, "a self-contained view of the pioneer California economy ignores many important international connections . . . . California quicksilver was produced with capital and entrepreneurship from Mexico and the United States, labor from the United States, Mexico, England, China and Chile, equipment from England, and coal from California and Australia. Output flowed into the Pacific economy, and Pacific regions in turn sent raw material and foodstuffs to

California."[7] Similar comments could be made about California's gold and silver production in the nineteenth century, which were geared to Pacific Rim trade more than to U.S. markets.[8] In the late nineteenth century, California was the center of world gold and quicksilver production, with more than half of it exported, mainly to China, Mexico and South America, in declining order. California's mercury was half the world's production from 1850 to 1880.[9] The gold rush also led to the development of foundries and mining technology, which quickly found customers in Canada, Mexico, Central and South America, China, Japan, Russia, Australia and New Zealand.[10]

International Population

The international demographic impact on California was particularly important. About one-fourth of California's estimated population of about 165,000 in 1850 was born outside what is now the United States, but by 1860 the foreign-born share of California's rapidly expanding population had risen to almost 40 percent, with substantial flows from China, Mexico, Chile, England, Germany, France, Ireland, Scandinavia and Italy.[11]

By 1860 the Chinese were the largest single immigrant group, composing nearly 10 percent of the state's population and contributing importantly to building the state's infrastructure. The rapid Chinese influx, particularly into the San Francisco area and the Central Valley, aroused hostility from other groups, leading by the 1860s and 1870s to anti-Chinese protests and violence, systematic legal discrimination against Chinese and then outright restrictions on Chinese immigration. Anti-Chinese agitation in the 1870s led to anti-immigration features in the 1879 state constitution and contributed in 1882 to the adoption of the racially based federal Chinese Exclusion Act, one of California's earliest impacts on American foreign policy.[12] California's relations with Japan were more complex, with positive mutual attraction and the forging of close economic and cultural ties in the late nineteenth century giving way to increasing anti-Japanese sentiment in the twentieth century.[13]

California's population more than doubled in the 1850s and continued to grow rapidly in the following several decades, driven both by the steady flow westward from the other American states and territories and by substantial international immigration. The foreign-born made up some 24 percent of California's population in 1850, 39 percent in 1860 and 38 percent in 1870, the highest share of foreign-born residents in the United States in the decades after the Civil War.[14] From 1890 to 1920, international immigrants—now increasingly from Mexico, Italy and Japan—were still nearly 30 percent of all newcomers to California, even as migration from elsewhere in the United States to California increased, in part due to the national restrictions on Asian immigration combined with the state's rapidly growing need for labor.[15] With the influx of Asian and then European immigrants, however, the number of persons who had resided in what had previously been Mexico (or Californios, as they were then called) declined rapidly as a share of the total population, falling to just 2.4 percent by 1910.[16]

The impact of international immigration was especially important in northern California. San Francisco (Yerba Buena then), a village of 800 inhabitants in 1848, was one of the world's fastest-growing cities from 1849 through the early 1850s; by the late 1860s, it was the informal capital of the western United States and the whole country's tenth-largest metropolis. The San Francisco Mining Exchange era briefly ranked as the world's largest stock market during the Comstock Mining bubble of the early 1870s.[17] International migration and investment were central to the city's rapid emergence. In the middle of the 1850s, San Francisco reportedly published more newspapers than London, with two daily papers printed in French and others in German, Italian, Swedish, Spanish and Chinese.[18] Robert Louis Stevenson commented in about 1880 on the cosmopolitan nature of San Francisco, with "airs of Marseilles and Berlin . . . you hear French, German, Italian, Spanish, and English indifferently."[19]

In the mid-nineteenth century, before the completion of the transcontinental railroad in 1869, California was still remote from the rest of the United States, separated by the great mountain ranges and growing outside the main framework of America's gradual westward expansion. As Carey McWilliams pointed out, perhaps exaggerating a bit for effect, "measured in terms of comfort, money and time, California was actually nearer to China and South America, prior to 1869, than it was to the Mississippi."[20]

California's Global Ties, 1870–1939

California's growing economy in the late nineteenth and early twentieth centuries was primarily based on mining, ranching and agriculture, with some incipient industry. Foreign-born labor, European investment and international markets were critical to much of this growth. Immigrant labor, mainly from Asia and Europe, surged into California during the Gold Rush, providing much of the manpower for gold, silver and quicksilver mining; iron foundries; railroad-building; and supportive activities. Immigrant labor was equally important to California's swift rise during the late nineteenth and early twentieth century as an agricultural producer, based on the state's combination of rich soils, bountiful sun, highly diverse ecology and climates, innovative techniques and research. California even became (albeit briefly) one of the world's most important granaries.[21] Its wheat trade depended so heavily on British finance that the California wheat industry was considered "almost a colonial appendage to Victorian Britain."[22]

California lost the international competition for wheat markets by the turn of the century but quickly developed other agricultural sectors. Cultivation of fruit exploded, and the export of canned and dried fruits to Europe and Asia took off. Citrus fruit, nut and vegetable farming; the dairy industry; and viticulture all expanded rapidly in the early twentieth century, some with significant international markets. By 1920 rice also became a major California crop, with exports to Japan, Europe and Latin America. Fish and lumber, both key to the early California economy, were also then international export products.

California's agriculture was internationally shaped in the late nineteenth and early twentieth centuries. Agricultural workers from China, Japan, Mexico and the Philippines played an indispensable role. Japanese farmers introduced intensive techniques that helped build California's rice and vegetable sectors; Chinese introduced celery and peas; and Slavonians played a major role in the apple industry. International contributions also facilitated California's agricultural specialization: double dwarf milo maize from Japan, flax from India, alfalfa from Chile, avocados and tomatoes from Mexico, pears from China, plums and prunes from France and Japan, figs from Greece and Turkey, navel orange budwood from Bahia, Brazil and viticulture from France and Hungary.[23] The stunning development of California agriculture and horticulture— stimulated immensely by the introduction of the refrigerated railcar, which permitted produce to reach more distant markets—was also aided by global markets in Asia and Europe.[24]

In the late nineteenth century, San Francisco's elite took a lead role in establishing additional lines of economic activity tied to international affairs, particularly shipbuilding and a modest but growing arms industry. San Francisco's press, led by William Randolph Hearst, by then a national figure, pushed avidly at the turn of the century for the United States to play an expanding world role. The conquest of the Philippines in 1898 consolidated and reinforced American power in the Pacific and made West Coast ports much more important both to the U.S. Navy and to the U.S. economy. Federal spending for warship production soon became a prime contributor to San Francisco's growth. Many of the ships in the Great White Fleet that President Theodore Roosevelt dispatched on a global circumnavigation in 1907 were built in San Francisco.[25] From 1914 through 1919, as a result of World War I, San Francisco's established shipbuilding industry experienced, albeit temporarily, a fourteenfold expansion of employment.[26]

The West Coast's importance in America's global trade and its world power position grew rapidly in the early twentieth century. The four principal West Coast ports, three of them in California, expanded their exports by 30 percent between 1901 and 1911, more than double the rate of expansion in those years of the top four East Coast ports.[27] San Francisco and San Diego beat out New Orleans as the national sites to celebrate the opening of the Panama Canal, a development of great significance for California's growth and for its global connections that was emphasized in the Panama-Pacific International Exhibition of 1915.

San Francisco's early success at building military and particularly navalrelated facilities was strongly reinforced right after World War I by the U.S. Navy's decision to divide the fleet into Atlantic and Pacific components. San Francisco's bet on defense-related investment was emulated from the 1920s on by Los Angeles and San Diego. San Francisco, Los Angeles and especially San Diego based a considerable part of their twentieth-century growth on building military, naval and related facilities, competing to attract federal funding and private investment to spur regional development by responding to and emphasizing the country's international security imperatives. A "metropolitan military complex" forged California's growth in large measure as a concerted and competitive response to international trends and perceived or plausible international threats.[28]

The petroleum sector, another important feature of California's early twentieth-century economy, also had strong international dimensions from the start. Edward L. Doheny, California's leading oil tycoon in the late nineteenth century, established the Mexico Petroleum Company of California, working fields near Tampico and launching Mexico's petroleum industry in the process.[29] Standard Oil of California developed its properties in large part for exports to East Asia. Oil exports played a major role in reinforcing the expansion of the Los Angeles harbor area at San Pedro Bay, which had begun to develop in the late nineteenth century on the expectation of coal trade from Utah and direct freight to and from the interior. By the 1930s, Los Angeles had become the world's largest oil-exporting port. U.S. exports in the late 1930s supplied some 60 percent of Japan's energy demand, and California provided most of it.[30]

The development in the early twentieth century of the motion picture industry, a quintessential feature of Southern California's economic growth, had key international components from the start. The leading initial entrepreneurs were such immigrants as Samuel Goldwyn (Poland), Louis Mayer (Russia), Harry Warner (Poland) and William Fox (Hungary). World War I devastated much of Europe's cinema industry, allowing California to capture international markets and talent. By the late 1930s, California supplied about 65 percent of the motion pictures shown in theaters around the world, and approximately 35 percent of all revenue received by American film producers came from foreign markets.[31]

International Visions

As early as the nineteenth century and with increasing frequency in the early twentieth, a few California leaders called for the state to play a larger international economic role. Wallace Alexander, of the sugar conglomerate Alexander and Baldwin; Wigginton Creed, president of Pacific Gas and Electric Company; E. W. Wilson, president of the Pacific National Bank of San Francisco; and others were active in the Foreign Trade Club in Northern California in putting international trade on the agenda of the San Francisco Chamber of Commerce and also in opposing anti-Japanese and anti-Chinese immigration and trade restrictions.[32] Some years later, Henry F. Grady, a UC Berkeley dean and adviser to the San Francisco Chamber of Commerce, took a leading role in promoting trade liberalization, which he argued would be good for California and the country, especially as Asian markets grew.[33]

In Southern California, a number of private capitalists and public entrepreneurs also promoted international trade and pushed for the development of the ports and trade infrastructure. Harry Chandler, Harrison Gray Otis, Henry Huntington and other business leaders articulated a bold international vision for Los Angeles. Among the most insistent champions of internationalism were Clarence Matson, manager of L.A.'s Harbor Department in the 1920s;

banker George Carpenter, cofounder with Matson of the World Trade Center for Los Angeles (later called the Foreign Trade Association of Southern California); and University of Southern California president Rufus von Kleinsmid.[34] Their emphasis was primarily on Asia, seen as the most promising region for vastly expanded commerce. But there was also strong interest in links with Mexico and Latin America, particularly after the Mexican Revolution (1910–1921) led some 10 percent of that country's population to enter the United States and after completion of the Panama Canal's transformed shipping routes and drastically reduced shipping and travel times to the West Coast from South America.

By the end of the 1930s, California, building on its nineteenth-century beginnings, had established itself as a substantial partner in trans-Pacific trade. A gigantic statue of Pacifica at the Golden Gate International Exposition on Treasure Island in San Francisco Bay in 1939 evoked a hopeful dawning era of even greater Asia-Pacific cooperation, commerce and culture.[35]

California had by the 1930s also clearly established its relevance to international affairs in another important but contrary respect. Anti-immigration sentiment in California, directed first against Chinese, then also against Japanese and Koreans, repeatedly flared, sparking international tensions from the 1870s on. The *San Francisco Chronicle* led the campaign against the "Yellow Peril" at the turn of the century and into the 1920s. In 1906, shortly after San Francisco received a generous gift of $250,000 from the Japanese Red Cross to assist in earthquake recovery, the city's Board of Education voted to segregate Chinese, Japanese and Korean children in an "Oriental Public School." The Japanese government strongly protested, and one major Tokyo newspaper called for a military response. President Theodore Roosevelt, mindful that Japan had just spectacularly defeated Russia and might well threaten the Philippines, a new American outpost, was enraged at the California "idiots" responsible for this provocation.[36]

The "Gentleman's Agreement" of 1907–1908 between Japan and the United States eased tensions by removing the segregation order in exchange for "voluntary" restrictions in Japanese migration, but conflict over immigration persisted. California politicians and labor unions readily used anti-Japanese sentiment to expand their popularity. In 1913, California's legislature forbade Japanese from owning land in the state, ignoring a visit to Sacramento and request to drop the measure by Secretary of State William Jennings Bryan and rebuffing President Woodrow Wilson's attempt to secure phrasing that would be less offensive to Japan.[37] Exclusionists in California, not satisfied with the anti-Japanese land laws in the state, turned toward prohibiting Japanese immigrants at the federal level. The Japanese Exclusion League of California, established in 1920, worked to incorporate anti-Japanese provisions in the new immigration law being considered by the Sixty-eighth Congress. Senator Hiram Johnson persuaded his fellow California senator, Samuel Shortridge, to drop an anti-lynching bill in order to win the support of senators from the South for this exclusion provision.[38] The federal Immigration Act of 1924, which made all Asians ineligible for U.S. citizenship, was thus prompted in part by pressure from California. It exacerbated U.S.-Japan tensions and fed anti-American sentiment in Japan. California pressures were also important in causing a suddenly more strict enforcement of various immigration law provisions to reduce the inflow from Mexico, which fell from an average of 58,747 a year in the 1920s to 12,703 in 1930 and 3,323 in 1931 and then gave way to forced repatriation of Mexicans during the 1930s.[39] California was not formally making its own foreign policy, but its impact on the international relations of the United States was undeniable.

California's Take-off: World War II and Its Aftermath

Another international event, the global Depression of the 1930s, slowed economic growth in California for a time, but the state began to recover faster than most of the country, relying on agriculture and increasingly on manufacturing as its engines of development. Internal migrations caused by the Great Depression and by the disastrous storms in the Dust Bowl produced the trek of hundreds of thousands to California during the 1930s. Almost all came from the other continental American states, especially the Great Plains, the Midwest and the Southeast; some 43 percent were farmers or agricultural laborers, but many of these soon became industrial or service workers in the newly emerging California industrial economy. By 1940, California's population had reached 6.9 million, larger than any other state but New York, Illinois, Pennsylvania and Ohio, and its rate of increase was accelerating.

Compared with the rest of the country, California's economy was relatively strong in 1940. California agriculture, especially its horticulture, had by then assumed a role of world leadership, looked to for its organizational and marketing practices as well as its successful research and extension system.[40] California agriculture and resource-based manufacturers were joined by the burgeoning motion picture industry, a developing aviation industry, a significant apparel business, a growing automobile sector and an incipient electronics industry. By 1937, Southern California had surpassed Long Island as the country's leading center for the manufacture of aircraft, and the California Institute of Technology (Caltech) in Pasadena was becoming recognized as the nation's best institution for aeronautical research and teaching.[41] Southern California became the main site, after Detroit, for U.S. automobile manufacture and assembly.

Although California by 1940 was clearly growing, its ambitions were "relatively modest and in many instances provincial." As Kevin Starr has put it, California was expected to "continue to grow at a steady pace, with agriculture remaining the lead element in the economy."[42] But the state was to move to a different and faster track soon thereafter, propelled by World War II.

California played a huge role in America's successful war effort in the early 1940s. The number of military bases in the state increased from sixteen to forty-one, more than those in the next five states combined.[43] A colossal expansion occurred in aircraft production, not only for the U.S. military but for Great Britain and other European countries as well. Airframe factories increased their employment in California to more than 280,000 by 1943. Shipbuilding boomed as well, and with it metal and electronics firms. California secured some 8.7 percent of all defense contracts during the war years, behind only New York and Michigan.[44] Federal expenditures for military and industrial facilities in California came to $19.7 billion between June 1940 and June 1945.[45]

The Second World War helped transform California demographically, economically, socially and politically. Trends that had already been evident in the 1920s and 30s, such as the buildup of defense-related facilities and the construction of an automobile freeway system, were greatly reinforced and magnified by World War II, while other trends were reversed or, in some cases, initiated. World War II's consequences greatly expanded California's population growth, changed its demographic makeup and reinforced the changing balance of demographic, economic and political power between northern and southern California. The forced repatriation of Mexicans that had occurred during the Depression years of the 1930s gave way to a new U.S.-Mexico guest worker program.[46] The Bracero program, as it was called, established in 1943 and renewed immediately after the war's close, again brought hundreds of thousands of Mexicans to California. The war also generally strengthened California's manufacturing sector, stimulated a powerful science-technology establishment and fostered a major expansion of the state's already impressive transportation infrastructure.

California's population grew by 53 percent during the 1940s, swelled by the millions who came to work in the defense-related industries: aircraft, ship-building, tank and automobile assembly, port development and production of steel, rubber, tires, garments and other products. Wartime production more than doubled the size of California's industrial sector. Beyond aircraft and ship production and the manufacture of arms, federal wartime spending was de-voted to military installations and personnel, science facilities and research, agriculture and infrastructure, including the considerable expansion of Los Angeles Municipal Airport and other airfields.[47]

By February 1945, as Starr reports, "*Fortune* was announcing that the Pacific Coast was no longer an economic colony of the East. Previously, the Coast had exported raw materials for manufacture elsewhere and was dependent upon outside financing. Now, as the War drew to a close, the Coast reveled in its new-found financial and industrial power."[48]

After a brief period of postwar readjustment, California resumed its rapid growth. The ports of Los Angeles, Long Beach, San Diego, San Francisco and Oakland all launched multimillion-dollar programs of improvement, build-ing facilities that were to spur California's further development as an indus-trial and commercial center. Investment greatly expanded in the University of California system, Stanford, Caltech, Scripps, the University of Southern California and other educational and research institutions. The state's infra-structure, already being rapidly developed in the first decades of the century, mushroomed further with new highways, energy production and distribu-tion facilities and mammoth water projects. The aircraft industry success-fully completed the transition (begun in the 1930s) from military back to primarily passenger aircraft production and soon entered a new generation of military production as well. California groups from north and south led the campaign to re-expand shipbuilding, based on security as well as commercial considerations.

Approximately 850,000 veterans, most of them formerly from elsewhere in the United States, settled in California in the 1940s, eager to take advantage of the opportunities California offered; many who had spent time in military training in California on their way to the front vowed to return after the war, and did. California's population surged to 9.3 million in 1945 and 10.6 million in 1950.

Los Angeles, a small town of 10,000 inhabitants in 1880, was still a modest city of about 100,000 at the dawn of the twentieth century. By the end of World War I, Los Angeles was growing fast, but L.A. County was still only the twenty-seventh-largest manufacturing center in the United States in 1919.[49] By 1929, spurred in part by the development of its harbor to facilitate trade, L.A. had become the country's fifth-largest metropolis, its third-largest manufacturing center and the West Coast's leading port. Los Angeles had by then already displaced San Francisco as California's main economic, commercial, demographic and political center. By 1949, Los Angeles was the country's third-largest metropolitan area, although Los Angeles County also remained the nation's top agricultural producer. Thirty-two percent of L.A.'s population had arrived since 1940, overwhelmingly from other American states, not from other countries.

Largely because of its military and naval installations, San Diego was also transformed from an isolated border town to a growing metropolis, though still in the shadow of Los Angeles. What was to become "Silicon Valley" (mostly Santa Clara County) and Orange County began their rapid growth as well, transitioning from rural and agricultural regions to industrial centers; the population of Santa Clara County in 1940 was less than 200,000 and that of Orange County about 140,000.

Although the influx of African Americans to Los Angeles during and after World War II had already begun to alter its hue, L.A. had been in the 1920s and 1930s and was still in the late 1940s and into the 1950s considered the country's most WASP (white Anglo-Saxon Protestant) big city, and most of the state was overwhelmingly both American-born and white.[50] Only 8 percent of California's population in 1960 had been born abroad. In sharp contrast with California's nineteenth-century heterogeneous and cosmopolitan makeup, California of the 1950s and early 1960s was relatively homogeneous and provincial. California was then so "Anglo" that the primary language even of its foreign-born residents was English.[51] In many ways the national and international image of California, and its prevalent self-image, was fashioned during this period, not on the basis of the state's earlier—or its later—realities.

Though spurred to its rapid growth to a great extent by international events, California's economy in the late 1940s was built mainly around agricultural and industrial production for the state's own expanding market and for the rest of the United States. International exports as a percentage of

California's economy almost certainly declined from the late nineteenth century to the mid-twentieth century.[52] In terms of energy resources, too, California in the mid-twentieth century was largely self-sufficient and regionally focused.[53]

As it grew, however, California was beginning to acquire greater international visibility, and some were beginning to imagine the emergence of California as a global actor. As McWilliams put it, presciently, in 1949:

> In the last century, California has steadily moved to a more central position in world affairs. In 1848, it was one of the most remote areas of the world, the last frontier of America, in a world in which the United States still occupied a subordinate position to Europe. Today, the United States is the world's first power, and California, no longer a frontier, occupies a more central position, in terms of our global interest, than the older settlements on the eastern seaboard. . . . California is destined to occupy in the future, not a marginal, but a central position in world affairs. The ports of the west coast will be the ports through which the expanding trade and commerce of the west will flow to ports throughout the entire vast area of the Pacific. . . . The Pacific as "the ocean of the future" is still merely an oratorical phrase, a rhetorical flourish, a theme for chamber of commerce bombast. . . . [but] the oratorical phrase of yesterday may become the economic reality of tomorrow. . . . The problem of the West. . . . is to build toward the future, toward the Pacific. [54]

As McWilliams implied, however, there was still too much focus on local projects, interregional conflicts and vested interests—all of which kept Californians provincial.

Lagging Concepts

Most of California's citizens in the mid-twentieth century, more than 90 percent of whom had been born in the United States, were primarily inward-looking, especially after the end of World War II. The same was largely true of California's media, many of which had probably been more focused on international matters in the late nineteenth and early twentieth century than they were in the late 1940s and early 1950s. California in the mid-twentieth century was no longer very internationally oriented, demographically and in economic terms—especially as compared with the leading Atlantic Coast states, or indeed with its own past.

Although California's dimensions in the mid-twentieth century were growing to national proportions, the vision, perspective and connections of its citizens were mainly domestic and indeed quite local. California's Mexican-origin population had grown, but forced-march assimilation was making the Latino population almost invisible, with Spanish instruction rooted out of schools, little media or marketing in Spanish and few ties between the immigrants from Mexico and their home country.[55] California's Japanese American population had suffered internment on national security grounds during World War II and now kept a very low profile, as did Chinese Americans.

California was beginning to be more visible internationally, yet few Californians were then thinking in global terms. A disjuncture was emerging between the state's growing international prominence and the lack of deep involvement or interest in world affairs by most Californians, even those in leadership circles.

The Cold War and California

As World War II had fueled California's rise after 1940, international factors also largely drove its further transformation in the 1950s and 1960s. California's robust growth in these years was based mainly on the Cold War military buildup. From 1950 to 1956, California secured 16.4 percent of all the rapidly expanding military spending in the United States, a share that grew even larger in the late 1950s and 1960s. From 1946 to 1965, the thirteen western states, with one-sixth of the U.S. population, accounted for one-fourth of all Department of Defense (DOD) military and civilian personnel, one-third of all military prime contract awards (including one-half of all DOD research and development contracts) and two-thirds of all missile contracts; California took the lion's share in all these categories.[56]

This trend accelerated again in connection with the Vietnam War buildup in the mid and late 1960s and intensified once more as the competition between the United States and the Soviet Union for supremacy in outer space took shape. Federal expenditures and contracts in California for the National Aeronautics and Space Administration and for the Atomic Energy Commission dwarfed those in any other state.

California's economic boom continued through most of the 1960s and 1970s and into the 1980s, stimulated in large measure by military-related spending: Defense Department procurements, expansion and modernization of military and naval installations and facilities, defense-related scientific enterprises and huge investments in university research and in the aerospace industry.

The major emphasis on infrastructure continued. Los Angeles Airport had the country's first jet passenger flight in 1959, and the expanded Los Angeles International Airport inaugurated the nation's first jet-age terminal in 1962. Oakland became the first major port on the West Coast to build terminals for the then-revolutionary container ships and soon became, for a time, the largest container-ship building facility (by tonnage) in the United States, second in the world only to Rotterdam. Not to be outdone, the ports of Los Angeles and Long Beach underwent huge capital-intensive improvement in the 1960s and 1970s and became, in turn, the country's best and most-used facilities for handling containerized trade. California's vast freeway system expanded greatly as well, as did the state's higher education establishment.

The Cold War military buildup prompted the rapid economic and population growth of Los Angeles, Long Beach, San Diego, Santa Clara County and Orange County. A DOD survey in 1984 reported that one-fifth of the total annual U.S. military budget, some $40 billion, was by then being spent in California; Texas was a distant second with $14.2 billion annually, followed by Virginia ($12 billion), New York ($10.7 billion) and Florida ($8.2 billion).[57] How crucial to California's economy the military-based sector had become was illustrated when significant cuts in the federal defense budget in 1969–1971 triggered California's brief recession in the early 1970s. This dependence was shown again when greatly expanded military spending in the Reagan years in turn stimulated a revival of California's rapid growth in the 1980s. California's real economic growth of almost 200 percent from 1963 to 1988 was mainly based on the U.S. response to perceived international challenges and was vulnerable to disruption after the U.S. withdrawal from Vietnam, and then again in the 1990s, when the Cold War came to an end and defense production soon plummeted.

The state's population grew by 2.4 million from 1950 through 1955 (to about 13 million) as tens of thousands of engineers and scientists and hundreds of thousands of laborers and service workers moved west to take advantage of the opportunities opening up in the Golden State. It then swelled again to almost 16 million by 1960. California became America's most populous state in 1962; by 1971, its population had reached twenty million, reflecting the "fastest long-run population growth of any advanced society in the world, including Japan or Israel."[58] The gap between California's population and that of the country's second-largest state (first New York, then Texas) continued to grow through the rest of the twentieth century.[59]

Growing International Consciousness

A few California business, professional and civic figures in the mid-twentieth century were devoting more attention to the world beyond America's borders. Several California political and community leaders, mainly in San Francisco, got quite interested in the United Nations, in part because the U.N.'s 1945 organizing conference was held there.[60] The Treaty of Peace with Japan was signed in San Francisco in 1951, again reinforcing an international vision and role for California. Prominent California politicians—particularly Governor Earl Warren, Senator William Knowland and U.S. Representative Richard M. Nixon—were taking a strong interest in world affairs: Warren mainly in Mexico, Knowland in China and Nixon in the Cold War rivalry with Soviet Russia.

Bank of America, then the state's largest financial institution, began in the late 1940s to develop an international presence, mostly in Asia; it established nine overseas branches, eight in Asia and one in Europe, between 1947 and 1951.[61] California's large engineering firms—Bechtel-McCone, Morrison-Knudsen and Kaiser—began to be more involved internationally than they had been previously. The state's major oil companies—including Union Oil, Getty Oil and Standard Oil of California—undertook new activities in the Persian Gulf and in Asia, particularly to supply postwar Japan's burgeoning requirements for petroleum, and to work with Japanese partners on developing Indonesia's petroleum resources. Energy trade with western Canada also increased significantly, especially after the construction in 1961 of a pipeline bringing natural gas from Alberta to California. With petroleum and natural gas imports from Sumatra, Venezuela, the Middle East and Canada, California became increasingly integrated into the global energy economy.[62] And California's agriculture began during this period to expand its international markets, especially across the Pacific, for rice, fruits, nuts and other products.[63]

As America's preeminent world power became obvious, and with growing California-based business interests abroad, Californians began organizing themselves to become better informed on global issues. The World Affairs Council of Northern California was founded in 1947, and the Los Angeles World Affairs Council in 1953; both were devoted to broad public education on international affairs. The RAND Corporation was established in Santa Monica by the U.S. Air Force after World War II as an international security research center, though it was sited in California primarily to remove it from day-to-day policy pressures in Washington, D.C., not to connect with California concerns and perspectives.

Various colleges and universities in California began programs on international affairs during this period. USC's School of International Relations, which had been founded by Von Kleinsmid in 1924 as the first such faculty west of the Mississippi, grew rapidly after World War II as a training ground for people entering the growing U.S. foreign and defense policy establishments. Occidental College in Los Angeles established its first lectureship on international affairs in 1948, and a program on diplomacy and world affairs in 1957. UC Berkeley started its International Studies Institute in 1955. The Monterey Institute of International Studies, a graduate program, was established that same year.

There were other signs of increasing interest in world affairs in the 1950s, 1960s and 1970s. California's major cities began developing sister-city relationships in 1957, taking up an initiative President Dwight Eisenhower had launched that year. The *Los Angeles Times* began in the 1970s to devote more attention to international issues, particularly to Asia, and to promote the idea of California as a Pacific Rim presence.

But California still lagged far behind the Atlantic Coast power centers in focusing leadership attention on international questions. California's international links and stakes were not generally salient, and not an object of concerted attention. A history of one of California's major law firms, O'Melveny and Myers, points out, for instance, that as of 1965 the firm's top clients were almost all Southern California corporations, and its practice was almost entirely confined to that region, with almost no international involvement.[64] There was no California or West Coast equivalent or counterpart to such Atlantic Coast organizations as the Council on Foreign Relations or the Carnegie Endowment on International Peace, nor were there important university research centers on international studies comparable to those at Harvard, Columbia or Princeton.[65]

The Emergence of Global California

By the time Los Angeles hosted the 1984 Olympics, California was by a considerable margin America's most populous and clearly one of its most prosperous states. San Francisco was headquarters for both Bank of America and Wells Fargo Bank, two of the nation's half dozen largest financial institutions;

each by then had strong international interests. Southern California dominated the nation's aerospace and military industrial sectors and played a leading role in the emerging information technology sector, as well as in cinema and television. Los Angeles was by now the country's second-largest metropolitan area and its largest manufacturing center. San Jose and the Silicon Valley emerged as the main site for the fast-growing computer industry. San Diego was expanding apace, developing various business ventures around its military and naval facilities and its research and educational institutions. Orange County was rapidly industrializing. The Central Valley's importance for agriculture continued to grow. The wine industry, based primarily in northern California, was fast expanding in size, quality and reputation. California's universities and research laboratories were becoming recognized as among the nation's premier intellectual centers. San Francisco-Oakland and especially Los Angeles-Long Beach had developed world-class trade portals, both seaports and airports, serving growing regional, national and international markets.

As California's economy, infrastructure and population grew, its political salience rose, in the United States and internationally. By 1973 California had the largest congressional delegation, and therefore the largest bloc in the electoral college. California became a major and sometimes decisive influence in U.S. presidential elections; an indispensable source for political campaign funding; and the political base for such prominent leaders as Mr. Nixon and Ronald W. Reagan, who became the thirty-seventh and fortieth presidents of the United States, respectively.

California's cultural impact also expanded. Notwithstanding Woody Allen's crack that turning right on red was California's only cultural contribution and Johnny Carson's quip that the only live culture in California was its yogurt, California increasingly came to be recognized as avant-garde in realms from clothes and cuisine to music, cinema, television and popular culture. In literature, architecture and technology—and in politics and public policy—California became a trendsetter, nationally and internationally.[66] Not all of California's influence was positive, to be sure, but the state's growing impact was recognized.

By the 1980s, California was not a remote hinterland but a recognized heartland, radiating nationally and internationally. And while California was reaching this stature, it was also changing dramatically in demography, economic structure, social stratification and international relationships.

The emergence of Global California in the 1970s, 1980s and 1990s was shaped primarily by two drivers: burgeoning international immigration and the rapidly changing international economy.

The Impact of Immigration

California's demography began to change radically in the late 1960s. Immigration from outside the United States exploded anew, primarily in response to two federal government actions: the 1964 termination of the Bracero program and the passage of the 1965 Immigration and Naturalization Act, the Hart-Celler legislation. Taken together, these federal decisions dramatically altered the composition and impact of immigration on America's population, first and especially in California.

Ending the Bracero program transformed the movement of agricultural workers between Mexico and the United States from a predominantly legal and seasonal flow to a mainly undocumented and largely more permanent one. It also vastly increased the size of the permanent Mexican population in the United States, largely concentrated at first in California, as thousands of former braceros chose to settle and bring in other family members, as allowed under the new legislation. The number of Mexican-born residents of California multiplied tenfold from 1960 to 1990: from nearly 250,000 to almost 2.5 million. By the year 2000, almost 3.93 million Mexican-born persons lived in California, and the massive flow continues, though it now goes not only to California, still the biggest single destination, but also throughout much of the United States.[67]

The 1965 Immigration and Naturalization Act in turn opened up a new era of Asian immigration to the United States, especially to California. By abolishing national quotas (which, with the provisions rendering Asians ineligible for citizenship, had nearly ended Asian immigration in the 1920s) and establishing family reunification and employment skills as policy priorities, the 1965 act spurred a tidal wave of new immigration from Asia, particularly from Korea, the Phillipines and Taiwan. This wave was soon reinforced by the denouement of the Vietnam War and the consequent adoption of the 1980 Refugee Act, which permitted immigration by many Southeast Asians. It was then further expanded by the major influx of South Asians and subsequently, with the implosion of the Soviet Union, of Russians. As with Mexico, so it was with Asia: the greatest impact of the increasing migration flow was in California, which in the mid-1970s replaced New York as the preferred destination for new immigrants. California's geographic position as a natural entry point from both Mexico and Asia, previous Latin American and Asian immigration, the resulting existence of established immigrant communities and networks from these regions and the state's booming economy all contributed to this huge influx. By the end of the 1990s, California had twice as many foreign-born residents as New York.

California had in several previous periods attracted international immigrants, but the scale, pace and nature of the flow after 1965 were unprecedented. During the 1970s, California added nearly 1.8 million foreign-born residents, more than had entered the state in the previous seventy years taken together. During the 1980s, an additional 2.82 million international immigrants settled in California. Another 2.4 million entered California in the 1990s. From 1930 to 1970, over 95 percent of California's population growth had come from those born in California or elsewhere in the contiguous United States, but in the 1970s, foreign-born immigrants accounted for 49 percent of the state's population growth.[68] For the first time, in fact, California experienced a net outflow of U.S.-born inhabitants, but the state's total population continued to increase on the basis of international immigration.

By the final years of the twentieth century, international immigration was responsible for most of California's population growth, as flows from California to other states expanded while international immigration into the state continued unabated. Despite net migration to other U.S. states of some 755,000, California's population grew by almost 2.16 million from 1995 to 2000.[69] International migration and births, mainly in immigrant families, accounted for the overall increase. Nearly half of all new births in California in the late 1990s were to Hispanic women, an increase from 20 percent in 1970, and births in Latino families became the majority in California by 2001. Although there is some evidence that immigration to California may have leveled off since the mid-1990s and that the new immigrant share of California's population may finally have begun to decline somewhat, the impact on California—its society, economy and culture—of massive immigration over the past forty years has already been immense.[70]

International migration into California after 1970 rapidly transformed the state's ethnic makeup. In that year, more than three-fourths of California's population was of European ancestry, and only one-sixth was either Hispanic or Asian. Whereas almost half of the immigrants to California in the 1950s came from Canada and Europe, the number of such European-heritage immigrants after 1970 fell to less than 10 percent. The share coming from Mexico and Central America climbed to over half, and those entering from Asia more than doubled. Seventy-eight percent of the foreign-born population in California in 1990 came from Asia and Latin America, compared with 41 percent of immigrants to the rest of the country. Seventy-four percent of California's legally documented immigrants in 2001 came from eleven countries, all in Asia or Latin America. (The United Kingdom, the source of 1.4 percent of California's immigrants, ranked twelfth). The share of documented immigrants coming to California from Latin America and the Caribbean plus Asia rose to an estimated 87 percent by 2001. These regions were the sources of the bulk of unauthorized immigration as well.[71]

Within California, immigrants clustered mainly in the Los Angeles region, where Mexicans and Central Americans, many of them undocumented, predominated; the San Francisco Bay Area, where Asians were the majority; rural California, especially the Central Valley, where less-educated Latin Americans and Asians settled; and the San Diego region, mainly a destination for less-educated Mexicans, Filipinos and Vietnamese.

As a result of this immigration, California by the 1990s had an internationally linked, culturally and linguistically diverse population. The state clearly was gaining in many respects from the availability of relatively inexpensive and productive immigrant labor and from its contribution to agriculture, manufacturing and services. California was profiting from the high skills of certain immigrant groups, especially those from South Asia, Taiwan, Hong Kong and other parts of China, Iran, Israel, Russia and other parts of the former Soviet Union and from the entrepreneurial spirit of many immigrants and their development of commerce and small industry. The state was beginning to benefit, further, from the role of immigrants in connecting California to markets, capital and investment opportunities in their home countries.[72] Immigration was giving California competitive advantages in a globalizing world.

But California's very large immigrant population also posed difficult policy challenges. The relatively low levels of educational attainment and income of most immigrants—particularly those from Mexico, Central America, the Philippines and the rest of Southeast Asia—exacerbated social problems and threatened competitiveness. The presence of a large and vulnerable population in the labor pool threatened the job opportunities and earnings of similar undereducated native-born workers, especially African Americans. The relative youth of the immigrant population vastly expanded demand for public services, especially for kindergarten through twelfth-grade education and for emergency room health care.[73] More generally, the rapid influx of immigrants contributed to unsettling and divisive issues of identity and community.

Debates about the implications of and appropriate responses to massive immigration grew intense during the late 1980s and the 1990s in California, especially during the severe economic downturn of the early 1990s, which was exacerbated by the rapid decline of the aerospace sector at the Cold War's end. As in the earlier episodes with respect to Asia, so in the late 1980s and early 1990s with regard mainly to Mexico and Central America, anti-immigrant sentiment (particularly focused on unauthorized immigrants) became a significant ingredient in California's politics—and consequently a factor in the international relations of the United States.

This was especially true in 1994, when the California electorate approved Proposition 187, the "Save Our State Initiative," which mandated severely restricting social services to undocumented immigrants and their children. Incumbent Governor Pete Wilson's support for Proposition 187 contributed to his landslide reelection that year, but it also heightened identity politics in California, helped mobilize and politicize the state's Mexican-American population and produced frictions with neighboring Mexico. These tendencies were reinforced and exacerbated by the campaigns in 1996 to adopt Proposition 209, mandating an end to "affirmative action" programs and in 1998 to enact Proposition 227, banning bilingual education.[74] After a lull at the turn of the century, anti-immigration sentiment began to rise again during the first years of the new millennium, though not as sharply as in other regions of the United States where increasing immigration was becoming a new reality.

The Globalization of California's Economy

The second aspect of California's growing internationalization during these decades was economic. A combination of East Asia's and later South Asia's rapid economic growth, the general liberalization of international commerce and the structural transformation of California's economy—with an increasing emphasis on export of manufactured goods and services—all combined to globalize California's economy.

In the mid-twentieth century, California was primarily producing goods and services for its own growing market, for the western region and for the rest of the continental United States. During the 1970s and 1980s, it became increasingly connected (or, more accurately, reconnected) to the world economy, a trend that accelerated further in the 1990s. Exports through California's ports grew more than 1,000 percent from 1975 to 1999, from $10.3 billion to more than $120 billion. Imports increased 1,700 percent during the same period, from less than $12 billion to more than $200 billion. The Los Angeles Customs District, once a trade backwater, saw its total trade multiply from $6.2 billion in 1972 to $122 billion in 1992 and fully $200 billion by 1999. It further grew to $214 billion in 2002, $264 billion in 2004 and more than $300 billion in 2005.[75]

Exports from San Diego and from the San Francisco Bay Area boomed as well, with the Bay Area emerging in the 1990s, together with Seattle-Tacoma in Washington, as the country's most export-intensive region, thanks primarily to worldwide demand for high-tech products from Silicon Valley. Foreign investment in California climbed sharply after 1970, reaching $115 billion by 1999, as Japanese, Chinese and Korean investors joined the European and Canadian firms and individuals that had previously purchased assets in California. International tourism also took off during these decades, as California garnered a growing share of the flow of overseas visitors to the United States. Estimates of the annual income in California derived directly from foreign tourists rose to $6 billion by the mid-1990s, to $10 billion by the year 2000 and to nearly $13 billion in 2004. Income from international activity by California's service firms ineluctably followed all this activity; by the end of the 1990s, for example, the O'Melveny and Myers law firm had engagements in thirty-seven countries, including all the leading industrial nations, and many of the firm's large clients were now foreign-based.[76]

The importance of the international economy for California was strongly reinforced during the 1990s. Six factors accelerated California's enhanced integration into the world economy during that decade: (1) the need to reorient business as a result of the downsizing of the military-industrial sector following the end of the Cold War and then the implosion of the Soviet Union, (2) the swift and enormous growth in international markets for California's entertainment and communications technology products, (3) the rapid expansion of Asia's economies and their emergence as the most dynamic markets for U.S. exports generally, (4) the explosive growth of the maquiladora sector and integrated production operations in Mexico, (5) the development of the North American Free Trade Agreement with Canada and Mexico and (6) the rapid development of other production-sharing arrangements and the outsourcing of services, especially in Asia.

By the end of the 1990s and into the twenty-first century, California's economy, though still producing mainly for U.S. markets, was much more linked to and shaped by the international economy. In all the four leading sectors that were propelling the California economy—information and communications technology, entertainment, tourism and professional services (including legal, accounting, financial, engineering and architectural services)—international markets were both key and growing.[77] In many of these sectors, immigrant entrepreneurs took leading roles.

Global California had come into its own by the early twenty-first century. What was in the mid-twentieth century a somewhat parochial, inward-oriented state is now decidedly an international player. A state that fifty years earlier was populated almost entirely by migrants from the other continental American states has become once again highly diverse and cosmopolitan—with 27 percent of its population (and a still growing share) born in other countries and with fully half its population of Asian, African, Middle Eastern or Hispanic (or Latino) background. Despite the efforts to root out bilingual education and mandate only English as California's official language, the state's largest radio and television stations operate in Spanish, the most widely viewed television programs are in Spanish and California also has strong Asian, Russian and Middle Eastern media, churches and business sectors. By the early twenty-first century, there were 289 foreign-language publications in California, forty-nine in Los Angeles alone, as well as hundreds of foreign radio and television stations.[78]

An economy that in the 1950s was overwhelmingly oriented toward agriculture and manufacturing production, as well as the provision of services for local markets in California and other American states, now again increasingly depends on international trade—both exports to and imports from the rest of the world, especially Asia, Canada and Mexico—and on international investment. A state that was nearly self-sufficient in energy and isolated from world and even from national energy markets has become once more closely integrated with the world energy economy and significantly (and increasingly) dependent on international sources of oil and gas.[79] An educational system geared previously toward training native-born students for roles in the U.S. economy and society is facing the urgent challenge of integrating immigrant children from all over the world, as well as preparing all its graduates for roles in a globalizing world of international production, markets, labor and investment.

By the early twenty-first century, California is not only larger, more productive and more powerful than any other American state, but also more internationally linked—with Asia, Canada and Latin America, the Middle East, Europe and Africa.[80] It seemed unexceptional in 2003 that four of the five leading candidates for election as California's governor, debating on statewide television, spoke foreign-accented English, and that an Austrian-born candidate, Arnold Schwarzenegger, became governor. No other American state has such diverse and significant international demographic, economic and cultural ties.

Envisioning Global California

Self-awareness, discussion, and promotion of California's international interests and links—a common aspect of the state's public discourse in the nineteenth and early twentieth centuries, then somewhat dormant in the mid-twentieth century—revived in the final decades of the century. During the 1970s, 1980s and 1990s, California's governmental, political, civic, business, media and academic leaders increasingly came to recognize, or to rediscover, the state's global interests and vocation.

Governor Edmund G. "Pat" Brown, whose energetic leadership accelerated the growth of California's highway, water and educational infrastructures, was the first California chief executive to grasp the importance of international trade and tourism for California's growth. By the time Governor Brown left office in 1967, California had foreign offices in Tokyo and London and another about to open in Frankfurt in 1968, though all were closed in 1968 by his successor, Ronald Reagan, in line with Reagan's general bias against public-sector expansion.

Reagan's successor in 1976, Edmund G. "Jerry" Brown Jr., took a major interest in California's foreign commerce, opening the state's first Office of International Trade in 1977 in the new Department of Economic and Business Development (transformed in 1980 into the California Commerce Department, and in 1992 into the Technology, Trade and Commerce Agency). Brown traveled to Mexico, Canada, Japan and Great Britain to promote California's economic interests. He articulated, long before other prominent U.S. leaders, the vision of a North American common market with Canada and Mexico and promoted the idea of California as a "Pacific Republic." Former Governor Reagan, by then a presidential candidate, joined Jerry Brown in the mid-1970s in calling for a free trade agreement with Mexico, again long before the notion became fashionable in the Boston-New York-Washington corridor.

Jerry Brown's immediate successors in Sacramento, George Deukmejian and then Pete Wilson, expanded California's overseas trade offices and traveled abroad tirelessly on behalf of the state, though Deukmejian showed little interest in international affairs before his second term, and he reportedly had no passport until that time.[81] Lieutenant Governor Leo McCarthy, himself an immigrant from New Zealand, also took a leading role in proposing a comprehensive state trade policy, though few of his recommendations were implemented.[82]

California opened trade offices in Tokyo and London in 1987, in Mexico and Frankfurt in 1989 and in Hong Kong in 1990. By the end of the century, there were thirteen such offices on three continents. Governor Wilson led state trade missions to Mexico and to Asia. Almost immediately upon taking office, his successor, Gray Davis, made a high-profile visit to Mexico to improve California's overall relations with Mexico in the aftermath of the Proposition 187 controversy and then welcomed Mexico's President Ernesto Zedillo to California for a state visit within three months of his own trip.

Governor Davis also took the unprecedented step in 1999 of creating the position of secretary of foreign affairs of California, to facilitate the governor's international relations by working with embassies, consulates and foreign officials to ensure better ties between California and many nations and to provide some coherence to the state's diffuse international program. The first incumbent in that post, Michael Flores, estimates that California's governors have made an average of five official foreign trips per term and have received more than twenty foreign dignitaries per year, a practical illustration of Global California's ties.[83] Governor Arnold Schwarzenegger has kept up this pace, concentrating particularly on China and Japan but also visiting Mexico immediately upon being reelected in November 2006.

The California Legislature, too, took an increasing interest in international affairs. Assembly Speaker Willie Brown introduced AB 3757, establishing the California State World Trade Commission, a bill that Governor Jerry Brown signed into law in 1982.[84] In 1985 the assembly and the senate adopted resolutions on human rights in South Africa and on compensation to survivors of the internment of Japanese in California; the state senate approved resolutions addressing the treatment of Jews in the Soviet Union, the U.S. trade embargo of

Nicaragua, famine in Ethiopia, Salvadoran refugees, immigrants from Hong Kong and the status of Orthodox Christians in Turkey.[85] The California Senate created a Select Committee on the Pacific Rim in 1986 and a Committee on California-Mexico relations in 1989.

In 1987 the Senate's Rules Committee established the Senate Office on International Relations to help foster strong cultural and economic ties between nations and California. The office receives foreign officials and delegations on their visits to the senate and collaborates with many California organizations in programming visitors' stays. In 1991 the senate further established a non-profit entity, the California International Relations Foundation, to facilitate international exchange and the hosting of international visitors. This latter organization is still modestly active, among other areas, in facilitating the California Japan Scholars Program, established in 1996.[86]

At the turn of the century, under the leadership of Assembly Speaker Robert Hertzberg, further innovations were introduced. The assembly elected a standing subcommittee on international trade and development, and select committees on Asian trade, California and Latin American affairs and ports. The assembly speaker established an Office of Protocol and International Relations, hiring staff from the U.S. Department of State. Assembly and senate committees began a series of hearings on the implications, positive and adverse, of international trade agreements for California and explored ideas for the state's greater participation in creating those agreements.[87] As he finished his term as speaker in 2002, Representative Hertzberg reported that he had "witnessed the evolution of the day to day agenda of the Assembly from one dominated by parochial interests void [sic] of international considerations, toward a reorganization of California's role in global affairs . . . The traditional policy domains of education, health, consumer protection, privacy and public safety were being discussed with a growing recognition of their international significance."[88]

What was true in Sacramento was also reflected at the municipal level. Los Angeles Mayor Tom Bradley in the 1970s and 1980s developed a Global Los Angeles project, strongly emphasized international trade promotion and spearheaded the 1984 Olympics in L.A. as part of an emphasis on global relationships. His successor, Richard Riordan, also undertook considerable international initiatives, establishing a Trade Advisory Board in 1997, which was later revived, after some atrophy, by his successor, James Hahn. Hahn's successor, Mayor Antonio Villaraigosa, set up an office for international trade and talked repeatedly of L.A.'s role as a world capital; he made extended trade promotion visits to Asia and to Central America and Mexico and announced plans to visit Europe and Israel. As mayor of San Francisco in the 1980s, Dianne Feinstein traveled to Shanghai, Leningrad, Haifa and other cities to negotiate trade pacts and sister-city relationships. San Francisco created and staffed an international affairs office, and San Diego and San Jose established comparable units. All four cities—Los Angeles, San Francisco, San Diego and San Jose—also developed more active sister-city relationships in the 1980s and 1990s.

Focus on East Asia and Mexico

The increasing California interest in international relationships tended to focus mainly on Japan, China, Korea, Mexico and Canada and primarily on trade and investment. Commercial and financial links with Japan expanded rapidly in the 1980s as California manufacturing, agricultural and service firms sought larger Japanese markets and investment, while Japanese investors came to see California as a key window into the whole United States. Korean investors, too, brought more than a billion dollars into the California economy, largely in their own financial institutions and companies.

Growing trade with and investment opportunities in China became a principal focus of interest, as that country's rapid growth took off, investment opportunities blossomed and favorable trade arrangements were negotiated. In contrast to their counterparts on the Atlantic Coast, California business and political leaders tended to see China much more consistently in terms of opportunity rather than threat. When China's President Jiang Zemin visited the United States in the fall of 1997, he was snubbed in New York by Governor George Pataki and Mayor Rudolph Giuliani on human rights grounds, but was warmly greeted in Los Angeles by Governor Wilson, Mayor Riordan and a bipartisan group of business and other leaders.[89] California firms from many sectors have since then aggressively sought opportunities in China. Indeed, the San Francisco Bay Area has positioned itself in many ways as this country's main portal for exchange with China.

The other major focal point of California's international interest in the last years of the twentieth century was Mexico, which became by the end of the millennium the state's leading export destination as well as by far the largest source of its immigrants. California in the last three decades of the twentieth century vigorously reestablished its unique Mexico connection in many dimensions: people and money, food and music, culture, trade, immigration, politics and social policy.[90] Even as politically manipulated wedge issues—over immigration and social services, affirmative action and bilingual education— caused major frictions between the governments of California and Mexico, markets and migration continued to integrate the two societies on the ground. California exports to Mexico doubled between 1994 and 2000, from $7.7 billion to $15 billion. Proposition 187 and other adverse reactions to Mexican immigration did not reverse the increasing importance of Mexico and Mexicans to the California economy, society, culture and politics, as is discussed more extensively in Chapter 4.

Growing Interest in World Affairs

The growing significance of foreign markets and international relations for California spurred greater interest in world affairs in the media and academia. James Goldsborough, a veteran foreign correspondent then with the *San Jose Mercury News*, published a brief essay in *Foreign Affairs* in 1993 proposing a separate foreign policy for California, to be fashioned for the most part around Pacific Rim commerce.[91] The *Los Angeles Times*, the state's largest and most influential newspaper, significantly beefed up its international presence in the 1990s, especially in Asia and Latin America, and substantially augmented the space it devoted to international news, especially regarding Mexico and East Asia.[92] The *San Jose Mercury News* devoted a special Sunday section in 2000 to California's global links and challenges and added a daily section on business in Asia. The *San Diego Union-Tribune* expanded its coverage of Mexico and the *San Francisco Chronicle* recruited a former foreign correspondent to write a weekly column on Global California.

California's professionals generally became more aware of and better informed about international affairs. Expanded concern with global affairs was especially evident in the university world. The University of California at San Diego (UCSD) set up a major research center on U.S.-Mexican relations in 1979 and the privately endowed Institute of the Americas, to promote inter-American business expansion, in 1984. In 1986, UCSD opened a new Graduate School of Pacific Studies and International Relations, the first graduate program in the country explicitly focused on Pacific Rim issues; in 1999 the same university established a new research center on comparative immigration studies, concentrating largely on Latin America and Asia. International programs were also strongly reinforced at UCLA, UC Berkeley, Stanford and the University of Southern California (USC). UCLA established its Center for International Relations (later called the Burkle Center for International Relations) in the 1970s; USC began its Center for International Studies in 1986; Stanford founded its Institute of International Studies in 1987; and the University of San Francisco inaugurated a Center for Pacific Rim Studies in 1988. The equivalent centers and institutes at Yale, Princeton and Harvard had opened in 1935, 1951 and 1958, respectively.

The emphasis on international studies in California's major universities accelerated during the 1990s and the early twenty-first century. USC's president, Steven Sample, championed the creation of an elite Association of Pacific Rim Universities to foster intellectual exchange around the entire Pacific Rim and became the association's first president in 1997. USC's 1994 strategic plan and its subsequent updates have focused attention on international studies, the Pacific Rim and Latin America; the University's Marshall School of Business became the first business school in the United States to require most of its MBA students to have field experience abroad. The University of California system established a California House in London in 1999 and announced a second California House (Casa California) in Mexico in March 2001. In 2005 Stanford announced a major expansion and substantial new funding for its International Institute, renamed the Freeman-Spogli Institute for International Studies, as a cornerstone of the university's strategic plan for the early twenty-first century.[93] International studies are today being emphasized throughout California's world of higher education.

A group of West Coast business and professional leaders, mainly from Los Angeles, began to work together in 1993 to establish the Pacific Council on International Policy, which was incorporated in 1995 as an independent leadership forum based at USC, dedicated to advancing the international interests of California and the other western states.[94] The Pacific Council grew quickly, attracting a leadership network of some 1,200 members, building links with the New York Council on Foreign Relations and other Atlantic Coast foreign policy fora and undertaking distinctive studies on Mexico, Japan, Korea, China and India; transnational relations in North America; and globalization's impact on the major city-regions of the American West, especially in California.[95]

The Milken Institute, a research center founded and funded by international financier Michael Milken, began to conduct an annual Global Conference in Los Angeles, attracting many hundreds of participants, and to devote attention to international issues in its annual "State of the State" conferences. The Hoover Institution at Stanford devoted considerably increased attention to international affairs. The Public Policy Institute of California (PPIC)—the state's leading think tank, established in 1994 with a major endowment gift from William Hewlett, the cofounder of Hewlett-Packard—instituted in 1999 a "Global California" project of research monographs focused on California's relations with the world economy. The California Council for International Trade, an export promotion lobby group established in 1957, initiated in 1998 an annual conference on international trade, aimed at engaging members of California's congressional delegation.[96]

But Lack of a Global Mindset

An institutional infrastructure to serve Global California began to develop by fits and starts in the late twentieth century and in the first years of the twenty-first, but explicit discussion of California's international interests and how they might best be advanced remains notably sparse. California is deeply affected by global trends and is capable of exerting considerable world influence. Yet for all its power—and despite its global dimensions, links and stakes—California still lacks concepts, strategies and policies to understand and respond to its international challenges and opportunities. California has reverted to its original DNA as a profoundly international place, but Californians have not yet adopted a global mindset.[97]

This paradox was dramatically illustrated early in the new century as California dismantled the Technology, Trade, and Commerce Agency, including its international trade and investment promotion programs as well as all of its overseas offices. This was done, to be sure, in the context of a huge state budget crisis and in the face of press articles suggesting that the state's foreign offices were not productive or effective and that false claims were being made about their accomplishments.[98] But the fact is that after closing the Technology, Trade and Commerce Agency in 2003, California became the only state in the nation with no formal broad-based international trade and investment promotion program.[99]

California's turn inward in the early twenty-first century was not limited to the closing of the Trade and Commerce Agency and the overseas offices. The Public Policy Institute of California terminated its Global California research program in 2007. The *Los Angeles Times*, under new ownership, reduced its international coverage as part of a reduction in staff costs. The *San Diego Union-Tribune* significantly reduced its international coverage and confined its Dialogue section to topics within the state, dropping previous attempts to incorporate transborder issues. The binational San Diego Dialogue between San Diego and Tijuana has all but atrophied. California has been ironically diminishing its limited capacity to identify and promote its international interests just as the realities of globalization and its impacts are intensifying.

3 California's Regions in a Globalizing World

EACH OF THE MAJOR REGIONS of California—Los Angeles, the San Francisco Bay Area (including Oakland, San Jose and the Silicon Valley as well as the city of San Francisco itself), San Diego, Orange County, the Inland Empire and the Central Valley—has its own characteristics, including a distinct relationship with the world beyond the United States.[1] Some California regions depend significantly on international markets, investment, imports and/or human resources; others less so. Many receive substantial international migration, but the flows come from different regions, and the immigrants vary greatly in socioeconomic background, education and levels of literacy and other skills. The ties California's regions have are different in nature and intensity with East, South and Southeast Asia; Mexico, Central and South America; Canada; Europe; the Middle East; and Africa. These differences, combined with the absence of adequate concepts, processes and institutions to assess and respond to global developments and their impact, have made it difficult to grasp, let alone act on, California's strong interests on international matters.[2]

Los Angeles: America's Most Global City

Despite its notable efforts in recent years to develop a downtown center, Los Angeles remains a bustling and sprawling mélange of separate and remarkably diverse local communities—ninety suburbs in search of a center, in the familiar cliché, or perhaps more accurately, ninety islands in a loosely connected archipelago, composing a new kind of megametropolis. It is also a cardinal point on the international compass, a bridge to both Asia and Latin America, and in many ways America's most global city. It incorporates huge and growing numbers of foreign-born immigrants and generates worldwide visibility and influence.

One hundred foreign consulates are based in Los Angeles, more official international representatives than anywhere else in the United States other than Washington, D.C. and New York City.[3] More nonstop international flights a day arrive at or depart from Los Angeles International Airport (LAX) than any other airport in the United States except New York's John F. Kennedy International. Los Angeles is the center of world cinema and a global leader in television, music, fashion and design. And it is a major center of international trade, the main gateway between the United States and Asia and a key link with Mexico.

Los Angeles cannot be understood without taking into account its many ties beyond the borders of the United States, not only with Asia and Latin America, but also with Canada, Europe, the Middle East and Africa. The demography of Los Angeles has been shaped and reshaped from the start by migration, but this is especially so since the massive flows of international immigrants began in the late 1960s. The region's economy depends significantly and increasingly on international trade, services, investment and especially human resources: from Hollywood talent, scientists, engineers, doctors, nurses and pharmacists to domestics, gardeners, construction workers, janitors and restaurant personnel.

The society and politics of Los Angeles have for many years been forged in large part by international influences. L.A. has been dubbed the "capital of the Pacific Rim," the "capital of the 21st century," the "Venice of the 21st century" and the "capital of the Third World."[4] If none of these labels is quite right, all capture aspects of its special global qualities.

Demography

Nearly 10 million people reside in Los Angeles County, and some 17.5 million people live in the entire five-county Los Angeles metropolitan area, made up of Los Angeles, Orange, San Bernardino, Riverside and Ventura counties. The Los Angeles region includes eighteen different cities, L.A. itself the largest among them, with more than 150,000 inhabitants each.[5]

Los Angeles is not only the most populous of California's regions, but its population is the most diverse in origin. Although the number of native-born Californians leaving Los Angeles for other parts of California or elsewhere in the United States has been larger in the past twenty years than the number of native-born Americans moving in, L.A.'s population has continued to grow, mainly because of international immigration as well as high fertility rates among Latinos and some other immigrant groups. Since 1980 the five counties of greater Los Angeles have absorbed nearly 4.5 million immigrants. Some 41 percent of the residents of the city of Los Angeles and 36 percent of the residents of Los Angeles County were foreign-born at the time of the 2000 census, and more than 30 percent of the residents of the entire five-county region were born abroad.[6]

Although Los Angeles has been a city of immigrants ever since its origins, the enormous expansion of L.A.'s international immigrant population has been recent. One out of every six foreign-born residents in the entire United States today lives in Southern California. For the past twenty years, the "Anglo" (i.e., white, non-Hispanic) population of Los Angeles has remained about the same, whereas the Latino population has more than doubled and the Asian-origin population has tripled. Nearly two-thirds of L.A.'s residents are of first- or second-generation international immigrant origin. Except for the Mexican and Japanese diasporas, in all of the major immigrant groups in Los Angeles a majority are first-generation immigrants who have resided in the region for fifteen years or less.[7]

The city of Los Angeles alone is home to the world's seventh-largest population of persons of Mexican origin and by far the largest outside Mexico; all of Los Angeles County has the world's second-largest Mexican population.[8] L.A. has the largest concentration in the world of Koreans and Salvadorans outside their home countries. Diasporas of more than 100,000 from eleven different countries in Asia and Latin America reside in Southern California.[9] Los Angeles has the largest communities in the United States of ethnic Armenians, Cambodians, Filipinos, Guatemalans, Iranians and Thais, as well.[10]

Broadway, in downtown L.A., just a block or two from the headquarters of the *Los Angeles Times*, looks and sounds like part of Mexico. Traditional Chinatown and Monterey Park, Koreatown, Latino East Los Angeles, Glendale's Armenian community, Iranian neighborhoods in Beverly Hills and Santa Monica, little Ethiopia, little Saigon, Thai Town, little Phnom Penh and little Tokyo all vividly illustrate how international L.A.'s population has become.

The number of individual communities in Los Angeles with a majority Asian-origin population increased from one in 1990 to seven in 2000, for example.[11] More than 10,000 Sikhs parade through downtown Los Angeles each year to celebrate Baisakhi, a Sikh harvest holiday, and there are many other national celebrations during the year, of which Cinco de Mayo, the Mexican holiday, is the largest.[12]

Although much of the region's foreign-born population, like its longer-established residents, still largely clusters in separate geographic enclaves, it is important that workplaces, schools and entertainment sites bring people together from different backgrounds. Tensions among the diverse foreign-born groups—and between them and whites and especially African Americans, as between African Americans and whites—undeniably exist and have become more evident at times like the Rodney King civil disorders of 1992 or during the murder trial of O. J. Simpson, the African American sports icon.[13] But L.A. is undergoing, on the whole, a remarkable experiment in international and interethnic integration. The politics, business, media, culture and cuisine of Los Angeles have become strikingly multicultural. Although ethnic tensions persist and burst forth from time to time, a big everyday story in Los Angeles is of multiethnic coexistence and gradual, if uneven, integration.[14]

Immigrants have contributed to high employment growth in Los Angeles and have provided a competitive advantage to Southern California employers because of their strong work ethic. They have also contributed entrepreneurial ability and motivation to the development of small and midsize businesses in Southern California, the region's fastest-growing sector and increasingly the source of jobs, and they have played a major role in bolstering labor organizing.[15] Like other great capitals, past and present, Los Angeles attracts ambitious and talented people from around the world. To be sure, however, many immigrants from less-advantaged backgrounds, particularly from Mexico and Central America and from some Asian countries, also bring with them low levels of education and literacy. The troubling fact that Los Angeles County has the lowest level of literacy among working-age adults of any significant-sized city in the United States owes primarily to international immigration.[16] This presents a major challenge to the city's future.

Latinos (or Hispanics and Hispanic Americans) are L.A.'s biggest population group, having grown from 15 percent of the county's population in 1970 to 28 percent in 1980, 38 percent in 1990, nearly 45 percent in the year 2000, and more than 47 percent as of 2006; soon they will be an absolute majority.[17] Mexicans and Mexican Americans are by far the largest segment, but there are also hundreds of thousands of Central Americans and tens of thousands from South America and the Caribbean. Asians and Asian Americans account for another 13–14 percent of the population of Los Angeles County, with 1.35 million persons: immigrants from China (including Taiwan and Hong Kong), the Philippines, Korea, Japan, Vietnam, India, Cambodia, Thailand, Indonesia, Pakistan, Sri Lanka, Laos, Bangladesh, Malaysia, the Pacific Islands, Iran and the Middle East.[18] In a city that was overwhelmingly white and native-born in the 1950s, non-Hispanic whites are now only about 29 percent of the population, down from more than 80 percent in 1960 and from some 70 percent in 1970.[19] Between 1970 and 1990, the population of Los Angeles County increased by nearly 2 million, while its non-Hispanic white population decreased by almost 1 million.[20]

The new majority of people of color—Latinos, Asians and Asian Americans, those from the Middle East and African Americans—are quite diverse among themselves, but many share international connections and orientations not present to the same extent among native-born "Anglos." Many have family ties and economic and social relationships in their countries of origin. Remittances sent back home from Mexicans, Central Americans, Filipinos and other immigrants in Los Angeles amount to many billions of dollars annually; facilitating these transfers has become a major business for California banks and other financial intermediaries. Newspapers, radio and television stations, churches and community organizations, based both in immigrant communities and in the original local communities of origin, are woven into L.A.'s social fabric. Juvenile gangs in Los Angeles have offshoots, counterparts and transnational links in Central America and Mexico. So do churches, political movements and community-based organizations—in Mexico and Central America as well as in Asia.

Hundreds of local associations in Los Angeles tie immigrants to their places of origin, including some two hundred Mexican Hometown Associations. These groups contribute to economic development and welfare programs in their communities of origin, advocate for U.S. policies favorable to their home countries and oppose measures they regard as detrimental, promote the naturalization of immigrants and their participation in the U.S. political process and help identify and develop opportunities for investment and profit that strengthen the Los Angeles economy.[21]

Los Angeles is the national headquarters for some of the most influential immigrant-based organizations in the United States, including the Mexican American Legal Defense and Education Fund, the National Association of Latino Elected and Appointed Officials, the Mexican American Opportunity Foundation, Leadership Education for Asian Pacific Americans, the Korean American Coalition, the Asian Pacific American Legal Center, the Muslim American Public Affairs Council, the United Neighborhoods Organization and others.[22] Some of the most important immigrant-based media organizations are based in Los Angeles, including Univision, the fourth-largest television network in the United States; *La Opinion*, the country's oldest and largest Spanish-language newspaper; the *Korea Times*; the *Chinese Daily News-World Journal*; *Sing Tao Daily*; and other Asian media.[23] Iranian American television stations in Los Angeles have become important in Iran's politics, as they transmit back to Tehran stories and information about Iran not otherwise available in that country's own media.[24] Los Angeles is also the home to important ethnically linked think tanks, including the Tomás Rivera Policy Institute (on Latinos) and the Korean Studies Institute, both at the University of Southern California.

Immigrants to Los Angeles have become integrated relatively quickly into American society and politics. Members of the Asian and Middle Eastern diasporas "naturalize" (become U.S. citizens) early and at high rates; some 62 percent of foreign-born Asian immigrants in Los Angeles were naturalized as of 2006, and the number continues to rise. Although Mexican immigrants take longer to naturalize, the rate of naturalization has recently been accelerating; in 2001, the percentage of eligible Mexican immigrants naturalizing reached 34 percent and has continued to climb.[25] Many immigrants are increasingly active politically and, after naturalization, as voters.

Business, civic, labor, cultural and political leaders of an international immigrant background are increasingly influential in L.A.'s mainstream circles. Toy magnate Charles Woo, CEO of Megatoys, from Hong Kong, was chairman of the Los Angeles Area Chamber of Commerce in 2001; Dominic Ng, chairman, CEO, and president of East West Bank, also from Hong Kong, was chairman of the United Way campaign in 2000–2001. Four of the voting trustees of the University of Southern California are Asians, residing in Tokyo, Hong Kong, Mumbai and Seoul; and two are Mexican American, residing in California. The late Miguel Contreras, who died in 2005, was selected in 1996 to head the Los Angeles Federation of Labor as its secretary-treasurer, the first Latino serving at that level; he has been succeeded by his widow, Maria Elena Durazo, who previously led the activist Hotel and Restaurant Employees Union International. Another Latino, Jose Huizar, headed the L.A. Unified School District from July 2003 to June 2005 and then was elected to the Los Angeles City Council. Lee Baca serves as L.A. County sheriff, Rocky Delgadillo is L.A. city attorney and was a candidate for California attorney general in 2006 and Thomas Saenz is general counsel to the mayor of Los Angeles; all three are Latino. The incoming director of the Los Angeles Philharmonic Orchestra, Gustavo Dudamel, is Venezuelan; he replaces Esa-Pekka Salonen, a Finn. The director of the Los Angeles Opera, Plácido Domingo, was born in Madrid and raised in Mexico. The director of the J. Paul Getty Museum, Michael Brand, is from Australia, as is the dean of UCLA's Anderson School of Business, Judith Olian. The dean of USC's School of Architecture, Qingyun Ma, is from China. And so it goes in a thoroughly international metropolis.

Recent immigrants and their descendants have begun to reshape L.A.'s politics and public policy. Latinos and Asian Americans are registering and voting each year in larger numbers and beginning to exert political power. The election of Antonio Villaraigosa as mayor of Los Angeles in 2005, the first Latino mayor in L.A. since the nineteenth century, brought national and international attention to this trend, but Villaraigosa's triumph was by no means isolated or merely personal. Until the mid-1980s, no Latino had served on the L.A. City Council in a quarter of a century, nor on the more powerful County Board of Supervisors in a full century. As of mid-2008, five of the fifteen members of the L.A. City Council were Latino, as were one of the five county supervisors, seven members of the U.S. Congress from greater Los Angeles and six state senators and ten members of the California Assembly from the Los Angeles region. The former speaker, Fabian Nuñez, who served from 2004 to 2008, was the third Latino speaker of the assembly in a decade. Statewide, Latino politicians, many from the Los Angeles region, held 25 percent of the seats in the California State Senate and 23 percent in the California Assembly.[26] The state's lieutenant governor from 1999 to 2006, Cruz Bustamante, is also Latino. The mayor of Beverly Hills, elected in 2007, is an Iranian immigrant; and the two leading candidates for the Orange County Board of Supervisors in 2007 were both Vietnamese.

Unsuccessful candidates for mayor of Los Angeles in previous years included Michael Woo, a Chinese American, and Villaraigosa himself, who finished second in 2001. Asian American voters are said to have, in effect, determined the 2001 election, in which Latinos mostly supported Villaraigosa,

African Americans mostly supported James Hahn, Anglos split their support about evenly but Asian Americans put Hahn over the top.

The impact of growing Latino and Asian American participation and success in electoral politics is not limited to office-holding and opportunities for political careers; there are effects on policy, as well. Foreign-born Angelenos, especially Latinos and Asian Americans, provide significant support for greater investment in education, more liberal and accommodating immigration policies, affirmative action programs of various kinds and an inclusionary commitment to multiculturalism.[27] The character and quality of Los Angeles are thus being shaped by recent immigrants.

Economy

The five-county Los Angeles metropolitan region would rank, by itself, as the world's sixteenth-largest economy in 2005, with an estimated gross domestic product of more than $814 billion, just behind Mexico and ahead of the Netherlands.[28] The regional economy is highly diversified, and each of its most important sectors includes a strong international component.

First and foremost, Los Angeles is a major trade hub for exports and especially for goods entering the U.S. economy from abroad, both those destined for local use and those to be transshipped elsewhere in the United States. Since 1990 trade through the Los Angeles customs district has more than tripled, from $107 billion in 1990 to $264 billion in 2004, $293.9 billion in 2005, $329.4 billion in 2006 and $349.4 billion in 2007 (all in nominal dollars). In each year it was more than that of all other West Coast trade centers combined.[29] The L.A. customs district surpassed New York as the nation's largest in 1994 and has relinquished this top spot in only one year since.[30] Between 1972 and 2000, L.A.'s share of U.S. global merchandise trade climbed from 6 percent to 14 percent, while New York's share fell from 21 percent to 12 percent; the 2006 figures were 11.4 percent and 10.2 percent, respectively.[31] In 2000, upwards of one-quarter of the Southern California economy was estimated to depend on global trade, up from 13 percent in 1972.[32] As of 2006, an estimated 485,100 jobs in the five-county Los Angeles area were directly tied to international commerce, with perhaps three or four times that many indirectly dependent on global trade.[33]

The ports of Los Angeles and Long Beach together have the most container traffic in the United States—more than 14 million TEUs (twenty-foot equivalent units) in 2005, and more than 15 million TEUs in 2006—and together rank globally behind only Hong Kong, Singapore, Shanghai and Shenzhen.[34] Cargo volume at Los Angeles–Long Beach reached 210.4 million tons in 2006, more than six times larger than that handled by the second-busiest West Coast port, Tacoma, and more than three times that of Tacoma and Seattle combined.[35] The two Los Angeles seaports handled more than one-quarter of all U.S. water-borne trade value in 2004 and some 36 percent of all U.S. container traffic.[36] LAX was in 2006 the world's fifth-busiest passenger gateway and eleventh in the world in terms of air cargo handled. LAX is one of the country's largest international trade gateways, by shipment values.[37] It handles more than half, by value, of California's enormous air cargo and more than 11 percent of the entire nation's at a time when air freight plays an increasingly large role in world trade, particularly in the high-tech sector.[38]

Investments to improve L.A.'s trade infrastructure were pushed forward strongly from the 1960s through the 1980s, particularly during the term of Mayor Tom Bradley (1973–1993), who envisioned Los Angeles as the prime link to an increasingly dynamic Pacific Rim and championed "Project World City" as a centerpiece of his tenure. In the last five years of the twentieth century, trade infrastructure investment in Los Angeles amounted to $4.3 billion, more than in any other metropolitan region: a billion dollars more than in the San Francisco-Oakland complex, twice the expenditure during those years in New York-New Jersey and three times the amount invested then in Seattle-Tacoma.

In the next two decades trade through Los Angeles may expand even faster, partly as a result of the completion in 2002 of the Alameda Corridor inter-modal transportation project, which links the seaports and LAX with the main railway trunk lines moving goods east and southeast. Because of these and other improvements, particularly the Alameda Corridor East project, the Southern California Association of Governments predicted that the growth of freight volume in Los Angeles from 1995 to 2020 would reach 240 percent by rail, 197 percent by air and 65 percent by truck.[39]

To meet this growing demand, however, Los Angeles would have to further enhance the cargo and passenger capacity of its airports and seaports. That would require L.A. to overcome mounting opposition by local communities and environmentalists to the expansion of LAX, the development of significant alternative regional airports and major improvements to the San Pedro Bay seaports. As Steven Erie has shown, these "mega-projects, designed to enhance regional competitiveness in the global economy, became objects of intense debate and opposition regarding their regional benefits and costs; they were ground zero for escalating conflicts that pitted the forces of globalization and the economy against community and the environment."[40]

This issue is difficult to resolve because the international trade community in Los Angeles is highly diverse and inadequately organized, consisting mainly of small and midsize entrepreneurs, many of them not very well connected to the region's political structure.[41] In addition, the environmental costs of the seaports and of LAX are geographically concentrated, whereas the benefits are highly dispersed, far beyond the region, thus making it much easier to organize opponents than proponents of infrastructure development. The "NIMBY" (not in my backyard) syndrome threatens to block further expansion of trade.

The jury is still out as to whether Southern California can execute the major infrastructure projects it needs to remain the West Coast's principal trade portal for the long-term future. This challenge has been compounded, moreover, by the need for stringent counterterrorism measures in the post-9/11 environment. A major and expensive reconfiguration of LAX is likely required, in part because the airport is considered one of the nation's prime and most vulnerable targets for terrorism. Specific proposals have encountered stout resistance from those likely to be adversely affected in an immediate way. Highly complex and demanding security measures are also required in the San Pedro Bay seaports.[42]

With the sharp decline of the aerospace and other defense-related industries in the late 1980s and early 1990s, the Los Angeles economy rebounded not only around foreign trade, but also around entertainment, including sports; tourism; business and health services; design, textiles and apparel; engineering, architectural, legal, financial and other services; as well as manufacturing, particularly of electronic goods, transportation equipment, chemical products, textiles, toys, cosmetics and furniture. In 1972, there were nearly two jobs in the aircraft, space and defense sector for every job in tourism and entertainment in Los Angeles. By 2001, there were twice as many jobs in tourism and entertainment as in aircraft, space and defense and three times as many jobs handling the region's foreign trade.[43] Los Angeles has become the country's fourth-largest cruise-line port, for example; the first three are all in Florida.

Los Angeles is the center of the world's entertainment industry, including cinema, television, music, multimedia, sports and theme parks. The industry predominance that Hollywood established early in the twentieth century and consolidated in the years after World War II was strongly reinforced during the 1990s as employment, production and profit all boomed in motion pictures, television, music and multimedia entertainment.[44] Some 80 percent of all U.S.-made feature films and television programs are made in California, mostly in Los Angeles. In addition to the large established studios (Disney, Sony, Fox, MGM, Universal, Paramount, Dreamworks-SKG and Warner Bros.), a great number of small and midsize enterprises have grown to serve the entertainment sector within a regional collaborative structure that draws on independent contractors, freelance artists, craftspeople and technicians in ever-changing combinations. Foreign markets, international investment and immigrant talent and labor are all central to this innovative and fast-changing business. Film and tape rental exports alone rose from $1.9 billion in 1991 to $9.3 billion in 2001, and Hollywood today relies more than ever on foreign box-office receipts and other exports.[45] International policy issues are key in this sector: competing with Canada and other sites of less-expensive production; securing international protection of intellectual property; countering restrictions on the use of non-national content in various markets; and overcoming political, social and cultural barriers to the export of films, television programs and music.

Los Angeles is one of the sports capitals of the world. It has two professional baseball teams (the Los Angeles Dodgers and the Los Angeles Angels of Anaheim); two professional men's basketball teams (the Lakers and the Clippers), and one women's team (the Sparks); two professional hockey teams (the Anaheim Ducks and the Los Angeles Kings); two professional soccer teams (Galaxy and Chivas USA); two of the country's perennial champion college football teams (USC and UCLA); UCLA's nationally ranked basketball teams; and two leading horserace tracks (Santa Anita and Hollywood Park). Los Angeles currently lacks a professional football franchise, but proposals to attract one again will almost certainly eventually succeed. All these sports have strong international connections: the talent is frequently from other countries and the fans are often immigrants.[46] When one of L.A.'s soccer teams plays a match against an international visitor, few in the crowd of 100,000 or more cheer in English.

Tourism, another mainstay of the contemporary Los Angeles economy, also has very important international aspects. Although 90 percent of tourism in the Los Angeles area is by people living elsewhere in the United States, the absolute numbers and relative share of international tourists, especially from Asia, Canada and Mexico but also importantly from the United Kingdom and other European countries, have both expanded significantly in recent years. International visitors contribute greatly to the region's economy, as they stay longer and spend more than local tourists; they are estimated to have spent $3.8

billion in Los Angeles County alone in 2005.[47] Tourism represents a major growth potential, particularly as Los Angeles develops new cultural facilities (such as the J. Paul Getty Museum, the expanded Los Angeles County Museum of Art and Walt Disney Concert Hall) and other attractions, including the new Roman Catholic Cathedral—and as increasing numbers of Chinese devote growing disposable income to international travel.

Los Angeles is also an important center for clothing design, the largest U.S. site for the manufacture of apparel, the nation's main locus for automobile design, a major place for the manufacture of electronic components and transportation equipment and the national leader in the toy industry. In the late 1990s, when manufacturing employment was falling nationwide, jobs in the manufacturing sector increased in the Los Angeles region. For all of L.A.'s manufacturing sectors, international markets are increasingly important. In many the entrepreneurial leaders as well as both skilled and unskilled labor are predominantly immigrants. In the apparel sector, for example, immigrants from Latin America and Asia, Korea especially, drive the region's industry—the country's largest—and Israelis are prominent in clothing design.[48]

In all these sectors—entertainment, textiles, tourism, technology, toys, trade infrastructure and logistics, finance and other services—international investment is important. Capital from China (including Hong Kong and Taiwan), Japan, Korea, the Philippines, Mexico, Canada and Europe is a significant component of L.A.'s growth.

Another important global link for Los Angeles is forged by students. In the 2005–2006 academic year, some 34,700 foreign students attended colleges and universities in the five-county Los Angeles region. This region alone has more international students than any state but New York and Texas and contributes almost half of California's total of some 75,000 foreign students, the nation's highest concentration.[49] These students are a major source of income—some $980 million, according to estimates—for Los Angeles educational institutions and for spending in the region's economy.[50] In a number of cases, they are "parachute" children, sent to the United States to establish a family business beachhead in this country as a means of insurance against home country difficulties. They also establish ties that facilitate current and future relations with the sending countries: in business, the media, government and the nongovernment sector. Some of them return to their home countries, bringing back know-how, intellectual property and capital, and creating a basis for expanded international trade.

L.A.'s future, in sum, will be very strongly influenced by international trends and by the region's capacity to manage their consequences.[51] In Los Angeles the mayor and other local officials, the superintendent of schools and other educators from kindergartens to universities, police officers, labor union leaders, executives of movie and television studios as well as the new Internet-based media, those in engineering and law firms, textile and toy manufacturers, doctors and hospital administrators, media leaders, clergy and political consultants: all have their work, challenges and opportunities structured in large part by international forces.

If all politics is local, the local is every year more transnational in contemporary Los Angeles. And if business is increasingly global, nowhere is this more evident than in L.A.—where trade is so important, and so much of the economy depends on international resources, markets, capital and labor.

Sharply contending visions of Los Angeles—the edge city; the post-metropolitan repressive, socially and racially divided dystopia; the fractal and carceral city; the multicultural heteropolis; a world city; the emerging high-tech universal city; and what Arnold Toynbee once called an "ecunemopolis"—all emphasize the central importance of immigration, international trade and other global connections for shaping Los Angeles. Commentators attribute different valences to the international insertion of Los Angeles, but all recognize that in L.A., global trends are central.[52]

The future of Los Angeles depends significantly on reinforcing the gains and mitigating the costs and risks of globalization.[53] Poverty, illiteracy and generally substandard educational performance, ethnic conflict, health issues, pollution, congestion, and gangs and crime are all closely related to the impacts of international flows on Los Angeles. But so are many of the best opportunities for Los Angeles in economic, commercial, political and cultural terms. Any viable strategy for L.A.'s future must take into account and respond to global forces and their local consequences, but this need is rarely, if ever, a focal point of in-depth political or policy discussion.[54] In the era of globalization, however, Los Angeles simply cannot afford to remain provincial.

The San Francisco Bay Area: Changing Realities

If Los Angeles is today America's most global city-region, the San Francisco Bay Area is certainly not far behind. The Bay Area is a much more traditional metropolitan region than Los Angeles, but like L.A., its population is international, its economy is globally integrated and significant worldwide, its fortunes are profoundly affected by international events and trends and its profile and impact abroad are great. The city of San Francisco and nearby Silicon Valley are themselves world capitals with stakes and links in many parts of the globe, especially in East and South Asia, and they contribute a great deal to making California in many ways the country's most internationally engaged state.

The San Francisco Bay Area comprises four main subregions: the city of San Francisco itself; the South Bay, including San Jose and Silicon Valley; the East Bay, including Oakland; and the North Bay, including the wine country. Each of these subregions is somewhat different in economic structure, demography, international relationships and overall character. The city of San Francisco remains the cultural, financial and professional services center; the South Bay is the largest population, economic and high-tech center; the East Bay combines heavy industry and the port of Oakland with growing knowledge-based industries; and the North Bay is mainly rural and agricultural but also now includes expanding suburbs and a burgeoning telecommunications sector. The four subregions are self-consciously connected and closely enough linked to treat them for some purposes as one large region: the country's fifth-biggest metropolitan area, with a total population of about 6.9 million in 2006.[55]

Consciousness of the importance of international links and relationships has been part of San Francisco's character ever since the 1849 gold rush. Japan opened a consulate in San Francisco in 1872, and the Japan Society of Northern California, still one of the strongest such organizations in the United States, was established in 1905, with the participation from the very start of members of San Francisco's elite. Relations with China were also cultivated by San Francisco's leaders from the late nineteenth century on, despite the friction over immigration. The 1915 Panama Pacific International Exposition in San Francisco left as a legacy not only the beautiful Palace of Fine Arts but also the Pan American Society of California, focusing on relations with Latin America.

San Francisco leaders lobbied to host the discussions leading to the formation of the United Nations in 1945 in the city's War Memorial Opera House, and San Francisco also provided the venue for the negotiation of the Japan-U.S. Mutual Security Treaty in 1951. The World Affairs Council of Northern California, founded in 1947, has for decades been one of the country's most successful such organizations, reflecting and contributing to the international orientation of the Bay Area's elite.

Chevron, Bechtel, and Levi Strauss—leading San Francisco area corporations since the 1960s—have all been visibly internationally minded, as was Bank of America, another major San Francisco-based institution until its merger and the movement of its corporate headquarters to North Carolina. UC Berkeley and Stanford rank among the nation's leaders in international and area studies, both of them with particular strength on both East Asia and Latin America. And several other universities, notably the University of San Francisco, also emphasize international studies. The city hosts a world-class Asian Arts Museum, with the largest collection of Chinese art outside greater China; the Asia Foundation, a leading nongovernmental organization with substantial U.S. government support; and numerous international business and cultural associations. Nearly seventy countries have consulates in the San Francisco Bay Area: some in San Francisco, others in San Jose or elsewhere in Silicon Valley.

The most dynamic city of California and indeed of the whole western United States in the late nineteenth and early twentieth centuries, San Francisco saw its relative stature decline in the second half of the twentieth century, when Los Angeles outpaced it as a population center, port and manufacturing region. A major proposal right after World War II to establish a world-class international trade promotion facility in San Francisco foundered and could not be fully implemented, as the city could not muster the necessary resources.[56] Hopes to build a thirty-story World Trade Center twenty years later were similarly dashed when the state legislature rejected funding for the project.[57]

By the 1970s, although suffering something of an economic decline relative not only to Southern California but also to its neighbors in the South and East Bay, San Francisco was emerging once again as a global urban center. The city not only boasted the cultural infrastructure of its prime, remaining an intellectual and professional oasis and a prime tourist attraction; it also took its place as a major West Coast financial and services center. Over the past thirty years, and especially during the 1990s, the Bay Area surged again in economic vitality, primarily due to venture capital investment in high-technology companies. Together with Seattle-Tacoma (home of Microsoft), the San Francisco Bay Area in the late 1990s became one of the most export-intensive regions in the United States. Although the bursting of the dot-com bubble in the spring of 2000 and subsequent softness in the computer sector slowed the region's growth somewhat, the Bay Area economy is still economically potent and diversified. It is also a national center of "progressive" politics, fusing liberalism, environmentalism and pluralism.[58]

The region's competitive advantages, particularly for knowledge-based industries, remain strong. The Bay Area is less important than Southern California as a media capital and entertainment center, but it has a very significant film industry (including Pixar, Lucasfilm Ltd. and beginning in 2008, Image Movers Digital); some predict it will become the third center of film production in the world.[59] The Bay Area is also one of the most "wired" regions in the United States, with a large online, broadband telecommunications capacity and a large number of commercial Internet domain names.[60] In 2004, Intel's "Most Unwired Cities" survey gave the Bay Area top national ranking in facilitation of wireless Internet access.[61]

The population of the San Francisco Bay Area, like that of the Los Angeles region, is highly connected internationally but with considerably differing emphases. The Bay Area has a large foreign-born population, which has grown from 14 percent of the region's population in 1980 to about 30 percent of the region's population in 2006, the second-highest percentage in the state, after Los Angeles.[62] The largest number of foreign-born residents in the Bay Area, however, are from Asia, not from Mexico and Central America. From 1984 through 2005, the San Francisco Bay Area took in some 869,000 legal immigrants, 25 percent of the state's total, with more than half the state's total from China, India and several Southeast Asian countries.[63] The demographic profile of the Bay Area has changed dramatically since 1980, when its population was counted as 69 percent non-Hispanic white, 12 percent Latino and 9 percent Asian; in the year 2006, the estimates were 46 percent, 22 percent and 22 percent respectively, with an increasing number of immigrants from the Middle East as well.[64] In the city of San Francisco itself, about one out of three residents by the year 2000 were Asian or Asian American, and by 2017 the city is projected to become the first major city in the nation to have an Asian American majority.[65]

The Bay Area is deeply involved in international trade, but less as an import center, transportation hub and transshipment node than as a point of export for high-technology goods and a base for international financial, architectural, engineering and other services. During the 1990s, trade in the San Francisco Bay Area increased by an average of 9.5 percent annually, largely due to Silicon Valley's commerce with Asia. The entire San Francisco Bay Area (including San Francisco, San Jose and Oakland) ranks as the second-largest exporting region in the United States by dollar value, after the New York-New Jersey metropolitan area. The San Jose metropolitan area alone exports more goods than do forty-five of the fifty U.S. states, and Bay Area exports as a whole are larger than those of all U.S. states except Texas and California itself. In 2004 some 46 percent of the Bay Area's exports went to Asia, 22.5 percent to Europe, 24 percent to NAFTA partners Canada and Mexico and less than 10 percent to the rest of the world.[66]

International exports are particularly vital for the Bay Area's strong information technology and biotech sectors. Early in the twenty-first century, international markets accounted for more than 75 percent of all semiconductor equipment sales.[67] The Semiconductor Industry Association projected that by 2007 only 17 percent of such sales would occur in the Americas.[68] International sales in 2006 produced 83 percent of the total revenue at Applied Materials, 61 percent at Advanced Micro Devices, 65 percent at Intel, about two-thirds at Agilent, over 65 percent at Hewlett-Packard and 57 percent at Sun Microsystems.[69] International markets account for a similar share of revenues for such Bay Area–based biotechnology firms as Chiron Corporation, Bio-Rad Laboratories and Gilead Science.

International markets are also crucial for the Bay Area's major apparel firms, Levi Strauss and The Gap; pharmaceutical leader McKesson Corporation and energy giant Chevron Texaco; the region's huge food and wine industry; Bechtel, the large engineering firm; and American President Lines, a maritime transport company largely focused on Asia and Latin America. Wells Fargo, Visa International, Charles Schwab and other financial services firms also have huge international business, as do a number of other companies providing legal, accounting, architectural, design, engineering and educational services. Bay Area architecture and urban planning firms are internationally prominent, with major signature projects in China, for example. Nearly 23,000 foreign students matriculated in Bay Area postsecondary institutions in 2005–2006, injecting some $682 million into the region's economy.[70]

Like Los Angeles, the San Francisco Bay Area has built a substantial infrastructure to facilitate international trade, and like Los Angeles it faces major challenges and severe constraints in keeping up with what is needed, especially in the post-9/11 environment. San Francisco Airport (SFO) serves thirty overseas destinations with nonstop service and thirty-six more with one-stop service, scheduling some 425 nonstop and 135 one-stop international flights weekly.[71] The opening of SFO's international passenger terminal in December 2000 greatly expanded the airport's capacity, but SFO is still sharply limited by inadequate runway capacity. San Jose International Airport and Oakland International Airport have both greatly enlarged their customs and cargo facilities, but troubling bottlenecks remain.

The port of Oakland, the fourth-largest container facility in the United States, undertook a $2 billion capital improvement program in the late 1990s to increase its capacity and efficiency. A joint international terminal, designated the Oakland International Gateway, opened in the spring of 2002 with a state-of-the-art transfer facility to permit containers to be moved more efficiently between shipping lines and transcontinental railroads. By 2005, Oakland's port was the fastest-growing maritime facility on the West Coast, with an increase of some 20 percent in a year in the number of imported containers moving through as the shipping industry reacted both to congestion in Southern California and to Oakland's improved facilities.[72] A major Oakland Harbor navigation project, scheduled to be completed in June 2009, is critical, however, for the Port of Oakland's ability to continue improving its competitiveness as a major shipping center; parts of the plan for port improvement have faced strenuous opposition from environmental groups and other local interests. Port security concerns have compounded these problems.

Many Bay Area companies depend on U.S. federal policies to advance their interests by facilitating exports, encouraging or reducing tariffs and other trade barriers, specifying accepted international labor standards and especially by making possible the entry into the United States of immigrant professionals and highly skilled personnel.

The importance of South Asian, Taiwanese, and other Asian engineers and technical personnel for the high-tech electronics, computer, telecommunications, biogenetic and biotech enterprises from the San Francisco Bay Area can hardly be exaggerated. Perhaps more than any other region of the United States, Silicon Valley firms (and Bay Area firms more generally) have had a vital interest in protecting and expanding the H-1B visa program (to make it relatively easy for technical personnel to enter the United States and hold jobs here) and in finding ways to facilitate the continuing inflow of highly qualified technical personnel and graduate students, despite tightened security pressures and their impact on immigration.[73]

The San Francisco Bay region and especially Silicon Valley have a unique set of international connections stemming from the large and increasing role of Chinese and South Asian immigrant entrepreneurs in the Valley, where more than one-third of the technology start-ups have been launched by immigrant entrepreneurs. These highly educated and technologically adept immigrant entrepreneurs are attracted to the Bay Area, and particularly to Silicon Valley, by its educational and economic opportunities and by its open and internationally diverse social climate. The Valley's lack of a strong and rigid preexisting social structure has been an asset for the open, communicative, innovative and international high-tech culture.[74]

Immigrant networks are playing an important role in circulating information, ideas, entrepreneurship and know-how back to their countries of origin. Asian entrepreneurs, many of them educated in Bay Area universities, have invested capital raised in the United States back in their home countries, creating and strengthening cross-border economic, business, commerce and social ties between Silicon Valley and growing high-tech sectors abroad. Many of them, the so-called argonauts, travel frequently between California and their home countries and maintain homes in each site, often cooperating with "sea turtles," that is, U.S.-educated professionals residing in China. The Indo-U.S. Entrepreneurs (TiE), the Monte Jade Science and Technology Association (founded by Taiwanese), the Hua Yuan Science and Technology Association, Hong Kong-SV.com, the California Asia Business Council and other formal and informal networking groups involving Chinese, South Asians, Koreans, Vietnamese, Iranians and others have all become important transnational organizations, linking northern California tightly to Asia.[75] What had once been considered a brain drain from Asian countries to the United States is better understood as a complex, multidirectional "brain-circulation."[76]

As in Los Angeles, the San Francisco Bay Area has seen its politics and governance reshaped by globalization and immigration. Latino politicians are not as prominent or successful in the Bay Area as their counterparts in the Los Angeles area, but Asian Americans have made strong inroads. Norman Mineta, a Japanese American, became the first Asian American mayor of a major city in the United States when he was elected mayor of San Jose in 1971; he went on to serve in the U.S. Congress from 1975 to 1995, and then as secretary of Transportation from 2001 to 2006. Robert Matsui, another Japanese American, served in Congress from 1978 until his death in 2005.[77] Frank Ogawa, also Japanese American, served twenty-eight years on the Oakland City Council. March Fong Eu, a Chinese American, rose through the ranks of local and state politics from the Alameda County Board of Education in the 1950s to the California Assembly and then to the post of California Secretary of State from 1974 to 1994. Her son, Matthew Fong, served as California state treasurer from 1995 to 1998 and was then the (unsuccessful) Republican candidate for the U.S. Senate in 1998.[78] Michael Chang, mayor of Cupertino until 2003, reflected the growing numbers and prominence of ethnic Chinese in that Silicon Valley city. Madison Nguyen, an immigrant from Vietnam, became the first Vietnamese American to serve on the San Jose City Council when she was elected in 2005.

Other recent Asian American political leaders from Northern California include Harry Low, a longtime judge and then state insurance commissioner; Wilma Chan, a California Assembly representative from Oakland who served as majority leader of the assembly from 2002 to 2004; Leland Yee, an assembly member from San Francisco; and Dennis Hayashi, former director of the California Department of Fair Employment and Housing and now a superior court judge.

Latino leaders in Northern California, though fewer thus far than in Southern California, include Ron Gonzales, former mayor of San Jose; Matt Gonzalez, former Green Party candidate for mayor of San Francisco who was president of the San Francisco Board of Supervisors until 2005; Sal Torres, a Mexican immigrant who was until recently mayor of Daly City, just south of San Francisco; and Ignacio de la Fuente, another Mexican immigrant, who became president of Oakland's City Council and was a candidate for mayor there in 2006.

In short, the San Francisco Bay Area has been greatly affected by its international ties and has a great deal at stake in the international arena. The links between the San Francisco Bay Area and China are particularly dense and significant, helping the region act as the premier U.S. portal for U.S.-China exchange.

A great deal of the growth and extraordinary prosperity of Silicon Valley and of the entire San Francisco Bay Area owes to the region's global reach and connections.[79] By the same token, however, some of the Bay Area's biggest challenges—highly uneven educational achievement, gross income disparities, growing drug trade and crime, housing shortages and infrastructure limits and particularly the trend toward outsourcing (or "offshoring") of both semiskilled jobs and engineering and technical work, especially to South Asia, are themselves strongly linked to global drivers and demands.[80] The region's recovery from the dot-com technology bust has to a significant extent been conditioned by the health of the international economy and remains dependent on sustained export expansion. And improvement in the governance and public policies of the San Francisco Bay Area will significantly depend on building transethnic cooperation in the region.

If the San Francisco Bay Area is to stay at "the head of the class," as Sarah Bachman has argued, it will have to succeed in fashioning and implementing a global strategy to manage the impacts of globalization as well as the region's myriad international relationships. Long attractively cosmopolitan in style and attitudes, the San Francisco Bay Area needs to become much more truly global in substance, strategy and outlook.[81]

San Diego: Lagging but Accelerating Globalization

San Diego, California's third large metropolitan region, appears on the map as a natural international gateway, situated both on the border between the United States and Mexico (and the rest of Latin America beyond) and on America's Pacific coast, facing Asia.[82]

In some senses, San Diego has always been internationally oriented: with intimate if complicated ties to neighboring Tijuana and Baja California; as a major port and base for the U.S. Navy and the Marines for more than sixty years; and with an economy largely built from the early decades of the twentieth century into the 1990s around military and naval facilities and contracts. Even after the very substantial post–Cold War downsizing of the Defense Department, San Diego is still home port for sixty-nine U.S. Navy ships and for more than 100,000 active-duty Navy and Marine personnel, and the Defense Department employs another 22,500 civilians in San Diego.[83] San Diego continues to garner many billions of dollars in defense procurement contracts. The defense establishment provides major research support for the region's universities and institutes, particularly for UC San Diego (UCSD), recognized by the National Research Council as one of the country's top ten research universities. Some 9–10 percent of the workforce in San Diego County still works on Defense Department-related matters.[84]

Military internationalism remains even today a defining feature of San Diego's reality; defense-related spending accounts for an estimated 15 percent of San Diego County's gross regional product.[85] But despite its border location, San Diego, paradoxically, has been less fully integrated than Los Angeles or the Bay Area into the world economy and international commerce, and it has also been less affected by international migration than either. One estimate in the late 1990s, for example, suggested that exports (manufacturing and services) accounted for no more than 8–10 percent of the San Diego regional economy, compared with 15 percent in the Los Angeles region and 25 percent in the San Francisco Bay Area.[86]

Until the early 1990s, San Diego's "international openness," measured by the ratio of exports to population, was at about the same level as the rest of the entire United States but substantially below that of California as a whole.[87] The San Diego economy was mainly organized around defense production, tourism, real estate and construction; none of these sectors have been primarily oriented historically toward international investment or exports.[88] A thriving fishing industry decades ago was quite international, but that has long since faded away.[89]

Two main developments in the 1990s internationalized the San Diego regional economy. Telecommunications giant Qualcomm spearheaded the rapid expansion of the high-tech industry, including other communications and electronics manufacturers as well as the fast-growing biomedical and biotechnical sectors. The leading segments of the San Diego private-sector economy during the past decade have all been knowledge based, high tech, internationally oriented and export dependent. In the late 1990s, San Diego numbered eighth in the nation (out of hundreds of regions) in securing utility patents, an indicator that technological innovation was driving the economy forward.[90] Indeed, San Diego has the third-largest concentration of telecommunications and biotechnology workers in the country.[91] During the 1990s, international exports from San Diego County doubled, with exports of electric and electronic equipment increasing more than 200 percent.[92] Although San Diego's share of California's total foreign trade remained modest compared with that of Los Angeles and the San Francisco Bay Area, foreign trade in the San Diego customs district grew faster in the mid-1990s than in any other California region (by 76 percent from 1994 through 1997).[93]

San Diego's economy was also becoming more globally integrated in the late 1990s because of NAFTA, which strongly reinforced the already-existing trend to link U.S.-based firms with production facilities just across the border. The *maquiladora* factories in Mexico, assembling items primarily for the U.S. market, employ Mexican workers at rates above prevailing local wages and are regulated by Mexican environmental and labor legislation, not by the more demanding U.S. standards. Tijuana has become a major world center for the manufacture and assembly of television sets and a major site for the manufacture of other consumer electronic products.

The rapid success of NAFTA in vertically integrating multinational production for the U.S. market, drawing on the maquiladoras, quickly expanded San Diego's trade figures, though the statistics tend to exaggerate the flows and particularly to exaggerate San Diego's role, in that they record as San Diego "exports" goods that simply pass through the region from elsewhere in the United States in order to be finished in Mexico and are then reimported to elsewhere in the United States. The actual manufacturing links between San Diego and Baja California are weaker than commonly assumed, because the maquiladoras often circumvent San Diego, obtaining their inputs elsewhere (often through Los Angeles) and distributing their products directly through channels in L.A., San Francisco, Texas or other places. The production and distribution patterns are not primarily determined by proximity but rather by corporate structures and market relationships. Commerce across the border at San Diego is restricted by severe infrastructure bottlenecks (in particular, insufficient cargo transportation facilities and a highly inadequate airport), as well as by cumbersome border-control complications. These problems were heightened after 9/11, when slowdowns in border traffic disrupted commerce significantly, causing severe dislocations. Although some immediate post-9/11 issues have been resolved, San Diego continues to face the tough problem that substantially augmented border security and immigration-control measures tend to conflict with economic openness.[94]

But even if San Diego has not been as closely integrated economically with neighboring Tijuana and Baja California as location alone might suggest, the San Diego region has certainly been greatly affected by the move of hundreds of production facilities from the United States and also from Asia and Europe to the Mexican side of the border. One major impact is the flow of Mexicans from Baja California into the San Diego region to work, shop, consume and vacation. The single most-traveled border crossing for people along any U.S. border is the San Ysidro Port of Entry, and it is complemented by Otay Mesa eight miles away; the two crossing points handled some 56 million individuals in 2005—nearly one-fifth of all U.S. border crossings.[95]

Demographically, San Diego has been transformed during the past thirty years by globalization and immigration, but in somewhat different ways and with somewhat distinct consequences from the patterns in Los Angeles and the San Francisco Bay Area. The Latino population of San Diego grew from 15 percent in 1970 to 20 percent in 1990 and 27 percent in 2000 and continues to increase. The Asian-origin population grew from 6 percent in 1970 to 8 percent in 1990 and about 10 percent in 2000, whereas the non-Hispanic white population declined steadily from 87 percent in 1980 to 55 percent in 2000 and is projected to be 51 percent in 2020.[96] San Diego's school system is fundamentally shaped by the challenge of integrating a largely Mexican-born student population, together with other immigrant children speaking nearly forty different languages.

San Diego's international character and global links are still substantially less developed than those of Los Angeles and the San Francisco Bay Area, however. San Diego's Latino population has much less organizational capacity and political clout than its counterpart in Los Angeles. Mexican and Latin American immigrants to the San Diego area have been slower to naturalize, to transform from sojourners to settlers and to exert political influence. Of San Diego's seventeen federal and state legislators in 2007—five members of Congress, two U.S. senators, three state senators and five members of the assembly—only three were of Hispanic background.[97] San Diego's Asian American population is predominantly Filipino and Vietnamese, rather than Chinese, Japanese or Korean, as in San Francisco and Los Angeles, and is much less connected to business and commercial activities in Asia than its San Francisco, Silicon Valley or Los Angeles counterparts.

Despite its location, San Diego has lagged behind Los Angeles and the San Francisco Bay Area and their pace of globally driven economic integration and demographic transformation. There are hardly any international banks in San Diego, for example, and much less civic infrastructure for global engagement than in Los Angeles or the Bay Area. The Institute for the Americas and the Graduate School of Pacific Rim and International Relations at UC San Diego find themselves with few strong local partners.

Globalization has been accelerating and its consequences multiplying, however, and awareness of the region's international policy challenge is consequently rising. Leaders in San Diego increasingly understand that the region must connect more effectively with Baja California's stunning economic growth and its growing ties to multinational corporations, particularly Asian firms. They recognize that San Diego and Baja California are linked by the dynamics of labor markets; the pattern of environmental pollution; drug-trafficking networks and small-arms exporters; auto theft and other crime; and especially by infrastructure needs ranging from the airports and the cruise-ship facilities in the seaport to energy grids and water resources. Opportunities exist to link research capabilities in the biomedical and other fields with manufacturing capacity in Baja California, but such linkages are slow to develop. Cross-border governmental and public-private cooperation has slowly begun to develop, encouraged by the UCSD-linked San Diego Dialogue and its Forum Fronterizo, but with many shortfalls.[98]

San Diego must substantially expand international markets for its products and services. Qualcomm's projected growth, for example, depends on seizing greater market share in China, India and Brazil. Sempra, the main energy company in San Diego, is also keenly interested in international activities, investments and markets, particularly in Mexico, South America and Asia; in 2003, Sempra announced a major joint venture with Shell that involves the conversion of gas for California and other U.S. markets at a facility in Baja California, using liquefied natural gas imported from Indonesia.[99]

If San Diego is to be successful in the twenty-first century, it will need to focus on responding to globalization. San Diego must radically improve its trade infrastructure facilities, particularly by building a larger, more globally connected airport, preferably jointly developed and managed with Tijuana. It will need to coordinate its airport development plans and the improvement of its highway and rail infrastructure with those of Los Angeles, the Inland Empire, and Orange County as well as Tijuana and Baja California. San Diego will have to learn how to cope with the rapidly changing demography of its schools, markets and communities. Improved educational performance is particularly urgent and would benefit from transnational cooperation with Mexico.

San Diego must find ways to turn its growing ethnic diversity into commercial comparative advantage. It must also work out means to assure that radically enhanced post-9/11 security measures at the international airport and border crossings do not permanently and significantly hamper commerce. As in Los Angeles and the San Francisco Bay Area, responding effectively to globalization and managing the region's international relations are absolutely central to San Diego's future.[100]

Several regional institutions are beginning to move forward. The San Diego Association of Governments, in partnership with the Tijuana City Council, has developed a binational corridor strategic plan that promotes the use of smart growth and sustainable practices for infrastructure planning on both sides of the border. On a larger scale, San Diego Regional Economic Development Corporation has partnered with the Imperial Valley Economic Development Corporation to develop an economic development strategy around five industry clusters for the mega-region that includes San Diego County, Imperial County and Baja California. The long-term goal is to create an identifiable "brand" for globally marketing the southwest binational mega-region as a competitive center for high-tech industries that take advantage of San Diego's well-developed high-tech industry clusters, Baja's lower labor and manufacturing costs and

Imperial's abundance of inexpensive land, dedicated water rights and wealth of renewable energy sources. Much work remains, however, to translate this attractive vision into implemented projects and programs.[101]

Orange County

Familiar national and international images of Orange County often still reflect the region as it was fifty or sixty years ago:[102] its largely Anglo population relatively homogeneous in ethnic background; conservative and somewhat isolationist in political orientation; a bit sleepy, at least by comparison with Los Angeles; and far from cosmopolitan or internationally minded.[103]

These images are no longer accurate, however. In the early twenty-first century, after six decades of relentless urbanization and suburbanization, Orange County is California's second-largest county by population and the fifth most populous in the entire United States.[104] Its economy has grown massively since the 1950s, first on the basis of military-industrial and aerospace firms during the Cold War, and more recently around internationally oriented high-technology companies in computer hardware and software, telecommunications, electronics, biotechnology and biomedical products and engineering as well as entertainment and tourism, much of it international.

Orange County today has more office space than any region in California but Los Angeles and San Francisco. The University of California at Irvine, a backwater campus when it opened in 1965, is today a major research university and Orange County's third-largest employer. Orange County's high-technology workforce of more than 75,000 is larger than those in Austin, Raleigh-Durham, San Diego or Seattle. Orange County's exports reached $16.3 billion in 2005, with major flows to Mexico, Canada, Japan, Taiwan, other Asian countries, Europe and Israel.[105] Orange County has become an economic powerhouse: dynamic, prosperous and increasingly international.

Equally dramatic, Orange County's demography has been transformed from the 1950s to the present, especially since 1980. Latinos made up 14.8 percent of Orange County's population in 1980, and Asians 4.8 percent; by the year 2000, Latinos were 30.8 percent and Asian and Pacific Islanders were 13.9 percent of Orange County's much-larger population. The foreign-born population of Orange County by the year 2000 was 850,000, nearly 30 percent of the total population; 41.4 percent of the country's residents who are five years of age or older speak a language other than English at home. Previously overwhelmingly concentrated in north Orange County, immigrant groups are now expanding in the county's southern communities as well.[106]

Orange County's Latino population, mainly from Mexico, reached 875,000 in the 2000 census, having increased during the 1990s by 55 percent, more than double the rate of Hispanic population growth in Los Angeles County during the same decade. Nearly 43 percent of public high school students in Orange County are Latino. Orange County's population of Asian immigrants, from South Asia, East Asia and Southeast Asia, has also exploded. The county has the largest concentration of Vietnamese outside that country, 136,000, according to the 2000 U.S. Census. In the 2007 elections, two Vietnamese American candidates with the same family name battled it out for a position on the Orange County Board of Supervisors; an Anglo candidate trailed both.[107]

Many of Orange County's small and midsize enterprises are minority-owned, including thousands of Latino-owned and Asian-immigrant-owned businesses, along with well-organized support groups, including the Hispanic Chamber of Commerce, the Orange County Minority Business Council and the Vietnamese Chamber of Commerce of Orange County.

Some Orange County leaders have understood the growing importance of international issues and relationships for the region.[108] The World Affairs Council of Orange County was founded in 1967, and the World Trade Association of Orange County in 1976. Orange County's International Business Center, opened in 2001, was a project spearheaded by the mayor of Santa Ana, Miguel Pulido, himself born in Mexico City; the center has a strong focus on the potential for expanding the county's trade with Mexico and Asia. International dignitaries—from Mexico and Latin America, and especially from South and Southeast Asia—frequently visit Orange County and connect these with their diasporas. Nowhere are Orange County's international links more evident than at Disneyland, a quintessentially American icon and a nearly obligatory stop for many foreign tourists.

Like Los Angeles, the San Francisco Bay Area and San Diego, Orange County has a lot at stake on the international front and must manage its global relationships more effectively. The region's general political complexion is more conservative than that of Los Angeles or the San Francisco Bay Area, but the need to develop international perspectives, policies and programs is equally evident and increasingly recognized. Orange County, too, has a great deal to gain from strategic thinking about Global California's challenges.

The Inland Empire

Of all of California's major regions, the fastest growing in population in the late twentieth and early twenty-first century was the "Inland Empire," to the east and southeast of Los Angeles, comprising Riverside and San Bernardino counties. During the 1990s, the Inland Empire's population grew by 25.7 percent, from 2.6 million to 3.3 million, and it had reached 3.8 million by 2005; it now has a larger population than metropolitan San Diego, St. Louis or Cleveland. From July 1, 2003 to June 30, 2004, the Inland Empire grew by 102,000 residents, more than forty-two of the fifty states grew in the same period.[109] The region is expected to add another 1.7 million residents in the next twenty years, an increase larger than that projected in any American state but Florida, Texas and California itself.[110]

This remarkable population growth, like that in California's other main regions, has had a strongly international flavor. The foreign-born population of the Inland Empire grew by 69.8 percent in the 1990s, from 360,000 to some 612,000 in 2000, with another 67,000 foreign-born residents added from 2000 to 2004—12 percent of the region's population growth during that period.[111] The percentage of residents five years of age or older speaking a language other than English at home increased by a reported 77.4 percent, with twenty-five different languages spoken. Although the share of foreign-born residents in the Inland Empire still lags behind the state as a whole (18.8 percent in 2000, compared to a statewide total of 27 percent), the demographic makeup of the Inland Empire is becoming increasingly international and diverse. By 2006, 44 percent of the residents of Riverside and San Bernardino counties were Latino, up from 13 percent in 1970.[112] By 2040, Latinos are expected to make up 70 percent of the population of San Bernardino County.[113]

The strong influx of people to the Inland Empire results from and contributes to strong economic growth. In 2003, the Inland Empire added more jobs than any other California region, adding more than 24,000 new jobs in a year when the state as a whole was losing some 45,000. And much of the growth in jobs and economic activity results from international trade, as the Inland Empire has become a major venue for the warehousing and transshipment of international imports. Most of the goods entering the Inland Empire at present arrive by train or truck from Southern California's ports on San Pedro Bay, but the region is projected also to become an "air cargo haven" by 2030, the second major air gateway of Southern California.[114] Already Ontario International

Airport is a major international hub for United Parcel Service (UPS), sorting and distributing a majority of UPS packages bound for delivery to the Pacific Rim. Four of the six direct weekly flights UPS sends to China originate at Ontario.[115]

Because of its strategic location—within easy reach of the San Pedro seaports and LAX, Ontario and San Bernardino international airports, and astride the main rail and motor vehicle arteries that connect with markets nationwide—the San Bernardino region has profited greatly from expanding international trade; in 2005, San Bernardino County alone processed $14.9 billion in imports and $917 million in exports, with another $2.5 billion in trade processed from Riverside County.[116]

Responding to these realities, the San Bernardino County established an International Trade Office and in 2007 held its first regional conference on global trade opportunities. The other main Inland Empire city, Riverside, adopted an "international strategic plan" in 2004, focusing on the need to expand exports, attract foreign investment, improve trade infrastructure, emphasize international education, foster international tourism and promote the visibility and awareness of the city as an international center. The Inland Empire has a Global Trade Center, a World Affairs Council, an International Business Association, a District Export Council and a Center for International Trade Development, primarily focused on Mexico and Asia.[117] The Inland Empire, too, is fast becoming an integral part of the world economy, with a lot at stake in expanding California's global commerce.

The Central Valley

California's Central Valley, the "other California" so often overlooked, accounts for about 27 percent of the state's territory and about 17 percent of its population. It comprises eighteen counties in four subregions—the Sacramento Valley, Sacramento Metro, the North San Joaquin Valley and the South San Joaquin Valley.[118] Taken together, the Central Valley is roughly the size of England.

With less than 1 percent of the farmland in the United States, the Central Valley produces more than 8 percent (by value) of the nation's entire agricultural output; it is California's most important agricultural region and one of the main agricultural centers of the world.[119] Six of the Valley's counties are among the country's most productive, including the nation's top three: Fresno, Kern and Tulare counties. Fresno County alone produces more agricultural value than twenty-four American states combined. Although much less visible in the national and international media than California's coastal regions, the Central Valley is a potent agricultural giant. The annual value of the Central Valley's agricultural crops plus the oil and gas from Kern County together exceed the value of all the gold ever mined in California. It is mainly due to the Central Valley that California has been the nation's leading agricultural producer for more than fifty years.

International immigration helped to populate the Central Valley from the start and to develop the region's agricultural prowess in the late nineteenth and especially the twentieth century. Italians, Germans, Portuguese, Swedes, Basques, Armenians, Russians, Iranians, Japanese, Cantonese, Sikhs and other South Asians, Hmong, Cambodians, Laotians, Filipinos, Mexicans and Central Americans have all made their marks on the Central Valley. They have introduced crops and techniques, built irrigation systems and introduced food processing and marketing innovations. And they have harvested the produce, from the early period on, and increasingly in recent years.

Although the Central Valley has long been importantly affected by international immigration, and by chronic labor conflict involving international migrant workers, it was otherwise relatively uninvolved internationally during most of the twentieth century. Most of the Valley's production was destined for California and other U.S. markets, though some of its rice and other products went to Asia. Unlike Los Angeles, San Francisco and San Diego, the inland Central Valley for many decades had few international commercial, political or cultural ties beyond those of its migrant workers. It has no international frontiers, and its only "international" airport (in Sacramento) for many years had no nonstop international flights. In a state otherwise notable for its rich and varied cosmopolitan connections, the Central Valley was somewhat different, organized mainly around family farms and increasingly on larger agricultural enterprises, both with decidedly local orientations and concerns for most of the twentieth century.[120]

During the last third of the twentieth century, however, the character of the Central Valley changed, with the accelerating expansion of large-scale commercial agriculture, much of it integrated with worldwide international companies and increasingly oriented toward international exports, and with the substantially expanded influx of foreign-born crop workers. By the end of the century, the Central Valley was exporting to foreign markets nearly $7.5 billion annually in agricultural products: almonds, walnuts and other tree nuts, cotton, wine, table grapes, dairy and beef products, processed tomatoes, rice and other fruits and vegetables.[121] About 40 percent of the valley's international exports go to East Asia (nearly half of that to Japan), 22 percent to Canada, 20 percent to the European Community and 7 percent to Russia. The development of large-scale agricultural enterprises has reinforced the transformation of the valley's labor market, drawing upon an ever-larger number of international migrant laborers, mainly from Mexico and Central America. Foreign-born laborers, more than half of them undocumented, are now 95 percent of the valley's crop workers.

The continuing flow of immigrant labor has swelled the valley's population, which has grown almost 25 percent faster than the rest of California's since 1975, doubling in the last thirty years. Projections for the future suggest that it will become the fastest-growing region of California, with the population likely to reach 12 million people by 2040. Immigrants from Mexico and Latin America, Asia and Eastern and Central Europe account for an increasing share of this expansion.

Immigration has been reshaping the valley's demography, schools, civic organizations and social service institutions. In the 1950s, the Central Valley was overwhelmingly populated by non-Hispanic whites, who still composed 73 percent of the population in 1980. By the year 2000, non-Hispanic whites were but 54 percent of the valley's population, Hispanics were 30 percent and still rapidly increasing and Asians were nearly 7 percent. Soon, if not already, no one ethnic group will constitute a majority of the valley's population.[122]

The Central Valley is by no means outside the international economy, nor is it exempt from the world economy's effects. Globalization's dual edge has become increasingly evident for the Central Valley in recent years. The valley's relatively strong growth over three decades has largely been based on agricultural exports, together with significant production of oil and natural gas in Kern County. Since the early 1990s, the valley has seen the entry of high-tech electronic, computer software and communications manufacturing and service enterprises seeking relatively lower housing costs and other positive lifestyle conditions that are no longer available at reasonable cost in Silicon Valley, the San Francisco Bay Area or along the Central Coast.

The Central Valley's agricultural producers, meanwhile, are increasingly encountering stiff competition, in third-world markets and even in the United States, from foreign growers able to produce and market at much lower costs many of the crops on which the valley has concentrated. The Central Valley's international competitiveness has been affected by the value of the dollar, strong until 2005 though dropping since then; by rising international opposition to the use of herbicides and pesticides; by the impact of the surging population on prices for land, water and energy; and by labor shortages exacerbated by tighter border controls in the post-9/11 environment. With the increasingly high costs of energy, water and (gradually) of immigrant labor, some Central Valley growers are finding that they cannot successfully compete with foreign producers of various fruits and vegetables: apples and apple juice, peaches, pears, apricots, raisins and other dried fruits, garlic, honey and other products. Imports from Colombia, Ecuador, Israel and other countries have also depressed prices for California's cut flowers. As commentator Jock O'Connell has succinctly stated, "The fundamental challenge for California growers operating in a worldwide market is that prices will be set globally but costs will still be set locally."[123]

To be successful in the twenty-first century, the Central Valley, like the rest of California, must understand and respond effectively to the international drivers of economic, social and demographic change. International trade today is estimated to account for about one-fifth of the jobs in the Central Valley, roughly comparable to the share of employment dependent on trade in Los Angeles or San Francisco. To stay competitive internationally, the Central Valley needs to improve its international airport access, for example.[124] Trade agreements, global agricultural subsidies, monetary policy and exchange rates, immigration laws and implementation and border management are all of direct concern.[125] From the perspective of Modesto, Sacramento, Stockton or Fresno, international policy issues are no longer esoteric or irrelevant, but increasingly important.

Parts and the Whole: The International Interests of California's Regions

Although the main regions of California differ greatly in exactly how they relate to the world beyond the United States, international links and influences significantly touch them all. Global markets, foreign investors and international immigrants are important to virtually every sector of California's economy: agricultural, industrial and services; high tech and low tech; entertainment, biotechnology, defense and other sectors. International flows profoundly affect the state's communities, schools, churches, health-care systems, business, labor, law enforcement, sports, culture and cuisine. Asia, Latin America, Canada and Europe are all important for California—in different ways and to different degrees that vary from region to region, but are nowhere insignificant.

Issues that range from tariffs and nontariff trade questions to immigration, from exchange rates to labor rights, from public health to crime, from airport and seaport security to congestion and pollution, from bilingual education to human rights—all put global questions at the very heart of California's various local concerns. If and when Californians from different regions and sectors better recognize and understand the many intersections of global and local concerns and perceive that they all share strong international stakes, their capacity together to address these concerns and advance their interests will grow.

Yet Global California's awareness of and pursuit of its global interests have up to now amounted, in practice, to less than the sum of its regions' stakes. The ports of Los Angeles-Long Beach and Oakland alone have probably done more than has the state government of California as a whole to identify global interests and advance them vigorously. California's response to flows of immigration has been confused and counterproductive, as discussed more extensively in Chapter 4. California's state government has over the past twenty-five years tried to promote commercial exports and foreign investment mainly by establishing trade offices in foreign capitals, but it has done so halfheartedly and ineffectively, often using these offices more for political plums than for strategic programs; as noted in Chapter 2, the offices were actually closed in 2003 in the face of press criticism and in response to the state's fiscal crisis.

California's congressional delegation has never pursued anything resembling a concerted approach even to identifying, let alone pursuing, the state's international interests. Interregional competition within the state has unfortunately been much more evident than broad statewide cooperation. Although each region recognizes that it has global stakes, no actor has articulated the state's overall international interests. California has not yet achieved an international vision, strategy or set of policies, nor good processes for developing these.

4 Promoting California's International Interests

C ONVENTIONAL DISCUSSIONS of U.S. foreign policy often suggest that it is the federal government's unique responsibility to formulate and conduct foreign policy. Politics, it is said, should stop at the water's edge; beyond our shores, the national government, under either party or any president, should seek to advance what is best for the whole country. The president and his advisors—not particular regions, states, sectors or pressure groups—should pursue the "national interest" in the international arena.

How the nation should respond to complex, uncertain, ambiguous and contradictory international realities is often unclear, however. On many issues, Americans from diverse economic sectors, regions and national backgrounds are affected in very different ways, and they have contrasting opinions about what should be done.

In truth, there is no unique "national interest" that only authoritative central governmental executives can fathom.[1] The national interest is contingent, contested and politically determined. It is not etched in tablets of stone, nor is foreign policy made only by the executive branch of the federal government. The other branches, especially the Congress, are important architects of American foreign policy. And that policy results not from rational calculation by a unitary actor but rather from a series of overlapping bargaining processes, involving both intra-governmental and extra-governmental actors that are frequently in conflict. These processes are informed, in turn, both by broad and diverging long-term visions and by concrete and immediate stakes, which may also be contradictory.[2]

Many different groups can and do participate, directly and indirectly, in identifying foreign policy goals and advocating approaches to pursue them. They include business enterprises and associations in commerce, industry, finance and other services; organized labor; farmers and agricultural workers; health care, law enforcement, educational and other professionals; and consumers of goods and services. People of different national, religious and ethnic backgrounds and in various diaspora communities with diverse links to their home countries—as well as anti-immigration lobbies—also participate. The media, foundations, faith-based groups and many other nongovernmental organizations focus on particular issues or try to represent the underrepresented. Local, state and regional government authorities and multiple public-private partnerships also play a role. So do individual voters, whose aggregate impact, at the ballot box or through opinion polls, can be important.

Each of these actors has a legitimate claim to participating in the interest-defining and policymaking processes. Each has influence, the extent of which depends on its resources; the substance of the particular issue; the skill of its representatives in the policy process; its relative access to diverse channels for decision-making and implementation in the executive, legislative and judicial branches of government; and its links to political leaders (through campaign contributions and other means) and to the communications media.

Divergent regional perspectives have long been an important source of American foreign policy. As Peter Trubowitz has argued, "Different parts of the country have different stakes in how the nation responds to international challenges and opportunities because of differences in what they produce, where they look for markets, their level of technological development, and, more generally, their position in the international economy."[3] Regional conflicts were at the heart of the main U.S. foreign policy debates of the 1890s, the 1930s and the 1980s. Changing coalitions pitted the industrial Northeast against the agrarian South in the 1890s, the urban internationalists of the Northeast and South against the nationalists of the rural West in the 1930s and the declining "Rust Belt" economies of the Northeast against the growing "Sun Belt" regions of the South and West in the 1980s. The preceding chapters of this book emphasize a long-standing but inadequately understood and therefore often ignored reality—that international trends, events, relationships and policies greatly affect California and its distinct regions, and that Californians therefore have important international interests.[4]

Identifying California's Main International Interests

As a single state in the U.S. federal union, California has no clear foreign policy mandate, however, nor does it have a dedicated international policymaking apparatus. It lacks, therefore, an accepted means for specifying its international interests or those of its citizens and for fashioning strategies and mobilizing resources to advance them. Although Californians have important international policy interests, we do not have systematic ways to identify, rank and pursue them.

Chapter 5 will discuss what Californians can do to strengthen our "cosmopolitan capacity"—that is, our ability to understand and respond effectively to international trends. California needs enhanced means to engage citizens, firms, labor unions, other nongovernmental organizations and political leaders in thinking about our international interests, weighing their relative priority and the trade-offs among them, considering the available means to advance these interests and evaluating the benefits and costs of alternative approaches. If Californians are to mobilize our resources more effectively, within constitutional limits, to promote our international interests, we will need to find ways to reach some agreement about what those interests are.

Californians from different regions, economic and employment sectors, socioeconomic and educational levels, ethnic and national backgrounds, faith traditions, generations, genders and political perspectives are all profoundly affected—both positively and adversely—by international forces.

Sometimes the impact of global events is direct, immediate and easy to comprehend. Foreign terrorist attacks or threats anywhere in the United States—or even in London, Madrid or elsewhere—can disrupt California's commerce, tourism, international student flows and sense of security. Middle East and Persian Gulf turbulence; instability in Colombia, Ecuador, Angola or Nigeria; political trends in Russia, Mexico, Venezuela or Indonesia; and rapid growth in China and India—all affect and often raise energy costs and the prices of gasoline at the pump and food in the supermarket. Financial crises in Asia, Mexico or elsewhere alter trade, investment and migration. International epidemics interfere with trade, tourism and educational exchange. Forest fires and industrial processes in East and Southeast Asia damage California's air quality, while sewage in Tijuana pollutes San Diego's beaches. Major defense industry buildups or downsizings in response to changing perceptions of international threats stimulate or cool off the state's economy and create or take away jobs. Wars and natural calamities abroad particularly affect California's large diaspora populations, who have family and friends in their home countries.

Most of the time, and for most Californians, international trends affect us in more diffuse but nonetheless significant ways. We are all affected by the world economy and by international regimes on trade, monetary, energy, intellectual property, environmental and other matters. California's consumers benefit from international imports, and many Californians gain from the export of goods and services, but some are hurt by outsourcing or by foreign competition. The overall balance of global military, technological and economic power shape the security and welfare of Californians. So do the underlying economics, politics and technologies of world energy and other markets. The lives of Californians are already and will be even more profoundly transformed by global warming, to which, as noted in Chapter 1, Californians themselves are contributors.[5]

Californians are subject to international threats to public health from defective produce and products.[6] They are also vulnerable to such internationally imported diseases as tuberculosis, HIV-AIDS, SARS, hepatitis, West Nile virus and potentially an avian flu virus. And they are hurt by the traffic in narcotics. Organized crime syndicates headquartered in Asia, Latin America and Russia prey on Californians. Californians—especially in the high-tech, biotechnology and entertainment sectors—are affected by international flows of intellectual property and by attempts to regulate these and to prevent and counter piracy. Those who work in the financial services sector, in telemarketing and in communications technology services are threatened, or may be made more efficient, by the outsourcing or offshoring of jobs to developing countries, and this challenge may well expand to other sectors.[7] California's agriculture depends as much on international trade negotiations and the growth of demand in foreign markets—and on economic, social and political conditions in the countries California's migrant agricultural workers come from—as on any circumstances within the state or the rest of this country. California is shaped by the changing currents of international migration and their underlying determinants and by the dramatic changes in world production and marketing processes. In today's globalized world, no Californian is without a stake in external affairs, whether or not he or she recognizes, understands or articulates this stake.

Some concerns of California's citizens are indistinguishable from those of citizens elsewhere in the country. All Americans want the United States to avoid being attacked by nuclear weapons or other weapons of mass destruction. Americans from every region want the U.S. government and other authorities to curb the proliferation of such weapons and to prevent them from becoming available to "rogue" states, failed states, extremist movements and other nonstate actors. All Americans want to have the threat from terrorism diminished, though California may be more exposed than most other states to this danger because of its location on land and sea borders, the prominence of its airports and seaports and Hollywood's iconic significance.

Similarly, Californians share with other Americans an interest in slowing, or if possible, reversing global warming; preserving global ecology and biodiversity; and making better use of the earth's resources, including those under the oceans and in outer space. Some of America's strongest nongovernmental environmental organizations have large and active memberships in California.[8] And many Californians join Americans from all over the country in supporting other goals: ending genocide, protecting fundamental human rights and the rights of workers, promoting democratic governance, alleviating world poverty, responding to natural disasters and pandemics, improving health, achieving greater equity, expanding the participation of women and ethnic minorities in politics and markets and enhancing the rule of law and equal access to justice. Of course, Californians themselves differ about the relative priority of these many objectives.

A few international trends, issues and relationships are unquestionably of special significance to California and its citizens, however. On some, such as curbing carbon emissions by changing automobile standards, California has, or might have, great and even disproportionate national and international influence. On others, such as the integration of immigrants, California has the potential for unique national leadership. In our own interest, Californians need to understand and identify the main international aims that are important to the citizens, firms and other organizations of our state and learn how to pursue these goals effectively.

Even in the absence of adequate institutional processes for authoritatively determining California's international interests, the analysis in previous chapters suggests three key goals that are surely worth pursuing: (1) expanding the gains and both minimizing and adjusting for the losses to Californians from participating in the world economy, (2) enhancing the benefits and mitigating the costs to Californians arising from international immigration and (3) managing the state's complex interdependence with neighboring Mexico in order to augment

the advantages and reduce the disadvantages of California's proximity to a relatively poor developing country. Many other international policy objectives also
concern Californians, but the importance of these three aims is evident.[9]

Expanding the Gains and Addressing the Costs to Californians of Participating in the World Economy

Participating in the global economy, like all economic activity, inevitably produces winners and losers; it brings greater benefits to some than to others, im-
poses greater costs on some than on others and often involves costs for some in
order to benefit others, as well as immediate costs absorbed to secure longer-
term gains. Californians as a whole have a strong interest in assuring that our
citizens, workers and firms, on balance and in the aggregate, gain as much as
possible from international economic activity. The aim of public policy should
be to enhance and more widely distribute the benefits of participating in a sustainable global economy while reducing, mitigating and compensating for the
adverse effects of doing so.[10]

Among the ways that Californians could work to gain more from international economic exchange are by promoting international economic growth
and sustainable development; by working to expand international exports; by
considering whether and how to expand the state's capacity to handle international imports; by working to assure access to international energy resources;
by promoting energy conservation and use of alternative energy sources; by encouraging education and cultural links with international economic partners;
by attracting foreign investment; by promoting protection of intellectual property rights; and by mitigating and compensating for the adverse consequences
of global economic engagement.

Facilitating Sustainable International Economic Growth

Californians should promote and facilitate international economic growth and
sustainable development, as well as fuller participation in the global economy,
especially by those countries and regions with the largest current or likely future significance for California as export markets for the state's goods and services and as sources of investment in our state.

Some countries and regions are particularly important for California's
economy because of the size of their markets, their dynamic growth and the

competitive advantages of California firms, arising from relative proximity or established demographic or business ties. Among these are China (including Hong Kong and Taiwan), India, Japan, Korea and other countries in East, Southeast and South Asia; Canada, Mexico, Central America and potentially South America in this hemisphere; and the European Community nations that remain important sources of foreign direct investment and of tourists for California. California should promote international trade by helping to shape U.S. financial, development and commercial policies, particularly through the influence of its large congressional delegation. (Steps that could be taken to mobilize the California congressional delegation in order to promote the state's international interests are discussed in Chapter 5).

Californians should also foster state, regional, private sector and other nongovernmental efforts—within constitutional parameters and in keeping with international law and practice—to facilitate international investment, nurture the rule of law and effective governance around the world, promote world commerce and protect the global environment. With the state's large share of U.S. trade and foreign investment, Californians should be vigorous champions of expanded positive-sum international economic exchange, especially with the countries of Asia and the Americas. At the same time, Californians should work to mitigate and manage the various costs of global economic engagement—including its impacts on labor, health and the environment—through regional and bilateral trade agreements, regulation and international regimes and by worker retraining and adjustment programs as well as other efforts to alleviate globalization's adverse consequences. As the largest and most internationally connected state of the American union, California can and should play a leadership role in seeking an appropriate balance between measures to facilitate globalization and to address its costs.

Expanding International Exports

Californians can expand their exports of goods and services in a number of ways.[11] Companies can improve the quality and competitiveness of their products and services. State agencies and public-private partnerships can promote global awareness of the merits of these exports as well as better inform California firms of international market opportunities. The state, the ports and regional agencies can improve the infrastructure for handling exports, particularly airport freight capacity and the intermodal transportation to air- and sea-ports. Chambers of commerce, regional development agencies and the state government can provide specialized training in export procedures and practices, targeted to "export-ready" and "export-willing" sectors. Educational institutions and professional and ethnic associations can develop and reinforce international business networks.[12] Public and private sector efforts can attract expanded international tourism, particularly from those countries that combine high potential for further growth of tourism with a demonstrated affinity for travel to California.[13]

At the federal level, Californians should promote improved international market access by harnessing the state's potential influence, through Congress and the executive branch, on bilateral and multilateral trade negotiations, especially in areas of importance to California, such as agriculture; entertainment; biomedical, environmental, communications and defense industry technologies; and electronic commerce.

Addressing the State's Import Capacity

Californians should carefully consider whether to expand further, and in any case how to make more efficient and environmentally sensitive, the state's capacity to handle international imports, while seeking to assure that neither the state nor its subregions bear a disproportionate share of the costs of processing flows that generate substantial national and international benefits but also some adverse consequences.[14]

Californians should promote sustained investment in more efficient, environmentally sound, and where appropriate, expanded state-of-the-art seaports and airports, in improved customs and on-land warehousing facilities and intermodal transportation systems, in better connections between ports and land transport systems and in more efficient and environmentally sensitive use of existing facilities and systems. As four former governors of California have jointly proposed, for example, California should enact an outright ban on the older, dirtier 25 percent of unregulated diesel engines that account for an estimated 65 percent of truck particulate matter pollution.[15] A recent California Air Resources Board ruling that diesel-fuel-burning harbor crafts must install new cleaner engines should be complemented by measures by the federal Environmental Protection Agency (EPA) to regulate emissions from oceangoing craft.[16]

Both the state government and the actual users of facilities should invest substantially in needed port improvements, rather than rely for investment, as in the past, primarily on municipal and regional governments and on autonomous port authorities.[17] In tandem, Californians should work to secure greater federal investment in facilities that are of national importance. We should also explore how to attract appropriate investment from those who will benefit most from facilitated trade, including those in China and other countries, and we should counter xenophobic resistance to properly regulated foreign investment in this sector. And California's air- and sea-ports should work closely with federal Homeland Security personnel, local law enforcement officials and the private sector to make security procedures more effective, with minimal disruption of traffic, and to improve first responder performance in the event of catastrophe.[18]

Californians should try in a coordinated fashion to strengthen the state's trade infrastructure and keep it competitive as product mixes and transportation modes evolve. We should carefully balance the various costs and benefits of expanded import capacity, especially in and around the already highly congested seaports. It is important to enhance California's air transport capacity, as air freight composes an ever more important share of goods exported from California, particularly of agricultural and high-technology products.[19] LAX and SFO have in recent years accounted for 95 percent of the state's air cargo, with evident limits on easy expansion, and neither airport adequately serves the needs of the Inland Empire or the Central Valley, California's two fastest-growing regions.[20]

To succeed in improving California's trade infrastructure, the state's public and private leaders should build trade-supportive political coalitions, drawing on those who stand to gain from imports as well as exports, in order to provide a statewide (and even broader) counterbalance to the intense local opposition that is understandably aroused by the various immediate transaction costs of handling air, sea and overland traffic, including congestion, pollution and noise. These important issues are often now confronted at the local community level, but these local decisions have strong statewide and indeed wider western regional, national and international repercussions. Clear state policies, regional and interregional cooperation—including alliances with other states that have similar interests—and concerted state influence on federal policies are all badly needed.[21] Although local impacts certainly cannot and should not be ignored, California's global interests are too crucial to have such key infrastructure policies as airport and seaport development decided, in effect, at the neighborhood level.

Ensuring Access to Energy Resources

Californians should work to assure secure and affordable access to international energy resources. Although some 40 percent of California's petroleum needs are produced in the state and an additional 20 percent comes from Alaska, the state is every year more dependent on foreign oil imports. Saudi Arabia, Ecuador and Iraq together account for nearly 70 percent of California's international oil imports, amounting in total to almost 30 percent of the state's fuel consumption; in recent years, California has been twice as dependent on Iraqi oil as the rest of the United States. California's dependence on foreign oil imports, moreover, is increasing each year, as in-state production declines by about 2 percent annually while demand for oil continues to grow, also at about 2 percent a year. This is occurring at a time when China, India and other major developing countries are steadily increasing their energy needs, thus causing upward pressure on prices. The spikes in California's gasoline prices in 2003, arising first from temporarily diminished oil production in Venezuela and then from the military conflict in Iraq, underlined the state's vulnerability to price shocks and interruptions of energy supplies, as did the immediate effects of Hurricanes Katrina and Rita in 2005.[22] Problems with BP's Alaska pipeline in 2006 further illustrated California's vulnerability.

Even in those times when world supplies are adequate, California's infrastructure for importing petroleum and petroleum products is severely strained, especially in Southern California, where storage capacity is normally very highly utilized, causing recurrent bottlenecks. California and the whole western region of the United States are vulnerable in the event of a disruption of energy supplies, because the U.S. Strategic Petroleum Reserve is located in Texas and Louisiana, with no pipeline to the West, and there is no comparable facility on the West Coast. In the event of a major international energy crisis requiring use of the Strategic Petroleum Reserve, California could well be subject to extraordinary costs, substantial delays and some panic buying.[23] While carefully evaluating environmental risks, Californians should consider promoting and helping to finance expanded petroleum storage facilities and even perhaps additional West Coast refineries, situated either in the United States or in Mexico's Baja California, and should consider pushing for a West Coast depot of the Strategic Petroleum Reserve.

Californians should take leading roles in promoting expanded North American energy independence with Canada and Mexico, involving petroleum, natural gas and liquefied natural gas.[24] Projects to build natural gas receiving terminals and regasification plants, either in California itself or in Baja California, merit careful study and quite possibly support and investment. Expanded energy infrastructure, increased pipeline capacity and more electric generation and transmission assets are also essential.

Investment in extracting petroleum from Alberta's vast tar sand reserves and perhaps in oil shale resources in Utah, Wyoming and Colorado likewise could perhaps directly benefit California, though the potentially large adverse environmental impact needs to be carefully evaluated.[25] So could innovative proposals to secure expanded and reliable petroleum supplies and natural gas from Mexico while channeling the resulting revenues to promote accelerated economic, educational and general development in Mexico, as well as efforts to strengthen that country's rule of law. Investment could be channeled through a proposed North American Energy Security Fund, under which the capital needed to develop Mexico's energy resources would be provided through loans backed by oil revenues and public sector loan guarantees (not involving ownership of subsoil rights), as political sensitivities in Mexico would need to be fully taken into account.[26] California's public, private sector and nongovernmental officials should take the lead in analyzing and perhaps promoting these and other ideas for enhancing energy security. California's huge public-sector pension funds could help mobilize the necessary investment.

Countering Global Warming

Californians should strongly promote greater conservation of energy, the expanded use of alternatives to fossil fuel and other efforts to stem global warming.

Californians have already begun to exercise leadership at the state, national and global levels on climate change. The state should continue to provide incentives for the production of wind, solar, biomass and other renewable energy sources; use state emissions standards to improve automobile fuel efficiency; and should vigorously promote national and international efforts to promote the development of sustainable energy sources. The agreement announced in 2004 between California and North Rhineland in Germany to share information about reducing emissions, undertaking other clean air initiatives and developing hydrogen cell technology illustrated what can be done. So did the cooperation announced by Governor Arnold Schwarzenegger and British Prime Minister Tony Blair in July 2006 to combat global warming. The order by the California Air Resources Board that automobile manufacturers must reduce the carbon emissions of cars sold in California in 2016 by at least 30 percent, beginning with substantial reductions in 2009, underlines the state's potentially decisive role. This measure has been challenged by the EPA as subject to federal supremacy, but the state may well prevail in asserting its legal authority to proceed.[27] Californians could consider taking initiatives toward a meaningful "carbon tax," using the state's influence to break through the political obstacles that have prevented national consideration of this crucial potential instrument for reducing greenhouse emissions and investing in alternative, renewable sources of energy.[28] California corporations are world leaders in developing energy-saving technologies; their work should be encouraged and exported. California has the stakes, the size and the likely clout to be a world leader on global warming, and its role is increasingly visible and potent internationally.[29]

Building Educational and Cultural Links

Californians should encourage positive educational and cultural links with current and potential international economic partners, not only for the intrinsic importance of expanded knowledge, understanding and cultural respect, but also to foster more beneficial international economic exchange.

Whatever Californians do to reinforce positive relationships with potential economic partners—in Asia and the Americas, but also in Europe, Africa and the Middle East—should help enlarge future gains from business, demographic and other flows. Educational programs that make Californians—students and adults—more aware of key countries and their ties with California are important. Study abroad programs should be expanded and extended, so that the next generation of California college graduates is better prepared to work in a global economy. California's colleges and universities should attract and educate additional foreign students, draw on more foreign-born researchers and further develop international partnerships and alumni networks.[30] Museum exhibitions, international concerts, dance recitals and other cultural activities can also play a role. Expanded international awareness would help Californians understand and cope better with a globalized world.

In an era when "soft power" is increasingly recognized as a major means to international success, California can do a great deal to build and employ the resources that come from values, culture, institutions and relationships.[31] California's entertainment and educational sectors are a major asset for the state. California's many diaspora populations can provide another important comparative advantage. California's firms and educational institutions should promote student and tourist visas that facilitate international ties, and California should invest at the state and local level in nurturing them. No other American state is as blessed with such a variety of natural bridge builders.[32]

Attracting Foreign Investment

Californians should work hard to attract foreign investment to the state, especially in the high-tech and biomedical sectors.

The investment climate in California, both for American and for foreign investors, has deteriorated in recent years. Extensive regulation, high real estate and other living costs, high and volatile energy prices, infrastructure limits, traffic congestion, the declining educational quality of the state's workforce and political gridlock that makes needed reforms difficult to enact have all combined to make California less business-friendly.

Californians need to muster the political will on a bipartisan and multisectoral basis to secure additional international investment, as well as to attract highly qualified scientific and technical personnel. Because of its globally recognized prowess in the communications and information industries, biomedical and biogenetic enterprises, environmental technology and the entertainment/multimedia sectors, California should be able to attract foreign investors and innovators wanting to participate at the cutting edge. To succeed consistently in attracting these capital and human resources, California and its citizens and firms need to invest effectively in the state's educational institutions—particularly in engineering, science and math—and in improving the quality of the workforce; in public-private partnership with universities and research laboratories; in steps to assure reliable and affordable energy and to expand the state's broadband connectivity and wireless sensor networks in the face of international competition; and in measures to improve the general quality of life and to strengthen governance. Only then can more effective communication with prospective international partners have a significant and sustained payoff. California representatives abroad cannot sell the state's virtues as a place to invest if these underlying conditions do not improve.

Protecting International Property Rights

Californians should promote effective international protection of the intellectual property rights that are essential to sectors crucially important to the California economy.

The information technology sector, biogenetic and biomedical industries, the clean tech sector and the entertainment and multimedia firms—all strong leaders of the California economy—share a concern with the effective international protection of various kinds of intellectual property.[33] Each faces enormous challenges from those in other countries who try to appropriate products that have huge development costs but then can be pirated and produced inexpensively in mass quantities. The specific issues faced in each sector are distinct and often highly technical, and the aims of each sector are therefore different, evolving and may sometimes be in conflict, but the underlying need to focus on this challenge is shared. Californians should continue to work with the state's congressional delegation, the executive branch and others to assure that the international protection of intellectual property and patents gets consistent high priority in U.S. foreign policy. At the same time, Californians can and should help develop policies to achieve other key objectives, including the important aim of making pharmaceutical products available at reasonable prices in developing countries.[34] Building crosscutting coalitions involving the state's agricultural, biomedical and information technology sectors could give California greater influence in building positive-sum solutions.

Addressing Globalization's Adverse Consequences

Finally, and importantly, Californians should focus concerted attention on mitigating the adverse consequences for some citizens of expanded global economic engagement.

International economic liberalization will be hindered as long as some sectors feel that they are being disadvantaged. If anxieties increase about diminished real incomes and about loss of jobs, traditional life and cultural identity, the political backlash against globalization will grow. Support for policies to expand international investment and trade will therefore be eroded. This trend is already clearly visible.[35]

When the North American Free Trade Agreement (NAFTA) passed the U.S. Congress in 1993, decisive bipartisan support from California's congressional delegation, 31 to 21, accounted for a substantial share of the 234–200 margin of victory by which the agreement passed. In 2005, when the Dominican Republic and Central American Free Trade Agreement (DR/CAFTA) squeaked through Congress by the narrowest of margins, 217–215 (on a postmidnight cliffhanger secured in the end only by intensive and personal lobbying by President George W. Bush on the Hill and vote-by-vote commitments on extraneous matters), 34 of California's 53 representatives opposed the agreement, including all 33 Democratic representatives. The difference between these two votes likely had little to do with precise distinctions between Mexico and the Central American nations, nor with the exact details of the two proposals. Rather, it reflected a substantial growth over time in public perceptions, in California as elsewhere in the country, that expanded international trade has adverse consequences for workers who are or might be displaced by international competition as a result of wage disparities as well as the relative lack of environmental protection abroad. Public opinion polls show that increasing numbers of Americans doubt the advantages of expanded trade.[36] The competitive dynamics of the Democratic 2008 primary campaigns in the Rust Belt states highlighted this sentiment.

Some Californians are adversely affected by the state's expanded participation in the global economy. In any case, the actual and perceived costs of globalization to California's citizens are undermining the political sustainability of expanded international economic engagement. Californians should work to mitigate and to the extent possible redress the adverse consequences of international trade for unskilled workers, the unemployed and others, including white-collar employees displaced by global production chains—both in this country and in the economies of our trade partners.[37] Emphasizing the benefits of global economic engagement and expanded trade for those who do receive its advantages, without addressing the concerns of those who feel themselves disadvantaged and dislocated, will not be enough to sustain the political support necessary for trade liberalization, especially as middle-level employees increasingly feel themselves vulnerable.[38]

Californians should give high priority at the national, state and local levels to enhanced unemployment insurance, to more effective worker retraining and other adjustment programs for those displaced, and to proposals for wage insurance.[39] Also important, investments in California's kindergarten through twelfth grade and postsecondary education system, child care and public health (including maternal, prenatal and infant care) are all crucial to developing a healthy and skilled labor force that can compete effectively in a globalized economy.

Improving the quality of California's whole workforce is absolutely crucial for the state's prospects. The children of immigrants will make up a large and growing share of California's future labor force; their education and training should therefore become a compelling priority.[40] No issue is more important for Global California's future; education programs merit expanded support even in the face of the state's renewed and difficult budget squeeze.

But programs to respond to immediate displacement and to improve educational skills for the medium and long term will not be enough to counter the actual and anticipated costs of globalization and to address the growing rupture between the fortunes of the U.S. economic elite and the rest of the country. Californians should be at the forefront of those who are seeking integrated new policies to restore a viable U.S. domestic social compact and to fashion international economic policies that are designed to improve equity and reduce poverty globally.

At home, growing anxieties should be addressed by an improved social safety net involving universal access to health insurance and fully portable and better-regulated private pension plans. Internationally, Californians should support efforts to end or substantially revise U.S. farm subsidy and agricultural trade policies under which high-income farmers in the United States and other advanced industrial countries are displacing low-income farmers in the developing world. More generally, Californians should support efforts to assure that potential trade agreements have a positive net impact on employment, wages and working conditions, both in this country and internationally. The compromise reached late in 2007 between the George W. Bush administration and the congressional Democratic leadership to revise the trade agreements with Peru and several other countries in order to improve basic worker rights and restore some balance between the rights of workers and those of investors suggests what could be done to help assure a more positive outcome from expanded commerce.[41] Californians and their representatives in Congress should be active in confronting this critical agenda.

Enhancing the Gains and Mitigating the Costs to California of International Immigration

From its earliest days, California has attracted international immigrants. As emphasized in Chapter 2, foreign-born immigrants were at the forefront of the gold rush. They developed California's agriculture; constructed the railroads, dams, aqueducts and highways that made possible the state's astounding growth; led the emergence of Hollywood as the world's cinema capital; and contributed greatly to military production during World War II, to California's rapid expansion after the war and to the rise of Global California.

In more recent decades, international immigrants have contributed considerably to California's economic production and expansion.[42] Immigrant engineers and entrepreneurs largely spearheaded Silicon Valley's transformation into the world's center for the computer.[43] Immigrant entrepreneurs, scientists and technicians are playing a similar role in the rise of the biomedical sector in the San Francisco Bay area, San Diego, Los Angeles, Santa Barbara and Orange County. California's health-care system relies heavily on immigrant doctors, dentists, nurses, pharmacists and other health-care professionals. The role of immigrant labor in providing services—in restaurants and hotels, child care, construction, building maintenance, landscaping, car washes, laundries and many other fields—has become central to the lives of California's middle and upper classes.[44]

But international immigration to California has never been without perceived costs and political controversy. Resistance to immigrant labor in the nineteenth century, then primarily coming from East Asia, has been mirrored throughout the state's history. It has waxed and waned with California's economic ups and downs, its shifting labor requirements, the changing ethnic and socioeconomic composition of immigrant flows and broader political currents that have affected notions of identity and community.

At various times in the last 125 years, Californians have been prominent in national efforts to curb immigration; at other times, Californians have been among those pressing for less restrictive and sometimes even pro-immigration policies. In recent years, both these currents have been evident. In 1994, a majority of California voters approved Proposition 187—which, as noted in Chapter 2, would have denied social services to unauthorized* migrants, mainly from Mexico and Central America. Yet California firms were at the same time in the lead of those pressing for expanded H-1B visas to import engineers and other skilled personnel, primarily from Asia.[45] More recently, California firms have continued to spearhead the fight to expand H-1B visas and streamline the acquisition of green cards for foreign-born graduates of U.S. colleges. Some Californians have led efforts for comprehensive immigration reforms that would expand services for unauthorized residents and provide them with legal status and an eventual path to citizenship. Others, however, have at the same time been heading the campaigns for much tougher border enforcement and for even more restrictive access to services, housing and other benefits by unauthorized residents.[46]

The unprecedented scale of international immigration into California since 1970 has produced major policy issues.[47] California's immigrant population today is extraordinary because of its size; its overwhelmingly Latin American and Asian origins; the substantial predominance of recent arrivals; and the large numbers of unauthorized entrants, especially from Mexico and Central America. It is also distinctive because of its educational and socioeconomic diversity—including numerous immigrants with advanced degrees but a much

---

* See discussion of the term "unauthorized" in Chapter 1, page 6;. Other terms, such as "undocumented" or "illegal," seem to me not precisely accurate, and tend to be used as political markers.

larger number with relatively low levels of education—and because of the comparatively slow rates and levels of naturalization, particularly among immigrants from Mexico and elsewhere in Latin America. These facts condition California's current realities and medium-term prospects.[48]

California's most concerted effort to respond to the growth of immigration was Proposition 187, the ballot initiative approved by the voters of the state in November 1994 by a 59–41 percent margin. Based explicitly on the argument that "the people of California have suffered and are suffering economic hardship caused by the presence of illegal aliens in this state," the initiative mandated officials of state and local government to identify such persons on the basis of reasonable suspicion and deny them access to various public services in the state of California, including health care, public education and other social services. Proponents of Proposition 187 argued that California was suffering an immense financial burden (estimated then at $2.7 billion annually, net of taxes paid by unauthorized immigrants) because of the federal government's failure to prevent such immigration, the high concentration of these immigrants in California and Washington's "failure to reimburse state and local governments for the services that they are mandated to provide to illegal immigrants."[49] The measure was strongly supported by Governor Pete Wilson, running for reelection against State Treasurer Kathleen Brown, who opposed the initiative, and it was widely considered a major reason for Wilson's successful campaign.

Upon public approval of Proposition 187, the U.S. District Court in the Central District of California entered a temporary restraining order enjoining the implementation of its operative sections and then granted injunctions, first preliminary and then permanent, precluding enforcement of the proposition's various specific provisions.[50] When Gray Davis succeeded Pete Wilson as governor in 1999, the State of California dropped its appeal to the permanent injunction, and the measure consequently became moot. For all the controversy and hoopla that surrounded its passage, Proposition 187 never actually went into effect.[51]

Had Proposition 187 been implemented, its impact on California would likely have been mixed at best, and most likely counterproductive. The costs to California of some social services might have been immediately reduced, thus alleviating immediate pressures on the state budget and on taxpayers.[52] But denial of health care and public education to unauthorized California residents arguably would also have endangered public health and diminished the quality of California's future workforce.

Enforcement of Proposition 187 might conceivably have led to more attention in Washington to the local fiscal costs of immigration. But its more direct impacts were to unnerve Mexican immigrants (many of whom naturalized subsequently, apparently in part in order to have a voice in U.S. politics) and to complicate relations with the government of Mexico, where Proposition 187 and the arguments employed on its behalf provoked deep resentment. The political backlash in Mexico interfered with positive trade and investment initiatives and at least temporarily damaged the prospects for cooperation on other issues. Governor Wilson was treated, in effect, as a *persona non grata* by Mexican officials, who compared him unfavorably to Texas officials, and Wilson did not visit Mexico again during his entire second term as governor.[53] Proposition 187 underlined California's need to deal with the impact of immigration, but it was not ultimately a successful way to promote California's interests.[54]

Although Proposition 187 was hotly debated at the time and extraordinarily divisive for some years thereafter, by now most sectors in California agree about the need to find effective ways of securing the advantages of immigration while mitigating its adverse consequences.

Extensive research by a number of different analysts has established at least latent consensus on a number of relevant propositions:

- High levels of immigration to California occur mainly when the state's economy is doing well and when the economies of sending countries are doing poorly. California, therefore, cannot realistically expect significantly reduced pressures to enter the state unless socioeconomic conditions, especially employment and wages, improve substantially in sending countries.

- Recurrent federal legislation to curb unauthorized entry into the United States has been hortatory at best and cynical at worst; it often seems intended primarily to calm domestic concerns without meaningfully affecting labor markets.[55] Politicians of both parties have highlighted visible but essentially symbolic demonstrations of their expressed commitment to control America's borders while at the same time permitting practices that predictably result in more unauthorized immigration.

- Periodic attempts by federal authorities to reduce immigration by more consistent and forceful protection of the border with Mexico have had little lasting effect on the flow of entrants. Such policies are unlikely to be effective as long as the strong underlying economic and social motivations for migration from Mexico and Central America are combined with high continuing demand for low-skilled labor in the United States. A 2002 study done for the Public Policy Institute of California (PPIC) showed that extensive and expensive efforts to step up border enforcement in the 1990s had little effect on flows of migration from Mexico beyond increasing the transaction costs, altering the points of entry and heightening the physical risks to immigrants. Other studies show that stepped-up border controls have enriched coyotes (people smugglers) and caused mortal risk or death to migrants who choose more remote and difficult routes to enter the United States, but have not significantly reduced the number of unauthorized migrants entering the United States.[56] One important impact of all these increased costs and risks, ironically, has probably been to induce unauthorized immigrants to remain in the United States longer than they did before, rather than risk apprehension at the border.[57] Circular migration has given way to quasi-permanent settlement.

- A combination of more persistent and better managed border controls—implemented both by more personnel and by greater investment in technology, together with improved documentation procedures (particularly secure identification cards with biometric features) and much more vigorous enforcement of existing or enhanced sanctions on employers for hiring undocumented workers— would probably reduce rates of unauthorized immigration somewhat. But the pressures for continuing immigration will persist, fundamentally because an aging and increasingly educated U.S. population will require more immigrant labor.[58] These underlying demographic and social facts will shape labor markets and invite immigration flows. Almost all of California's workforce growth between 2005 and 2030 is likely to come from immigrants and their children.[59] California's agricultural regions are suffering severe shortages of farm workers and are every year more dependent on immigrant labor.[60] The textile and construction industries, as well as hotels, restaurants and many other services, similarly depend on unskilled or low-skilled immigrant labor, much of it unauthorized. Large numbers of migrants are coming to California and elsewhere in the United States without legal authorization because there is high demand for their labor but currently no legal way to connect them with the available jobs.[61]

- Immigrant workers, equally productive at each level of skill and education as native-born labor but characteristically paid less, have made undeniably important contributions to the California economy over the years. Various studies show as well that immigrants have produced a net fiscal surplus for the federal government, paying more taxes than they receive in federal services and benefits.[62] Within Southern California, too, studies show that immigrants are an overall economic and fiscal benefit.[63] Public opinion polls show that most Californians understand and appreciate that immigrants contribute significantly in California.[64]

- By the same token, however, the huge concentration of low-income recent immigrants, often unauthorized, are large users of California's emergency health services, education and other public goods. These signify substantial fiscal costs, paid for the most part by the state and localities, not by federal agencies. The financial burden on Californians and a few other "gateway" states is understandably resented and is likely ultimately unsustainable in political terms.[65]

- Various studies, both at the national level and in California, suggest that immigrant workers, including unauthorized immigrants, produce net economic benefits to native-born residents, and that there is, at most, only a small adverse impact on the wage and employment opportunities of low-skilled native-born workers.[66] But immigrant workers with low educational achievement almost certainly have *some* adverse impact on the earnings of low-skilled native-born workers, often African American, thus contributing at the margin to a deterioration of earnings at lower levels of the economy that has exacerbated California's income distribution problems and fueled racial tensions. The educational deficit of many recent immigrants, moreover, has not only hurt their own prospects for advancement but may reduce California's overall productivity and its competitive position relative to other states in a knowledge economy. Although there is evidence that recent Mexican immigrants are somewhat better educated than those in the past and are beginning to take more diverse and higher-income jobs in the American economy, the gap between them and the requirements of an increasingly technological economy remains huge and may even be growing. The educational deficit of Mexican and Central American immigrants, mostly unauthorized, who come to California after age ten is particularly troubling, for programs to provide services and schooling to immigrants tend not to reach these people.[67]

The immense and widely recognized historic contributions of immigrants notwithstanding, therefore, California today confronts a serious challenge caused by massive and largely unauthorized immigration of relatively uneducated and unskilled persons. This wave of immigrants presents mounting immediate and medium-term fiscal costs at the state and local level and poses tough social and educational questions. It fosters a corrosive disconnect between law and practice and exacerbates latent (and sometimes overt) ethnic and racial tensions that tend to flare in periods of economic stress and/or security concerns.

The policy conundrum California consequently needs to address is quintessentially "intermestic,"—combining aspects and facets of both international and domestic processes and policies.[68] Such issues are notoriously difficult to manage, in part because the means for responding to them are so diffuse. The domestic imperatives on each side of the border, moreover, often run contrary to what would be needed to secure the international cooperation necessary to deal with the issue.[69] A border fence might make sense in domestic U.S. politics, but it surely complicates the process of securing cooperation from Mexico on this and other issues.

A central question for California is how to mobilize its considerable resources—at the local, regional, state, federal and international levels—to help turn immigration once again into a positive resource, rather than allow it to become a growing perceived and actual burden and a source of worsening societal divisions. This is not a simple matter, particularly as making and implementing immigration policy are obviously and necessarily federal responsibilities, but the issue is so central to California's future that the state and its citizens should try to find ways to identify and promote its interests.

Specifying California's interests regarding immigration would require defining, and to the extent possible, reconciling the different and sometimes conflicting perceived needs of many parties: employers in different sectors of production; organized labor; nonunion, unemployed and underemployed workers; previously incorporated immigrants; authorized and unauthorized recent immigrants; social service and advocacy organizations linked to the immigrant communities; those who provide educational, health and other social services; law enforcement officers; Homeland Security officials; and the general citizens, taxpayers, consumers and voters of California. Only an open and deliberative process, conducted skillfully by effective political leadership, could adequately ventilate all these perspectives, consider them and shape policies and compromises to meet the core requirements of all parties. But instead these issues are typically aired in today's California through strident rhetoric, the shrill discourse of talk radio discussion, bumper sticker slogans and facile pronouncements—not through deliberation or by consensus.

One of California's most important needs is to develop processes by which defining and promoting California's interests with regard to immigration can be considered. The state requires a credible way, widely accepted as legitimate, for taking into account disparate interests on immigration. Subject to such processes being constructed, as discussed below and especially in Chapter 5, some broad principles that might help Californians formulate a perspective on immigration can be tentatively advanced:

First, there is overwhelming consensus in California (as elsewhere) that current U.S. immigration policies are badly flawed. They tend to reinforce labor shortages; interfere with scientific and technical progress; keep families separated for extended periods; provide income to criminal people-smugglers; cause risks and even deaths to immigrants; facilitate labor exploitation; allow what often seem like sudden and uncontrolled surges of immigration; present severe fiscal challenges to locales and states with large clusters of unauthorized immigrants; lower the average educational level and productivity of the workforce; and significantly contribute to eroding the rule of law. These results are the opposite of what Californians want.

Second, because of its aging population as well as the increased educational level of its residents, California in the coming years will probably require more immigrant labor, both skilled and unskilled, not less. The evolving demography of Mexico, in turn, means that Mexico will face strong pressures to export workers for another decade or so, but that within about fifteen years the number of Mexicans entering the workforce may well begin to fall. The creation of jobs in Mexico should increase, and the pressures for migration should begin to diminish.[70] In California and nationally, the policy challenge in dealing with Mexican immigration—the largest, most visible and most controversial flow—

is essentially how to manage this issue until migration pressures predictably subside within fifteen years.

Third, Californians with divergent perspectives share an interest in transferring to the federal government more of the costs of providing education, health and other social services to unauthorized immigrants.[71] As unauthorized immigrant concentrations spread to several other gateway states, it should be possible to build a winning multistate coalition in support of such transfers. California's political leaders should be aggressively exploring that prospect.

Fourth, most Californians appreciate that all will benefit if those immigrants who do establish long-term residency, whether authorized or not, can become healthy, educated, English-speaking, taxpaying, credit-worthy, property-owning and law-abiding naturalized citizens, contributing positively to the state's development and welfare. The successful incorporation of immigrants into the economic, social, political and cultural future of California, in turn, requires investing in the education of immigrants and their children at all levels; expanding efforts to support English language instruction; promoting naturalization, voter registration and suffrage; facilitating immigrants' access to credit and other financial services; and supporting community-based agencies providing social services to immigrants.[72]

These issues should be high on California's agenda, not mainly out of charity but mostly from enlightened self-interest. California's economic competitiveness and social cohesion for decades to come will depend significantly on the educational and vocational achievement of its foreign-born immigrants and their children and on their identification with and commitment to the communities where they reside.[73]

Fifth, a viable approach to national immigration policy must be balanced and pragmatic. It should foster regularization of the volume and composition of immigrant flows so that they mesh more closely with labor market requirements, family unification and other goals. Policymakers should try to maximize the benefits and mitigate the adverse consequences of a deep and powerful current that is ultimately responsive mainly to family and market considerations and thus cannot be simply turned on or off by government policy at any level, much less by mere rhetoric and symbols.

Several proposals for new federal immigration legislation have been introduced in Congress in recent years, both by the George W. Bush administration and by varying combinations of members from both parties. These proposals have differed in nature and emphasis on such issues as the priority, approaches toward and resources devoted to border enforcement; the goal and procedures for temporary guest worker programs; and especially the possibilities and procedures for earned legalization by long-term unauthorized residents.

In December 2005, the House of Representatives approved a highly restrictionist measure, HR 4437, "The Border Protection, Antiterrorism and Illegal Immigration Control Act of 2005." This bill (among other provisions) called for some seven hundred miles of high-technology fences to be constructed along the border, with additional checkpoints, vehicle barriers and expanded Border Patrol personnel; broadened the definition of aggravated felony to include all smuggling offenses, illegal entry, solicitation and assistance; and tightened verification procedures to determine employment eligibility.[74] The Senate, in May 2006, passed S.2611, the "Comprehensive Immigration Reform Act," which combined strengthened enforcement measures with substantially expanded opportunities for legal immigration and earned legal status, including a "path to citizenship" for unauthorized immigrants.

Unable to agree in conference on how to reconcile these two very different approaches in the context of increasing politicization of the issue in the election year, the two sides agreed in August 2006 on "The Secure Fence Act of 2006," a bill focused sharply on border security, authorizing the seven-hundred-mile fence, projected to cost $70 billion, but appropriating only $1.2 billion for preliminary studies; President Bush signed this legislation on October 26, 2006. Virtually all observers concurred that the approved measure was simply a political stopgap, intended to dampen partisan pressures for the time being, but that it was by no means an effective and sufficient policy response.

After weeks of quiet and informal efforts in 2007 to reconcile differences, in close consultation with senior administration officials, a bipartisan group of senators submitted in May the "Secure Borders Economic Opportunity and Immigration Reform Act of 2007." This comprehensive proposal attempted to address the main concerns of employers, labor unions, unauthorized residents and their families as well as those who are concerned about border security and those who are outraged that "illegal" immigrants flout the law. The proposed legislation offered current unauthorized residents who have no criminal record clear paths to legalization and eventual possible citizenship, through a process that would have required them to pay fines, file applications and undergo background checks, thus precluding the simple "amnesty" to which majority public opinion objects. The bill would also have increased legal immigration, especially of skilled workers, through application of a point system designed to give priority to those most likely to strengthen the U.S. economy, though perhaps at the expense of the goal of family reunification. It also would have established a guest worker program to meet the need for unskilled labor, and it aimed to strengthen border enforcement through a combination of additional fencing, more investment in technology and increased numbers of Border Patrol agents. This proposed reform fundamentally recognized immigration as a necessary and irreversible flow and sought agreed means to channel and regularize it. It also sought to confront the issues posed by the existence of a large unauthorized and vulnerable population very unlikely to return to their countries of origin: it provided a means toward achieving legal residency without earning automatic citizenship ahead of those who follow the established immigration procedures.

Despite the elaborate efforts to respond to the core interests of several parties, the proposal was sharply attacked from several directions. Conservative opponents attacked the bill for offering "virtual amnesty" to millions of "illegal aliens." Immigrants' rights advocates charged that family reunification would be drastically curtailed. Representatives of Latino and other immigrant groups attacked the provisions of the proposed temporary work program—entry for a year, return to the home country for a year, back to the United States for two years, for a limit of three such visits and then permanent return to the home country—as utterly unrealistic. Even if it were feasible, they argued, it would be likely to institutionalize a permanent and exploited underclass. Employers, for their part, were concerned that the bill's provisions would entail serious labor discontinuities and would undercut their investment in training, skills and experience.

With the political climate heating up again, competing Republican aspirants for the party's presidential nomination scrambled to disassociate themselves from a proposal that was unattractive to the party's base, which is so important in the party's candidate selection process. A severely weakened President Bush proved unable to deliver votes in support of a proposal he strongly supported, and the bill's bipartisan proponents found themselves unable to advance the legislation; it was eventually supported by a majority of senators but not by the necessary sixty to preclude a filibuster. Consideration of comprehensive national immigration reform was deferred to yet another day, perhaps in the next Congress, possibly later than that.[75] A spate of local and state proposals and actions then predictably emerged throughout the country, attempting to help fill the policy vacuum, though legal and practical difficulties are likely to render these of limited effect, as discussed in Chapter 5.[76]

The future of California's society, economy and politics will be significantly shaped by how the issues of immigration and the integration of immigrants are handled in the months and years to come. With the failure of the Senate's efforts in 2007 to adopt comprehensive immigration reform, California's congressional delegation should, as a matter of high priority, deliberate the pros and cons of possible new proposals for federal legislation from the standpoint of the state's interests and should try to weigh in collectively, to the extent possible, when the opportunity is right for new legislation. This would be a realistic way for Californians to affect a major issue that has a direct and important impact on our lives. It would also allow California to exercise national leadership on a major issue for which California's unique experience and perspectives are highly relevant.

A potential concerted California approach to national immigration policy should be based on extensive public discussion and deliberation, convened by the state's civic and political leaders. Forging a broad consensus on the state's interest with regard to immigration would surely take considerable time and strenuous effort, and it could indeed ultimately prove to be impossible. But achieving and promoting a California perspective on immigration policy is worth attempting, for it could pay very large dividends. Governor Schwarzenegger and Assembly Speaker Karen Bass should consider taking the lead in exploring whether a consensual approach can be developed on an issue of such vital importance for the state.

Californians should try to play a leadership role in shifting the terms of the often strident and destructive national debate on immigration and moving it toward more pragmatic responses, including positive efforts to integrate immigrants. A first step in this direction, presented in Chapter 5, might be to convene a nongovernmental high-level California Commission on Immigration and Integration to make recommendations to the governor, the California Senate and Assembly, municipalities, the members of California's congressional delegation and to the citizens, firms, labor unions and other nongovernmental organizations of the state.[77]

Managing Complex Interdependence with Mexico

During the extensive public and congressional debates in the early 1990s about the NAFTA proposal, proponents and opponents argued as if the United States had a policy choice: whether or not to have an increasingly close economic, demographic, social, cultural, and political relationship with Mexico. Proponents of NAFTA favored closer interdependence; opponents did not.

By the time NAFTA was being debated, however, California actually had no such choice. Complex interdependence between Mexico and California was by then an irreversible reality—the result of millions of individual decisions over the years by migrants, investors, consumers and employers, much more than those by public officials. The flow of people, capital, goods, services and ideas back and forth between Mexico and California has been going on for many decades.[78] But these flows have accelerated in recent years, establishing transnational citizens, groups and processes on both sides of an increasingly porous legal frontier.[79]

The most important tie between Mexico and California is demographic. Authorized and unauthorized immigrants from Mexico and their descendants compose some 25 percent of California's population today, up from 12 percent in 1970. Thirty-seven percent of all Mexican immigration to the United States since 1850 occurred in the 1990s, and much of it was to California. Thirty-eight percent of the authorized immigrants to California during the 1980s and 40.2 percent during the 1990s, amounting to more than 2.6 million persons in those twenty years, were from Mexico, and an estimated 2.5 million to 2.8 million unauthorized Mexican immigrants now reside in California.[80] Mexicans in California remit at least $6 billion a year, probably quite a bit more, back to family members at home, accounting for a substantial share of Mexico's foreign exchange earnings.[81] The state of Zacatecas, from which much more than 100,000 persons have emigrated to California, primarily to the Los Angeles area, receives considerably more revenue from such remittances than from the Mexican federal budget.[82]

These strong demographic links are paralleled by expanding commercial and financial relations.[83] The export of goods to Mexico from California producers grew by almost 13 percent a year from 1988 through 2003, a rate of growth considerably higher than that of California's exports to the rest of the world, or from the rest of the United States to Mexico. By 2003, Mexico had surpassed Japan and Canada to become California's principal export market. California's exports to Mexico were $18.3 billion in 2007, 13.6 percent of all California exports, up from 6.8 percent (and $3.2 billion) in 1988.[84] Some of this flow, to be sure, reflects intra-firm shipments of materials for processing and re-export back into the United States, but this fact itself underlines growing economic integration.

Imports from Mexico by California-based firms more than doubled between 1995 (just after the enactment of NAFTA) and 2002, from $9.1 billion to $20.3 billion, an increase of 124 percent, outpacing imports from Mexico in the rest of the United States, which rose by 108 percent. Truck crossings into California from Mexico have grown nearly every year since 1994—from 657,000 to over 1.12 million in 2005. Crossings of people have risen most years as well, with some 62.5 million entries in 2004 at Otay Mesa and San Ysidro alone.[85] Striking increases have also been registered over time in expenditures by Mexican tourists in California and by California tourists in Mexico, as well as in direct investment in both directions. Baja California peninsula has become a prime vacation destination for Californians; even as real estate development has begun to slump in California, Californians are still buying property and building houses, golf courses, malls and real estate complexes in Baja.[86]

The mutual social, cultural and political impacts of Mexico and California on each other have grown, reinforced by political participation across borders and by transnational coalitions of various sorts. Mexicans residing in California are a force in their home country's politics, just as Mexican-American voters are an increasing factor in California's elections. Mexican state governors and national political leaders campaign, address the concerns of their U.S.-based constituents and raise campaign money in California. Many California political leaders travel to Mexico in order to enhance support at home.[87] Hundreds of Mexican hometown associations organize immigrants to advance their interests both in California and in Mexico.[88] Mexican-American organizations, many of them headquartered in California, are active and influential in both countries. Mexican, Californian, binational and transnational individuals and groups use instruments and approaches on both sides of the border to advance their interests, as migrants seek political representation and leverage both in Mexico and in California.[89]

Mexico's proximity and presence affect virtually every aspect of life in California: not just production, trade, investment and politics but education, health, the environment, religion, law enforcement, sports and the media. The close California-Mexico connection is a striking fact—not a theory, a possibility or an option.

California's substantial Mexico connection and its multiple effects have never led, however, to systematic California policies toward Mexico. On the contrary, efforts by Californians to deal with the specific impacts of Mexico on the state have been piecemeal, ad hoc and often counterproductive. The predictable consequences for California of trends in Mexico have rarely been anticipated; when they have, the approach adopted has often failed to resolve or has even exacerbated the problem. Proposition 187 was a classic example of this tendency.

To more effectively manage its relations with Mexico, Californians should concentrate on five objectives.

First, as discussed above, Californians should in a concerted way promote efforts at the federal level to regularize and manage migration flows in order to address and reconcile California's labor requirements and those of other states; confront the human needs of immigrants and their families; and improve the overall impacts of migration on California, including its fiscal effects and its consequences for productivity, public health, welfare and community. Californians have a vital interest in a comprehensive reform of U.S. immigration policy; we should work at the federal level to promote such a reform and should adopt measures at the state and local level that can complement and reinforce improved federal policy by addressing the challenges of integrating immigrants. Above all, Californians should try to change the national paradigm for discussing immigration: from exclusion and denigration to effective management and integration.

This imperative is much broader than policy toward Mexico, of course, but Mexico is a very large part of the immigration equation. And there are Mexico-specific issues that require attention in California. The special educational and health needs of migrant workers and their children require flexible approaches and augmented resources, for example. One key need is a joint California-Mexico online database for the school records of the children of migrant workers, an important means of keeping such children in school and learning; pilot programs have foundered for lack of funding.

Second, Californians have a strong long-term stake in incorporating and integrating Mexican (as well as other) immigrants in ways that strengthen California's human resources, contribute to a growing state economy, bolster effective governance and foster mutually beneficial relations with Mexico and other sending countries as well as between immigrants and other Californians. Whatever federal immigration policy may be or become, California already has a large Mexican immigrant population and will surely continue to attract large numbers in coming years, a smaller share of the U.S. total than in recent decades but still an appreciable flow. Measures to force or encourage Mexican immigrants to return to Mexico and to deter others from coming are bound to be mostly ineffective as long as the root causes of migration remain. Rather than focus only or even primarily on deterring unauthorized Mexican immigrants or promoting their return to Mexico, therefore, Californians should concentrate more on efforts to better integrate those who stay.

- Californians should invest across the board in developing the human talents of the substantial (mostly of Mexican origin) immigrant workforce in order to reduce and eventually eliminate the educational gap between them and other citizens. As David Hayes-Bautista predicted twenty years ago and Dowell Myers has recently documented, the retirement and health needs of California's older generation today and tomorrow depend on the productivity and commitment of today's immigrants and their successors and their children.[90] Studies of the educational and socioeconomic progress of Mexican and other immigrants to California show both that many immigrants learn English, acquire skills and achieve relative success, and that some do not, particularly those who migrate after age ten; these should be the subject of specially designed and targeted programs.[91]

- Californians should invest more in health care and human services for the immigrant population, in expanded health insurance coverage, and in public-private cooperation to develop binational health-care policies. Such investments are undeniably costly, but the price of inattention includes public health risks, an unhealthy and therefore less productive labor force and exorbitant charges for emergency care services. Studies show that the health of the second generation of Mexican Americans in California, the children of immigrants, typically becomes worse than that of their immigrant parents; reversing this disturbing tendency should be a priority for California's health-care system.[92] Failure to address the health issues of the Mexican American community by instilling good nutritional and exercise habits could eventually have profound costs and consequences.

Among the steps Californians should consider are a statewide screening and prevention program in the public schools aimed at identifying and preventing cases of obesity and diabetes, which are especially prevalent among the children of Hispanic immigrants. Nutritional and exercise counseling programs are particularly vital for the Hispanic population, because the children of immigrants are actually adopting worse habits and practices in this country than their immigrant parents brought here. As Governor Schwarzenegger has proposed, health insurance should be provided for all children in California, regardless of residential status. Consideration should be given to establishing a basic health-care provider license to enable trained individuals without full medical education to conduct basic preventive care counseling, common screening procedures and the most frequent emergency care procedures. This would provide needed services to recent immigrants and other low-income populations in a far less expensive way than the current frequent recourse to emergency-room treatment.[93]

- California should undertake more investments in civic education, naturalization and voter registration for adults. The surest way to turn immigration back into a widely recognized asset for California is to accelerate "buy in" by the immigrants themselves, while also enhancing the self-interest of the native-born population in building positive relations and thus their disposition to do so.

The temptation to isolate and punish unauthorized Mexican immigrants, illustrated by the campaign to deny driver's licenses to those who cannot show documentation establishing their legal right to residence—however understandable in political and symbolic terms—is self-defeating, both with regard to traffic safety and to the economic losses suffered as a result of lack of insurance. Governor Schwarzenegger's decision to reverse the earlier procedure by which unauthorized residents could obtain driver's licenses by presenting solid evidence both of identity (such as a foreign passport or a consular identification card) and of local residence was no doubt responsive to public opinion, but it was counterproductive public policy.[94]

The same is true of efforts to forbid banks and other financial-service providers from recognizing Mexican consular identity cards as a valid means of identification, a prohibition that would deprive unauthorized residents of access to bank accounts as well as credit and debit cards. Such measures will not significantly reduce the numbers of unauthorized residents but will force them to use less efficient and less secure means of handling money and remittances. Instead of adopting such measures on the false premise that they will deter unauthorized migration, California should focus on encouraging its current resident immigrants to integrate.

- A proposal some years ago by the Little Hoover Commission, called the Golden State Diplomacy Program, suggested giving immigrants access to a driver's license, in-state tuition, health care, job training and housing in exchange for their paying taxes, learning English, making sure their children attend school, staying out of the criminal justice system and demonstrating a willingness to become citizens; proposals in this vein deserve active consideration, development and support.[95] A good example of such an approach was the decision in 2001 by California's legislature to apply resident tuition rates at state colleges and universities to undocumented immigrants who have attended California high schools for three years and meet residency standards; these students may not (yet) be citizens, but they will likely be important contributors to California's human resources.[96] Rather than try to ostracize immigrants who are, in effect, here to stay, California will gain more from engaging them, at the local and state levels, in improving education, health, transportation, law enforcement and other aspects of community building.

- Californians should work with leaders of the Mexican immigrant and Mexican-American communities to build expanded economic, tourist, cultural and educational ties between California and Mexico and to enhance mutual understanding. Mexican immigrants and their descendants can be a significant asset in forging more positive California-Mexico links.[97] All Californians should be encouraged, in this regard, to appreciate the contribution of Mexican immigrants and to recognize the worth of Mexican society, history and culture.

Third, Californians should strive to assure that the intense interaction of Mexico and California in the border region is better managed in pursuit of shared goals. Californians should harness regional, state, national and binational efforts with Mexico to upgrade water treatment plants, improve water conservation and reclamation, better process hazardous waste, reduce pollution and improve air quality. Regional efforts are also needed in the border area to expand electricity production and ensure more efficient distribution. Plans to build natural gas import and regasification facilities in Tijuana and Ensenada to serve a binational energy market require close bilateral cooperation on controlling environmental impacts. Focused bilateral attention is required as well on the treatment of communicable diseases on both sides of the border, on coordinated approaches to providing emergency and other health care, on the special health problems of Mexican immigrants, on greater access to and portability of medical insurance by this population and indeed on the portability of medical insurance and Medicare benefits to U.S. retirees in Mexico.[98]

California and Mexico have a shared interest in streamlining procedures to facilitate trade, tourism and cross-border engagement. Customs and immigration procedures should expedite flows of goods and people while enhancing homeland security through such cooperative techniques as dedicated trade lanes, electronic transponders and NAFTA transportation identity cards with encoded biometric information for frequent travelers.[99] All these measures primarily require federal government action, but more consistent cooperation is also needed between law enforcement officials on both sides of the border, including local and state police. California can and should improve its performance in this regard.

Californians should devote high priority, at the federal, state, regional and binational levels, to turning the border with Mexico from a looming potential disaster into a dynamic zone of expanded progress. The potential exists to fashion synergy between California's design and management capacities and the labor of Baja California, but this will take careful planning and execution. Greater emphasis should be given to such efforts as the nongovernmental San Diego Dialogue, the San Diego-Tijuana binational planning and coordination committee, the regional transportation committee and the Mega-Region project of the San Diego Economic Development Corporation.

Fourth, Californians should work to foster greater economic exchange with Mexico. This underlying objective—which recognizes and builds on the fundamental fact that modes of production and labor markets are both, to an increasing and probably irreversible extent, becoming functionally integrated—can be advanced over time in a number of ways. At the federal, state and local levels, through public policy and private initiatives, Californians can work to improve the physical infrastructure and human services to handle bilateral trade and can help make rail transportation, trucking and other aspects of trade infrastructure more compatible across the political boundary. Californians can promote tourism in both directions and improve facilities and procedures to accommodate these flows. As suggested above, Californians can work with private enterprises and public agencies to develop mutual advantage in the energy sector, where California's needs and Mexico's potential may well fit closely.

All these efforts to promote greater economic exchange will be most beneficial for California if they are accompanied by greater socioeconomic equity and by improved labor and environmental practices in Mexico. These are not only worthy objectives in terms of the values of Californians, but progress on them also alleviates competitive pressures on California producers and reduces the pressure for migration from Mexico. Californians have a self-interested stake in finding appropriate ways, short of intrusive and counterproductive intervention, to promote and reinforce these progressive tendencies in Mexico. To some extent this can be done through federal policies and influence, but quite likely more can be and is being done by California's foundations, trade unions, corporations, the media and environmental and human rights organizations than by federal or state government action.

Finally, Californians have a long-term and legitimate interest in Mexico's improved governance and accountability. More effective democratic governance and the more consistent application of the rule of law in Mexico would, perhaps more than anything else, improve the business environment there and thus the overall prospects for positive economic exchange. This in turn would mitigate pressures in Mexico to migrate. Californians should do what we can, while fully respecting Mexican sovereignty, to promote the emergence of policies and institutions that will help Mexico strengthen the rule of law and equal access to justice. This aim should be pursued through influencing U.S. government policies and U.S. positions in multilateral institutions. But it should also and indeed especially be advanced by California's state policies and particularly by nongovernmental organizations, both from the Mexican-American community and from many other sectors: trade unions, chambers of commerce, foundations, the media, universities and professional associations. Considering whether and how Californians can appropriately, without undue and unwanted intrusive interventionism, reinforce Mexico's evolution toward effective democratic governance should be a priority theme in some of the state's social science research and public policy centers.[100]

No policy or set of policies will resolve all the issues that arise from California's proximity to a large developing country with intense demographic pressures, deep economic challenges, profound regional and social inequities and long-standing difficulties in achieving, strengthening and consolidating effective democratic governance.[101] The juxtaposition of an aging industrial society with a youthful developing country on its border involves opportunities for synergy, but it also engenders inevitable frictions. Economic, commercial, political and cultural conflicts will recur, exacerbated at times by historical resentments, lingering racism, vested interests and political point-scoring. As mutual interdependence between the two societies continues to deepen, some points of tension may well become more bothersome. But thorny issues can be better managed, resolved or at least attenuated by improving the understanding of their sources, thereby facilitating effective responses.

More satisfactory outcomes are likely if Californians and Mexicans jointly nurture relationships at many levels on a long-term basis. Much of Mexico's and California's future will be shaped by the unique California-Mexico connection, yet civic, political, educational and business leaders in each society have little systematic contact. Californians should consider developing a leadership cadre of professionals well-versed on Mexico and committed to building more effective relations with that country, and Mexicans should consider undertaking reciprocal efforts. A California-Mexico graduate fellows program, preferably designed and implemented on a mutual basis and modeled on the very successful Rhodes scholarship program (which has contributed so enormously to Anglo-American ties) would help improve the long-term California-Mexico connection.[102]

Mexican authorities have long understood the prime importance of California, where Mexico has established ten consulates, consistently posts top diplomatic personnel and representatives of numerous government agencies, arranges frequent visits by governors and other senior federal officials and devotes sustained high-level attention.[103] Developing similar concepts, strategies and capacity to manage its unique Mexico connection is part of what Global California needs to do, in turn, to succeed in the twenty-first century.

Promoting California's Other International Interests

Expanding the net gains and alleviating the undoubted adjustment costs from participating in the world economy, enhancing the benefits and reducing the costs of international immigration and effectively managing complex interdependence with neighboring Mexico are but three of California's important international policy interests. Many Californians would also give high priority to strengthening relations with China, Japan, Korea, India, Pakistan, Vietnam, Israel, Palestine, Iran, Russia and Brazil, to mention a few obvious examples.[104]

Others would particularly stress such aims as protecting the world's ecology; promoting human rights and democratic governance; curbing the trade in narcotics, arms, sex workers and other undesirable flows; combating racism, ethnic cleansing and religious intolerance; peacefully resolving various international conflicts; combating HIV-AIDS, tuberculosis and malaria, and otherwise protecting public health; and fostering greater international socioeconomic and gender equity.

Pursuing such legitimate goals effectively would require ordering priorities, making choices and fashioning appropriate and accessible instruments. None of this is or will be easy, especially at the state and local level and in the face of constitutional constraints. But the necessary first step is to think through long-term and more immediate objectives and to consider precisely how each goal might be promoted, as this chapter has done, by way of illustration, on three issues. Californians—citizens, firms, nongovernmental organizations, municipalities and the state government—need to build better capability for this kind of thinking and develop the habit of doing so. We need to develop cosmopolitan capacity commensurate with our interests and resources. That need is addressed in Chapter 5.

5 Building Cosmopolitan Capacity

DURING THE PAST TWENTY-FIVE YEARS, the international policy agenda of the United States has been fundamentally reshaped. The Cold War emphases on classic military security issues and on political and ideological competition with Soviet communism have given way to greater concern with economic, social and environmental questions; issues of ethnicity and identity; and since September 11, 2001, the threat of terrorist attacks by "rogue" states or nonstate groups.

Globalization—the intensification of transnational and international linkages, facilitated both by dramatic technological changes in transport and communications and by the opening of commercial and financial regimes—has transformed the world economy, politics and culture. From early-morning coffee to late-night television, Americans today live in a highly interdependent world. International trade, finance and labor affect much more of the U.S. economy than ever before. Americans, including Californians, are increasingly engaged internationally. They gain a great deal from this global involvement, but they are also more vulnerable to its risks.

Globalization has strongly reinforced the local impacts, both positive and adverse, of what happens abroad. Americans no longer feel themselves insulated from events overseas: from Afghanistan to Zimbabwe, China to Venezuela and India to Iraq. The lines between domestic and foreign policy have increasingly blurred. On such questions as trade, investment, intellectual property, the environment, public health, narcotics, migration, labor and consumer standards and human rights, much of the initiative, participation in and support for U.S. foreign policy comes from citizens in their communities. By the same token, the effects of national foreign policies are felt today all across nations, often far from the locus of central government decision making. As a result, there has been increasing involvement in international policy in recent decades by municipalities, regions, provinces and states, in the United States and elsewhere.[1] The role and impact of nonstate actors have also greatly enlarged.[2]

Thinking Globally but Acting Locally: The Growth of State and Municipal Activism

During the 1970s, many states and municipalities across the United States began to engage in unprecedentedly direct efforts to promote international aims based on local perspectives. "Think global, act local" became shorthand for this new emphasis on pursuing international objectives from vantage points much closer to individual citizens than traditional foreign policy had permitted. Many American states established their own international departments and sent missions abroad to expand exports and attract investment. Cities likewise began to undertake trade and investment promotion programs, established or strongly reinforced "sister city" relationships and touted their distinct virtues as production venues or tourist attractions.

States, governments, state legislatures and municipalities have increasingly engaged in efforts to influence policy on a wide variety of other economic, social and political issues. They have expressed opposition to apartheid in South Africa, genocide in Darfur and the Arab economic boycott of Israel. They have sought to protect the rights of Holocaust survivors, of refugees and migrants and of the victims of human trafficking. They have tried to promote human rights from Myanmar to Sudan, Northern Ireland to Palestine, Cuba to Nigeria and Armenia to Tibet. They have adopted codes of international corporate responsibility. They have pushed measures to oppose the proliferation of nuclear weapons and ban land mines, protect the environment, fight global warming, combat HIV/AIDS and other diseases, restrict offshoring and reduce the cost of prescription drugs.[3] They have worked to promote individual products from avocados to wine, adopted local laws to promote ecologically sound forestry practices and required special fishing procedures to protect dolphins, sharks and whales.

Many state and municipal efforts to engage in foreign policymaking have been more hortatory than practical; a typical illustration was the unanimous resolution of the Oakland City Council in November 2007 calling on Congress to ban a U.S. attack on Iran.[4] Berkeley is probably the national champion in this regard. Since the mid-1980s, the Berkeley City Council has, among other actions, expressed its opposition to the Nicaraguan contras and its support for the Contadora peace process in Central America, declared its sympathy for the East Timor independence movement and opposed NAFTA. In 1990, the Berkeley Council adopted Ordinance 5985, pledging to take joint and separate (but unspecified) action in cooperation with Alameda County, the Association of Bay Area Governments the State of California and the United States government to achieve "a) higher standards of living, full employment and conditions of economic and social progress and development; b) solutions of local economic, social, health and related problems; and regional, cultural and educational cooperation; and universal respect for and observance of human rights and fundamental freedoms for all without distinction as to race, sex, language or religion."[5]

In some cases, however, local involvement in foreign affairs has gone beyond purely verbal declarations to include economic sanctions and other tangible measures. During the 1980s, for example, several U.S. municipalities (Berkeley among them) offered physical sanctuary to refugees from the Central American civil wars, in direct contradiction to restrictive federal policies, and local officials formally withheld cooperation from federal officials to protect such refugees.[6] More recently, various states sought to interfere with the deployment of National Guard units to Iraq, in response to citizen opposition to the U.S. war effort there. And many states and municipalities have used purchasing procedures, investment and trade restrictions and other economic instruments to express various international policy preferences.[7] Several states, including California, have forced divestment by public employees' pension funds in any company doing business in Iran.[8] Similar provisions were earlier adopted by several states, also including California, regarding Sudan.[9]

Filling the Federal Vacuum on Immigration Policy

Perhaps the most active arena for state and local government action on international policy in recent years, and especially since early 2007, has been in response to immigration. State efforts to deal with the costs of immigration have grown in tandem with the worsening federal legislative gridlock on immigration policy. States and cities in different regions of the United States and with varying degrees of exposure to immigrants and especially to unauthorized residents, have reacted to the congressional impasse on immigration reform by enacting a number of laws and ordinances. Between January 1 and December 31, 2007, no fewer than 1,562 pieces of legislation related to immigrants and immigration were introduced in the fifty state legislatures; 240 bills in forty-six states became laws during this period.[10] Some of these laws have been rendered inoperative, as they have been held to be unconstitutional for infringing on federal supremacy.[11] In other instances, local communities and states have backed away from these initiatives for a variety of reasons, including the evident need for immigrant workers and the high cost of litigation, but the level of state activity in this arena remains unprecedentedly high.[12]

Most of these recent state and municipal measures regarding immigration have been efforts to deter or reverse inflows of unauthorized migrants. The Texas legislature, for example, approved a $43 million state appropriation to redouble state vigilance on the border with Mexico by stationing state police agents and sheriffs, with sensory equipment, along the frontier.[13] Other steps taken include requiring state identification cards for access to government services; allowing or even instructing local police to check the immigration status of all suspects; directing health, education and other government employees to report on the immigration status of clients; and denying driver's licenses (and therefore, in effect, automobile insurance) to those who cannot show proof of lawful residence. Several states have prohibited employers from hiring unauthorized migrants and have threatened suspension or revocation of business licenses to those who do not comply.

Perhaps the toughest such measure was signed into law by Governor Janet Napolitano, a Democrat, in Arizona in July 2007. Under this law, Arizona employers who knowingly hire unauthorized migrants face suspension of their business licenses for the first offense and the permanent loss of their business license for the second offense within three years. Employers must verify the status of job applicants using a federal immigration database known earlier as "Basic Pilot," and now called "E-Verify." Business and immigrant rights groups have filed lawsuits challenging the law, but it took effect on January 2, 2008.[14]

A few states and communities have moved in the opposite direction, providing greater openness and accommodation to immigrants. In Illinois, for example, the state legislature ruled in 2007 that the state could not require employers to check on the residency status of job applicants through the federal Basic Pilot/E-Verify system because the legislature considered the system error-prone. The state ruled that employers could ignore the system until the U.S. government showed that its data was at least 99 percent accurate, which is currently very far from the case.[15] Some states have adopted measures to protect immigrants from exploitation and to extend education and health care to their children. At least fifteen states have adopted laws to punish immigrant smugglers, especially if their clients were coerced into sex work. A number of states have recognized the "matricula consular," the consular identification card issued by the Mexican and some other governments, as a valid means of identification, thus facilitating the opening of bank accounts and access to some social services by unauthorized immigrants. Acceptance of the matricula consular has also made it possible for states who wish to do so to issue driver's licenses to anyone who has valid proof of identity and of local residence, regardless of immigration status.

The decision by Governor Eliot Spitzer of New York in September 2007 to allow unauthorized residents of that state to obtain driver's licenses upon presenting proof of identity and local residence, without regard to their immigration status, stirred immediate and intense controversy. Strident and unrelenting criticism came from CNN's Lou Dobbs and Fox TV's Bill O'Reilly, whereas fervent editorial support was provided by the *New York Times* and immigrant support groups. Republican lawmakers in New York, all the Republican presidential aspirants and some of their Democratic counterparts expressed opposition.[16] Within weeks, the governor was forced to withdraw his plan.[17] San Francisco, meanwhile, followed the example of New Haven and its own Left Coast tradition by going in the opposite direction, approving a local identity card that is valid for various purposes and available to any person with photo identification and a document (such as a utility bill) verifying residence in the city.[18]

California's International Policy Efforts

As the largest and most internationally connected American state, California from an early stage played a prominent role in the trend toward greater state and municipal activism on international policy.

Ever since the 1950s, when Governor Edmund G. ("Pat") Brown announced that his administration would aggressively seek international customers for its products, the state of California, under both Democratic and Republican leadership, has promoted international exports and made concerted efforts to attract foreign investment and overseas tourism. From the 1970s through the 1990s and into this century, California was one of the most active states in establishing international trade and investment promotion offices around the world, with some twelve such offices abroad in 2003 at the height of these activities—just before the decision, discussed in Chapter 2, to dismantle these offices.

During these years, as noted in Chapter 2, California also established its Technology, Trade and Commerce Agency (with Offices of Export Development, Export Finance and Foreign Direct Investment), the California Export Finance Council and the World Trade Commission as well as a number of committees in the California Assembly, to promote the state's expanded participation in the global economy. California entered into bilateral memoranda of understanding with Singapore, Israel, Taiwan and Mexico to foster cooperation on research and development, technology, communication, trade, emergency management and other issues, and it has arranged or hosted official visits by numerous international dignitaries.[19] Governor Arnold Schwarzenegger has emulated the practice of his recent predecessors by traveling abroad—to Japan, China, Israel and Mexico—to develop economic partnerships, promote exports and attract investment, adding his personal "star" power to more traditional approaches.[20]

As of 1999, California had the largest trade and investment program of the fifty states. Five California state agencies—Trade and Commerce, Food and Agriculture, Environmental Protection, the Energy Commission and the Community College System—were then spending about $16.1 million annually to promote California exports, attract foreign investment and operate the state's network of foreign offices. These agencies offered a wide range of consulting services to small and midsize California businesses, organized trade shows and delegations, recruited foreign corporations to invest in California and provided guarantees for loans from private banks to facilitate international trade and investment.[21]

California's major cities have also actively promoted trade and foreign investment. Richard Riordan, James Hahn and Antonio Villaraigosa—the three most recent mayors of Los Angeles—have all traveled abroad extensively on behalf of the city, and each established an International Trade Advisory Council; Mayor Villaraigosa has also established an Office of International Trade and

Development.[22] San Francisco, San Jose and San Diego all have similar offices, as well as extensive sister-city relationships.[23]

It is difficult to evaluate the impact of California's state and municipal efforts to promote exports and to attract investment and tourism. Barnstorming trips by governors and mayors have reportedly had modest concrete results. Limited research elsewhere suggests that state promotion programs generally have few significant effects on overall exports, although that may be due in part to the fact that state programs concentrate on small and midsize enterprises, whereas large companies still account for most U.S. exports. The number of years a state has had a foreign office in a country reportedly correlates positively with the level of foreign direct investment attracted to the state from that country, but the number of variables determining investment flows is too high to attribute specific investments to state programs. Professionally staffed and professionally enhanced efforts, carried out on a selective and tailored basis, appear to be modestly helpful, particularly when executed on the basis of public-private partnerships, with fees charged for services and with systematic and consistent evaluative follow-up.[24] The supposed benefits of California's offices were grossly oversold, however, leading to intense media criticism, and all of them were closed, as previously noted, during the major state budget crunch of 2003.[25]

California's international policy activism has not been limited to promoting trade and investment. State legislation has also regulated or prohibited the trade of endangered plants and animals, hazardous waste and improperly prepared or packaged foods and pharmaceutical products, for instance. The California Public Employees Retirement System (CalPERs) and the California Teachers Retirement System, with combined assets of more than $400 billion, have adopted policies to ban investment of their funds in countries with records of human rights violations or inadequate labor or environmental standards.[26] With respect to firms based in the United States and other advanced industrial nations, the policies limit investment by California's public pension giants to firms adhering to the global "Sullivan principles," a voluntary code of conduct barring U.S. corporate abuses abroad. Companies based in emerging-market countries have been evaluated since August 2002 through a complex formula that measures each country's compliance with standards regarding human rights, labor, preventing corruption and protecting investors.[27] California has also banned the state's procurement of clothing, such as uniforms, from sources found to use child or slave labor or to engage in "sweatshop" labor practices.

Several California municipalities—including San Francisco, Los Angeles, Berkeley, Oakland, Davis, Santa Cruz, Palo Alto, Santa Monica and West Hollywood—have gone further by prohibiting the use of public funds to invest in or procure goods from any company that does business with a number of countries (such as Myanmar, Indonesia and Nigeria) with gross human rights violations or other practices deemed appropriate for such sanctions. San Francisco, for example, pushed by Bay Area liberals and college campus activists, has adopted strict anti-sweatshop provisions.[28]

Perhaps the most innovative and potentially important attempt by California's state and municipal governments to make international policy has been on the environment. As noted in Chapter 4, in 2006 the California Air Resources Board (CARB), responding to the California Clean Air Act of 2002 and citing concerns about global warming as its reason for this action, ordered automobile manufacturers to reduce the carbon emissions of cars sold in California by 30 percent, starting in 2009 and culminating in 2016.[29] Unless federal courts definitively reverse the new rules as an impermissible intrusion on federal authority, the CARB action may well have the ultimate practical result of causing automobile manufacturers to adapt their entire U.S. fleet to the California standard, thus in practical effect determining national policy.[30]

California's Public Utilities Commission instructed private utility companies to use a "carbon adder," a formula to calculate greenhouse gas emissions, in weighing bids for electricity supply from power generators, and soon thereafter the California Climate Action Registry issued its first report measuring such emissions by utilities and power generators. This step sets the stage for possible adoption by California of the mandatory "cap and trade" system already enacted by the European Union and by eight states of the U.S. Northeast, and mentioned favorably by several presidential aspirants in the 2008 primary campaigns. CalPERs has also required all companies in its investment program to join the Carbon Disclosure Project, which requires companies to publicly disclose data on their carbon emissions.[31]

Various California municipalities have also been active on environmental issues. Most prominent perhaps has been San Francisco, which has established a Clean Technology Advisory Council and a Clean Technology manager for the city and enacted environmentally sensitive purchasing legislation, and which hosts one of the country's largest alternative fuel municipal vehicle fleets. San Francisco is striving to become a magnet for innovative, environmentally minded citizens and businesses.[32]

In addition, experts from CARB, the California Energy Commission, Lawrence Berkeley National Laboratory and the Energy Foundation in San Francisco have together undertaken consultations with China's national and local governments to improve energy conservation there and to counter atmospheric pollution and slow global warming by cutting China's carbon emissions. Governor Schwarzenegger has explicitly argued that California and other states must take the initiative on measures to stop or slow global warming because the federal government is not doing enough, and he has been highly visible internationally in this connection.[33]

Backing Off a Bit

Except on climate change, however, California has in recent years backed off somewhat from its earlier international activism. Citing favorably California's increasingly strong state stance on environmental issues, California's Assembly pushed in 2007 for a statewide referendum on "whether the president should end the United States occupation of Iraq." Some three hundred towns across the country had adopted measures to this effect, but no state had yet done so. Governor Schwarzenegger vetoed the legislation, however, on the grounds that Iraq policy was not a state issue and that the people's vote would carry no practical weight.[34]

Having taken a national lead, however ultimately unproductive, on efforts at the state level to curb immigration through Proposition 187 in 1994, California has not recently been particularly active in undertaking state actions to affect immigration policy. Former Governor Gray Davis had favored and signed into law a bill allowing unauthorized migrants to obtain driver's licenses upon documentation of their identity, through the matricula consular or otherwise, as well as proof of their local residence. Governor Schwarzenegger campaigned for the governorship in the special recall election in part, however, by promising to nullify this provision. Once elected, he promptly did so.

Aside from the driver's license issue, California has kept a relatively low profile on immigration policy since the mid-1990s and has been fairly accommodating to immigrants in practical terms. The California legislature approved and Governor Schwarzenegger signed into law in October 2007 a measure that prohibits cities from requiring landlords to check whether tenants are in the United States without legal authorization, making California the first state in the nation to adopt this preemptive policy.[35] California continues to offer in-state resident tuition rates to California high school graduates entering the state university system, regardless of immigration status, and several communities offer social services to unauthorized migrants. Despite pressures to change its practices, the Los Angeles Police Department has kept in effect Special Order 40, barring police from inquiring about the immigration status of arrestees.[36] On immigration policy and the integration of immigrants, Californians clearly have important interests and they articulate diverse and strongly held opinions, but the state at present has no explicit overall policy or agreed approach.

Stakes Without Standing

That California's state government has backed away somewhat both from its earlier efforts to promote exports and foreign investment by establishing offices abroad and from its direct attempt to affect immigration policy by denying state social services to immigrants underlines an important reality. The instruments available to the government of California (and those of other states) to promote the international interests of its citizens are far from clear, given constitutional doctrines and judicial determinations (noted in Chapter 1) that bar state interference with federal supremacy on matters of foreign affairs and international policy. California is faced with a structural gap between its high stakes in the realm of international policy and the modest scope for authorized direct state action.

Californians have important international interests but cannot pursue most of them effectively through state public policies. This constraint has become self-fulfilling, as California's state government, in the face of these limits, has to some extent abandoned earlier efforts to directly promote the international objectives of its citizens. The impact of international trends on California's citizens has been rising, but the state's efforts to respond to these trends have weakened. Because they have global links without sovereign power or international standing, Californians are ever more vulnerable to globalization.

What Can Californians Do?

This book has argued both that Californians have substantial international interests and that we have the resources necessary to advance them. Californians need to find the ways, within constitutional constraints, to draw on our assets more effectively to increase the benefits and manage the risks of global engagement.

Californians can do this in three ways that could complement each other: by better mobilizing our potential influence on federal policies, especially through Congress; by taking more concerted advantage of the available scope for state and local action; and, perhaps most important, by building enhanced capacity to help our citizens, firms, unions and other nongovernmental organizations better understand and pursue their own interests.

Mobilizing California's Congressional Delegation

To promote our international policy interests at the federal level, Californians have a powerful potential resource in our congressional delegation, the nation's largest. California has fifty-three representatives in the House, more than 12 percent of the total, and our two senators are veterans with substantial seniority. On a wide range of international policy issues—from trade to immigration, environmental protection to human rights and infrastructure to narcotics—Californians could achieve great influence if our congressional delegation acted in a more unified manner to advance the state's global interests.

The impact on U.S. foreign policy that Californians might achieve through our congressional delegation goes beyond the sheer size and voting power of the delegation, for a number of members of the delegation have influential leadership positions. In the Democratic-controlled 110th Congress, Californians chaired or were ranking minority members of seven of the twenty standing committees; they chaired or ranked on ten of twenty standing committees in the Republican-controlled 109th Congress. In the past twenty years, California has had more representatives on the House Foreign Affairs Committee (previously called International Relations) than any other state, more than 20 percent in some years, exactly 20 percent in 2007–2008.[37]

Perhaps California's most significant current congressional resource is Speaker of the House Nancy Pelosi, D-San Francisco, whose path to national prominence began in the 1990s with highly publicized stances on human rights in China, including strong opposition to the granting of most favored nation status. Ms. Pelosi took the lead in 2007 in establishing the creation of a new House Select Committee on Energy Independence and Global Warming (including Californians Hilda Solis and Jerry McNerney). She is a powerful leader of the U.S. government's legislative branch. Among the many other influential members of the House of Representatives from California (discussed in detail in Chapter 5 endnote 35), another who deserves special mention is Representative Howard Berman, who chairs the Foreign Affairs Committee, succeeding Tom Lantos, also from California, upon the latter's death in February 2008.[38]

In the Senate, Dianne Feinstein chairs the Committee on Rules and Administration and the Judiciary Committee's subcommittee on Terrorism, Technology and Homeland Security; she serves on the Select Committee on Intelligence, and in the past has served often on the Foreign Relations Committee. Senator Barbara Boxer is a member of the Committee on Foreign Relations and chairs the Committee on the Environment and Public Works, which reviews questions related to global warming, among others.

California is thus well placed to exercise leadership in Congress on international issues, but the delegation has never addressed this challenge, and California opinion leaders and voters have never persuasively called on them to do so. The California Institute for Federal Policy Research, established to help the California congressional delegation become more effective, does not emphasize international policy issues. Very few of the institute's frequent briefings have dealt with international questions.[39] The California Chamber Council on International Trade (formerly the California Council on International Trade) has never succeeded in attracting more than a handful of members of the state's congressional delegation to its annual conference. By all accounts, the California congressional delegation—divided both by party and by region—has never convened to consider the state's international policy interests and their legislative implications.

Leveraging the state's potential influence in Congress to advance the international interests of Californians, and doing so on the basis of in-state research and analytic capacity as well as bipartisan deliberation, should be a high priority for Global California. To jump-start this process, Governor Schwarzenegger and Assembly Speaker Karen Bass should consider inviting the entire California congressional delegation to join them, members of the governor's cabinet, selected senate and assembly members and a few invited experts to a special seminar to assess California's international policy interests and how to advance them. The aim should be to determine what the most important international policy issues are for Californians and whether and how the state should attempt to wield its congressional influence, through bipartisan and transregional cooperation as well as by cooperation with other states that share some of

California's interests. Using this volume and other available sources, background memoranda could be prepared in advance by the Governor's Office, members of the senate and the assembly and invited experts.

If members of California's congressional delegation were to find this exercise useful, such organizations as the California Institute for Federal Policy Research, the California Policy Research Center, the California Research Bureau, the Pacific Council on International Policy, the Bay Area Council Economic Institute, the Public Policy Institute of California (PPIC), the California Chamber Council on International Trade and the Graduate School of Pacific Rim and International Relations at UC San Diego could be sources of expertise. They could be invited to develop plans for further periodic and regularly scheduled international policy briefings for the California congressional delegation.

It would also be useful to establish an ongoing capacity to respond to ad hoc inquiries by California's members of Congress on international policy issues. This might be done by the California Research Bureau, perhaps in cooperation with the California Institute for Federal Policy Research, the Public Policy Institute of California and/or one or more of the university centers. The state should have a robust and continuing capacity to analyze international trends that affect Californians and to identify specific ways to advance the interests of its citizens. That capacity should be a must for a state with so much riding on international engagement.

Thinking Strategically: Institutionalizing a State Capacity to Assess and Review the State's International Policy Interests

The governor should make an annual statement on Global California and its international interests, either as part of his "state of the state" address or as a separate report. The Governor's Office, in consultation with others, should develop and periodically update a comprehensive and strategic vision of the international issues on which Californians have an important stake and report to the citizens of California on whether and how their interests are being advanced. Such a summary review of California's international interests could help guide decisions both by public sector and by nongovernmental actors on a variety of issues—from infrastructure to education, health care to intellectual property and trade to climate change. This could be immensely helpful, not only to the state government and the congressional delegation, but to munici-

TABLE 5.1 State and city-region metrics for assessing levels of "global engagement" and "cosmopolitan capacity"

Measures of global engagement

- Exports and imports, volumes and values—by markets and sources, compared to other state and city-regions
- Exports per capita
- Foreign direct investment: amount, by country of origin
- Number of nonstop international flights weekly
- International tourism: number, by country of origin
- Number of international passengers per year disembarking and spending at least one night
- Annual expenditure by international tourists
- Long distance telephone and telecommunications volume
- Foreign-born residents: total and by country of origin
- Number of Hometown Associations and of other international diaspora organizations, and number of members of these organizations
- Remittances: total amounts, by country
- Share of workforce employed by foreign-owned companies
- Percentage of manufacturing workforce employed by foreign-owned companies
- Number of state-licensed foreign bank agencies and amounts of assets on deposit
- Number of Edge Act Banks, and total amount on deposit
- Deposits on foreign bank agencies and Edge Act Banks as a percentage of all bank deposits
- Public opinion data (especially on priority concerns, salience of different issues and countries and level of support for active U.S. role in the world)

Measures of cosmopolitan capacity

- Percentage of college and university students in study-abroad programs, by country
- International students enrolled in higher education institutes: number, percentage of total enrollment and countries of origin
- Number of consulates
- Number and activity level of sister-cities relationships
- Languages taught at kindergarten through twelfth grade schools
- Percentage of population that speaks a second language
- Number and audience/circulation of foreign-language news media (print and electronic)
- International content in local mainstream media (print and electronic), measured in column inches and minutes on evening news.
- Number of foreign reporters and overseas bureaus of locally based newspapers and other media enterprises
- Number, membership and level of activity of World Affairs Councils, leadership fora on international affairs (such as Pacific Council on International Policy) and related or similar organizations
- Number and quality of university area studies and international studies centers
- Number and amounts of international grants by locally based foundations
- Number and activity level of internationally oriented business associations

palities, regional development associations, nongovernmental organizations and even individual citizens.

To develop such a strategic vision, the governor and the California legislature should establish an ongoing capacity to assess the state's international policy interests and to take into account the views of California's citizens on international policy issues. Their views should be tapped on the basis of systematic public opinion surveys, polls and focus groups, as well as periodic issue-specific study and discussion groups, rather than on the fragmentary and often tendentious product of talk radio programs or facile bumper stickers. Such organizations as the Bay Area Council Economic Institute, the San Diego and Los Angeles Economic Development Corporations, the Pacific Council on International Policy and the Public Policy Institute of California should be consulted about and if possible engaged in this process.

As part of California's efforts to build the capacity to assess the state's international policy interests, the state might prepare or commission annual or at least periodic measures of California's global engagement and of the state's cosmopolitan capacity: that is, its ability to compete effectively in the world economy and to protect the interests of its citizens and firms in a globalizing world. Table 5.1 provides suggested metrics for such a systematic appraisal.

A California Commission on Immigration and Integration

Governor Schwarzenegger and Assembly Speaker Bass should consider jointly convening a nonpartisan blue-ribbon California Commission on Immigration and Integration. The aim of such a proposed nongovernmental commission would be to develop and build public support for a comprehensive medium- and long-term bipartisan approach by California to the fundamental challenge posed to the state by international immigration: how to continue securing the benefits that immigrants bring while reducing the costs and stresses associated with major inflows, especially by unauthorized immigrants.

Immigration policy must ultimately be acted on at the federal level, of course. The 2007 impasse on the proposed comprehensive reform bill shows how difficult it will be to reach consensus soon in Washington. Conceptual and political breakthroughs will be required to overcome Washington's gridlock.

The chances for such national breakthroughs would be significantly enhanced, however, if California—the country's largest state, with the largest international immigrant population, long experience with foreign-born residents and the largest congressional delegation—could suggest constructive approaches. This would be entirely consistent with Governor Schwarzenegger's emphasis, broadly popular in California, that on such issues as combating global warming or assuring health insurance for children, California should not passively wait for national action but should instead try to show the way.

A bipartisan, statewide, diverse and multisectoral commission of civic leaders could work together, free of the pressures of partisan politics and immediate political advantage, to craft approaches to immigration and integration that would best serve the interests of most Californians. Properly staffed by recognized experts and with enough resources to contract for special studies, such a commission could assess the costs and benefits of current and projected immigration flows and of current and proposed policies and practices. It could rank the diverse concerns and priorities of Californians, try to reconcile these and examine possible compromises. Finally, it could recommend approaches and policies—on the federal, international, state and local levels—to improve the net impact on California of international immigration and especially to enhance the integration of recent, current and future immigrants into California's workforce, electorate and communities.

It would undoubtedly be challenging to develop consensus recommendations from a genuine cross section of California's leadership, but the very exercise of shared analysis and collective deliberation could be immensely productive and might well lead to concrete and constructive results. California should prepare itself to play a leadership role nationally on this vital issue. Drawing on the state's experience and the attitudes of the majority of its citizens, Californians can help the country move past the toxic politics of immigration by focusing on medium- and longer-term interests. And California should take the lead in developing the policies and practices for integrating immigrants that need to be part of any sustainable immigration reform.

A Commission on California's Global Economy

The governor and assembly speaker should consider organizing a comparable commission to assess the interests of diverse Californians in responding to the changing global economy, again to fashion consensual analysis and recommendations. Broadly discussed and widely supported specific recommendations on how Californians could enhance the benefits and both mitigate and compensate for the costs of participation in the world economy could help members of the state's congressional delegation play more effective roles on a number of issues of international economic policy.

The real choices today are not between favoring or opposing globalization, which is an underlying trend, not a policy option. Nor is the current debate between advocates and opponents of trade particularly helpful; the core practical issues are how to manage trade for the broadest benefits and how to reduce, mitigate and compensate for its risks. Thoughtful deliberation and concrete recommendations on these questions from a California perspective could help show the way forward for the country as a whole. An ongoing advisory committee on California and the global economy might then be appointed by the governor and the legislature to review and update this vision on a periodic basis, taking into account new developments as they occur.

Acting Effectively: Taking Full Advantage of the Space for State and Local Action

Within a strategic vision for clarifying the international interests of Californians, and with priority attention devoted to mobilizing the influence of the state's congressional delegation, both the state government and California's municipal authorities could do much more than they have in the past to advance these interests. The constitutional constraint on actions by nonfederal government authorities operates only where state or municipal conduct violates or threatens federal supremacy, a line that is drawn in practice by federal courts, and which is still fluid in some areas.

State and local governments can act without judicial interference on a wide variety of issues.[40] Clearly permissible activities include the following:

- Bolstering the state's infrastructure (including air- and sea-ports, transportation, storage and widespread broadband and wireless availability) to handle international commerce, investment and tourism. This aim necessitates, among other tasks, exploring whether and how cooperation with Mexican authorities in the border region could be fostered to facilitate expanded legal commerce and to fight crime.

- Confronting the issues of water management, waste disposal and pollution. This, too, requires transnational and international consultations and cooperation on local and statewide issues with transborder actors.

- Enhancing domestic efforts to increase the conservation and more efficient use of energy as well as the expansion of available supplies by improving the state's energy infrastructure and policies. Among the issues to be considered is whether and how cooperation on energy with California's neighbors in Canada and Mexico could be forged, as discussed in Chapter 4.

- Promoting the advantages of California for international investment and promoting California's exports of goods and especially of services.
- Improving educational institutions and programs to foster global awareness, international competitiveness and civic integration.
- Improving the health of Californians by undertaking a variety of programs and interventions at the state and local level, some of them addressed to the special needs of immigrants and the public health implications of their arrival.

Further along a spectrum, where the lines of permissible action are not yet settled, are efforts to affect trade and investment by state procurement policies and by the investment policies of public pension funds; attempts to affect environmental policy by such measures as emissions controls, investment in clean energy and subsidies for energy conservation and the use of renewable resources; and possible binational cooperative efforts with Mexico to deal broadly with border management issues, including health, education and infrastructure. In all these domains, considerable space surely exists for permissible state and local actions. These could be much more effective if they were more strategic, better integrated and more coordinated, with consistent leadership from the governor.

Immigration policy is a highly contested area, in which state and local efforts to fill the vacuum caused by failed attempts at federal policy reform are currently being tested in the courts for their compatibility with federal supremacy. As previously noted, some of the most recent state and local efforts to regulate the employment of unauthorized residents and their access to social services have been or may well be struck down. Neither California nor the rest of the country benefit, in any case, from a crazy-quilt pattern of inconsistent policies in different jurisdictions. Californians have strong reason to work for comprehensive national immigration reform. A great deal can be done at the state and local level, moreover, to improve the integration, English language skills, naturalization, education and health of immigrants, as is emphasized in Chapter 4. California can and should be the national leader in this important realm.

Building Cosmopolitan Capacity

The recommended efforts to mobilize California's congressional delegation and to leverage the state's potential influence on national policy, as well as the

TABLE 5.2 A partial list of actors whose decisions and actions affect California's international interests and influence

---

Federal government

Executive branch

President	Treasury Department
National Security Council	Commerce Department
Office of Management and Budget	Trade Representative
State Department	Homeland Security Department
Defense Department	Drug Enforcement Agency
Energy Department	Environmental Protection Agency
Labor Department	

Congress

Judiciary

California congressional delegation
Congressional delegations of other states
  with similar interests
NGOs serving California congressional
  delegation (California Institute for Federal
  Policy Research, California Council on
  International Trade and Public Policy
  Institute of California)

California state government

Executive branch

Offices of the Governor and Lt. Governor	University of California
Business, Transportation and Housing Agency	California State University system
Department of Food and Agriculture	California Economic Strategy Panel
Environmental Protection Agency	California World Trade Commission
Energy Commission	Trade and Tourism Commission
Community College System	California state pension funds

Legislative branch

California judiciary

California Senate and Assembly
Senate and Assembly committees

Other public sector

Regional governance organizations	County supervisors
Regional and municipal economic	Municipal governments—mayors and city
development corporations and similar	councils
organizations	Law enforcement authorities at state, county
Centers for International Trade Development	and municipal levels
California Association for Local Economic	Seaport and airport authorities
Development	

Nongovernmental actors

Trade promotion organizations, such as	Political parties
California Chamber Council on International	Diaspora and immigrant organizations and
Trade, California Chamber of Commerce	hometown associations
and local chambers and World Trade Centers	Professional associations
Business associations, such as Semiconductor	Foundations
Industry Association and Motion Picture	Universities, community colleges, research
Association of America	institutions, think tanks and international
Trade associations	policy fora

Individual corporations—large, medium and small, including information technology, entertainment, biotech and environmental technology companies; venture capital firms; and firms that provide financial, engineering, architectural, legal, accounting and other services
Labor unions

Environmental, health, immigration, human rights, ethnic, fair trade and other nongovernmental organizations
Individual citizens

---

recommendations for state and local activities to promote our international interests within the bounds of constitutionally acceptable state action, are only part of what can and must be done to enhance California's cosmopolitan capacity—that is, the ability of individuals, firms and nongovernmental organizations to respond effectively to global challenges. Much of what Californians can do in the international arena must in fact be undertaken by individuals, firms, communities and nongovernmental organizations, such as those listed in Table 5.2, and it is important that they be better qualified to understand and respond effectively to international change.

Helping California's individuals, firms and nongovernmental organizations become more effective in grappling directly with international issues may ultimately be the most important way to advance the international interests of Californians.

International Education

California should develop the ability of its citizens to understand and respond more effectively to international trends by undertaking a high priority statewide emphasis on international education from kindergarten–twelfth grade through graduate and continuing education. An integrated statewide effort along these lines should include

- greater emphasis on foreign language competence, geography and cultural awareness at the elementary, middle school, high school and college levels, with special emphasis on Asia and Latin America, regions likely to be increasingly important for California's future;

- significantly expanded study-abroad programs for California students, especially in Asia and Latin America;

- focused efforts to draw on the state's large international student population as a resource for improved international understanding and networking;

- special programs to build improved awareness, understanding and business and professional networks with key countries, such as the proposed California-Mexico Fellows program mentioned in Chapter 4, as well as other special opportunities for high school, college and graduate students to connect with such other strategic nations as China, India, Japan, Korea, Brazil, Germany and Canada;

- public-private partnerships to reinforce the participation of California institutions of higher education in the Association of Pacific Rim Universities and in other specialized efforts to build transnational and international cooperation and foster continuing networks; and

- corporate programs to enhance employee awareness of the issues posed by globalization and of the opportunities and challenges associated with engaging in the world economy.

Research on International Relationships and Policy Challenges
Public and nongovernmental institutions in California, including private foundations and corporations as well as universities and think tanks, should facilitate and support advanced research on California's key international relationships and policy challenges. They should undertake and facilitate analyses comparable to the discussion of the California-Mexico relationship presented in Chapter 4 on California's links and stakes with such other countries as China, India, Korea, Vietnam, Japan, Canada, Germany, Iran and Brazil, to mention some of the most obvious choices. Research projects should also be undertaken and supported on the specific impacts of trade, foreign investment, outsourcing and migration on particular regions and communities of California.

Bilateral consultations should be organized and sustained on a number of key relationships; the Pacific Council's series of exchanges with Atlantik Bruecke on German-West Coast relations, the Council's joint project with the Indian Federation of Chambers of Commerce and Industry and the initiative announced in Sacramento in June 2008 by Governor Schwarzenegger and Chilean President Michelle Bachelet for Chile-California cooperation on a variety of issues illustrate the kinds of initiatives that should be encouraged and reinforced.[41]

California's government, corporations and foundations should support research on how to enhance the gains and mitigate the costs of globalization on such challenges as employment, wages, port and harbor improvements and other transportation infrastructure. Each region of California should develop the kinds of studies that the Bay Area Council Economic Institute (previously the Bay Area Economic Forum) has produced on that region's international assets and opportunities. Those who lead such research should assure that each region's stakeholders participate both in conducting the analysis and implementing the resulting recommendations.

Enhancing Global Awareness

California's decision-makers and opinion-shapers, both in the public sector and in nongovernmental organizations, should be encouraged and helped to think more systematically and consistently about the state's international stakes and to become better informed about decisions and actions that can be taken at the national, state and local governmental levels and in business and nongovernmental domains. The growing infrastructure for gaining information and exchanging data and perspectives noted in Chapter 2 represents undoubted advance over California's earlier very limited degree of global awareness, but much remains to be done.

It is crucial to reinforce the work of the Pacific Council on International Policy, the Bay Area Council Economic Institute, the several World Affairs Councils and those university-based international research centers that try to link research and analysis on international issues with the worlds of decisions and actions, as well as to expand the impact of such relevant research organizations as RAND, SRI International and the Institute for the Future. The Public Policy Institute of California should promptly restore an emphasis on the state's international challenges as a central aspect of what the state must confront if it is to achieve its potential for growth, competitiveness, equity and good governance. And California's media—print and electronic—have a crucially important potential for enhancing global awareness and cosmopolitan capacity. California's philanthropic foundations should support innovative and effective programs in this realm.

California has a long way to go to develop the strong internationally oriented leadership cadres that have made New York, Washington and London such important capitals. Exceptional individual policymakers from California such as Warren Christopher, George Shultz, Condoleezza Rice and William Perry are not yet consistently supported in our state by deep networks of business and professional leaders who are fully engaged and broadly knowledgeable about the wider world, like those in the Northeast corridor. Civic and business leaders who understand and act on international imperatives, and who can persuasively explain their importance to others, are vitally important in an increasingly globalized world. So are attentive publics who are well-informed about the world and internationally aware citizens empowered to respond effectively to global transformations. Nothing less will be enough for Californians to succeed in the twenty-first century.

Changing Our Mindset: Embracing Global Engagement

It is a truism that we live today in an era of globalization, as this volume has documented in detail. But it is not enough simply to be aware of globalization, or merely to cheer globalization or else condemn it. We must respond proactively and effectively to the many challenges, risks, costs and opportunities that globalization presents. Nowhere is this more obvious or more important than in California.

Californians got by during the twentieth century without concerning themselves much with foreign policy or international relationships. But in the twenty-first century, we cannot continue to leave these questions to Washington. Californians today have global stakes that require actions at the federal, state and local levels, and by nongovernmental actors ranging from corporations to unions, foundations to faith-based organizations, universities and research institutions to the media and professions.

Governor Schwarzenegger has taken some important first steps to recognize California's need to face climate change and to seize the state's opportunities to exert international influence on the environment. But these initiatives must be followed up, paralleled by comparable efforts on other questions, further developed and persistently coordinated, year in and year out.

California has a highly globalized and enormously dynamic economy, a richly diverse population and strong international links. We need to expand and better use our capacity to understand and meet the challenges of global engagement. Above all, we need to change our mindset—from living in a parochial place with the dimensions of a country to participating in a truly cosmopolitan center, ready to provide important leadership in the twenty-first century.

REFERENCE MATTER

Appendix: Global California—A Graphic Display

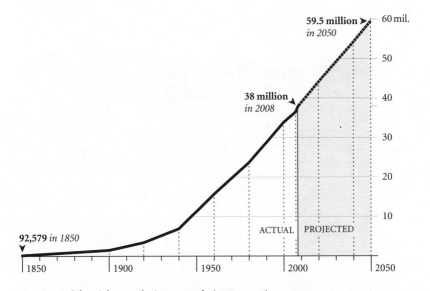

59.5 million *in 2050*

38 million *in 2008*

92,579 *in 1850*

ACTUAL   PROJECTED

60 mil.

50

40

30

20

10

1850   1900   1950   2000   2050

FIGURE 1 California's population growth (1850–2050)

SOURCES: 1850–2007 data: U.S. Bureau of the Census, Population Division, Estimates, July 1, 2007. 2020–2050 data: State of California, Department of Finance, Population Projections for California and Its Counties 2000–2050, Sacramento, California, July 2007. 2008 estimate: State of California, Department of Finance, Population Estimates for Cities, Counties and the State, Sacramento, California, May 2008.

All information graphics in this appendix were created by Tommy McCall.

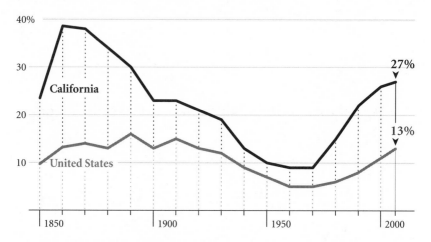

FIGURE 2 Percentage of foreign-born residents (1850–2006)

SOURCES: 1850 and 1860: Campbell J. Gibson and Emily Lennon, "Historical Census Statistics on the Foreign-born Population of the United States: 1850–1990," Population Division Working Paper No. 29 (February 1999), U.S. Bureau of the Census. 1870–2006 graph from The Public Policy Institute of California: www.ppic.org/content/pubs/jtf/JTF_ImmigrantsJTF.pdf.

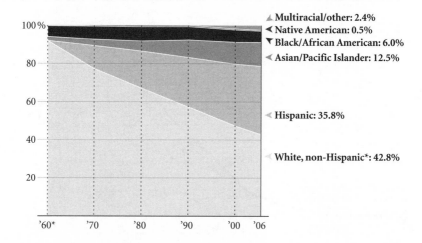

FIGURE 3 California's ethnic composition (1960–2006)

SOURCES: 1960: U.S. Department of Commerce, Bureau of the Census, Census of Population: 1960; Volume 1, Part 6, California. U.S. Government Printing Office, Washington DC, 1963. 1970–2000: California Department of Finance, Demographic Research Unit: California Race/Ethnic Population Estimates, July 1970–July 1990 and 2000–2004. 2006: American Community Survey 2006.

*Hispanic category did not exist in 1960; the Hispanic population was lumped into the white population. Ethnic categories have changed slightly under each census, including the addition of a Hispanic category in 1970, and multiracial/other category after 1990.

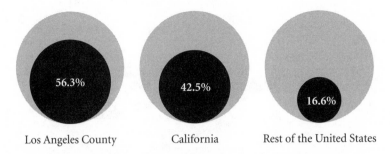

Los Angeles County   California   Rest of the United States

FIGURE 4 Percentage of persons aged five years and older speaking a language other than English at home, 2006
SOURCE: Census Bureau, American Community Survey, 2006.

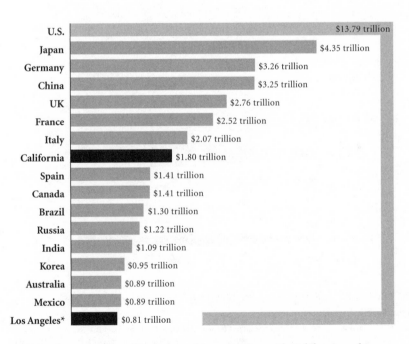

FIGURE 5 Gross product of leading world economies, with California and Los Angeles comparisons
SOURCE: Taken from Jack Kyser, Nancy D. Sidhu, Eduardo J. Martinez and Candice Flor Hynek, 2008–2009 Economic Forecast and Industry Outlook, for California and Southern California, including the National and International Setting. Los Angeles: Los Angeles Economic Development Corporation, February 2008.
*Five-county area.

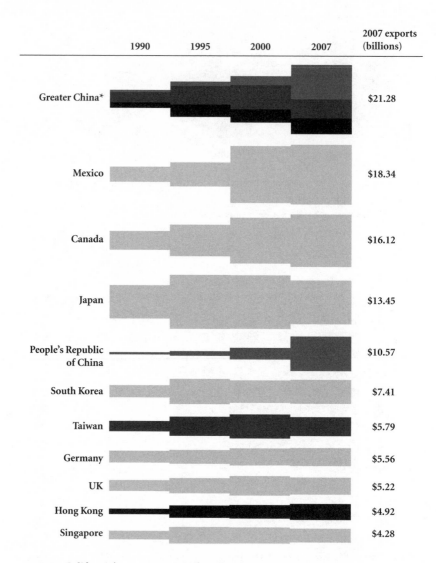

	1990	1995	2000	2007	2007 exports (billions)
Greater China*					$21.28
Mexico					$18.34
Canada					$16.12
Japan					$13.45
People's Republic of China					$10.57
South Korea					$7.41
Taiwan					$5.79
Germany					$5.56
UK					$5.22
Hong Kong					$4.92
Singapore					$4.28

FIGURE 6 California's top export markets (2007) with historical exports (1990–2000) for those markets

SOURCES: For 1987–1998, the data are from the the California Trade and Commerce Agency, with special thanks to Brian Bugsch. For 1999–2007, the data are from TradeStats Express™, http://tse. export.gov. The two series are not strictly comparable, but are based on very similar sources and measures.

*Total for People's Republic of China, Tiawan and Hong Kong.

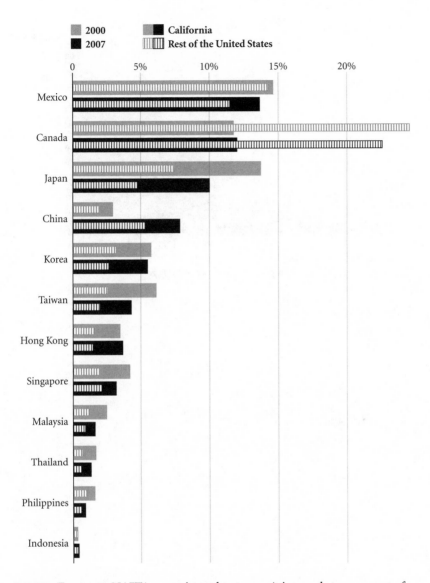

FIGURE 7 Exports to NAFTA countries and to top-10 Asian markets as percent of total exports, compared with the rest of the United States (2007)

SOURCE: Trade Stats Express State Export Data and National Trade Data from the International Trade Association, U.S. Department of Commerce at http://trade.gov.

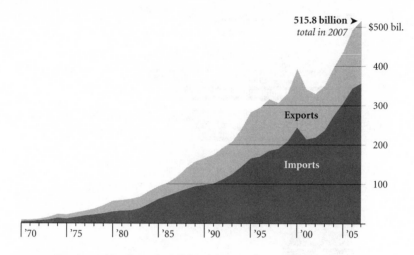

FIGURE 8 Foreign trade through California's ports (1970–2007)

Notes

To keep up on this subject and update information, I recommend the national, state, regional, port and municipal Web sites that are mentioned in the notes; the publications of the Public Policy Institute of California, the Milken Institute, the Pacific Council on International Policy and the many university research centers and institutes cited in the notes; the publications of the various regional economic development corporations and chambers of commerce; and the state's major newspapers, particularly the *Los Angeles Times*, *San Francisco Chronicle*, *San Diego Union-Tribune*, *San Jose Mercury News*, *Oakland Tribune*, *Orange County Register*, *Sacramento Bee*, *Fresno Bee* and *Riverside Press Enterprise*.

Chapter 1

1. See California Department of Finance, "Population Estimates for Cities, Counties and the State, 2001–2008 with 2000 Benchmark," May 2008, at www.dof.ca.gov/research/demographic/reports. As of January 1, 2008, the department estimated the state's population as 38,049,462.

2. Projections from PPIC predict that California's population in 2025 will be between 43.9 million in the low-growth scenario and 48.2 million in the high-growth scenario. See Hans P. Johnson, "California's Population in 2025," in *California 2025: Taking on the Future*, eds. Ellen Hanak and Mark Baldassare (San Francisco: PPIC, 2005), 27–28. The Census Bureau has predicted 44.3 million Californians in 2025, constituting upwards of 13 percent of the country's population for that year. See U.S. Census Bureau, Population Division, Interim State Population Projections, "Interim Projections of the Total Population for the United States and States: April 1, 2000 to July 1, 2030," 2005, Table A1, at www.census.gov/population/www/projections/projectionsagesex.html, accessed July 13, 2007.

3. California Department of Finance, "New State Projections Show 25 Million More Californians by 2050; Hispanics to Be State's Majority Ethnic Group by 2042," press release, n.d., www.dof.ca.gov/html/DEMOGRAP/ReportsPapers/Projections/P1/documents/P1 _Press_Release_7-07.pdf. The report prompted Jack Kyser, lead economist with the Los Angeles County Economic Development Corporation, to remark that California is "a country masquerading as a state." See Maria L. Lagana and Sara Lin, "60 Million Californians by Mid-Century; Riverside Will Become the Second Most Populous County behind Los Angeles and Latinos the Dominant Ethnic Group, Study Says," *Los Angeles Times*, July 10, 2007.

4. Data on country GDP are available from a number of online sources, including that of the International Monetary Fund, www.imf.org, as well as that of the World Bank, www.worldbank.org. The California state data is from the U.S. Bureau of Economic Analysis. See www.bea.gov.

5. For goods export statistics by country, see the World Bank, http://econ. worldbank.org. Statistics on country exports of goods and services are computable from the percentages of GDP constituted by such exports, available through the World Bank's data query facility. For merchandise exports by U.S. state, see the World Institute of Strategic Economic Research, www.wisertrade.org. On California's export of services, see Ashok Bardhan and Cynthia Kroll, "Services Export Opportunities for California—A Preliminary Assessment," Fisher Center Working Paper 300 (Berkeley: Fisher Center for Real Estate and Urban Economics, University of California, 2006).

6. The national figure is reported at $13,841.3 billion. See www.bea.gov. Also see Jon D. Haveman, Ethan M. Jennings and Howard J. Shatz, *California and the Global Economy: Recent Facts and Figures, 2006 Edition* (San Francisco: PPIC, Occasional Papers, 2006), iii, 23.

7. *Fortune* publishes its lists in April or May. Company rankings by revenue rely on data from the previous fiscal year. Texas hosted more companies in 2008 (58) and 2006 (56); New York ranked first in 2007 (57) and 2005 (54). California was runner-up with 52 firms in 2005 (third-place Texas registered 44), and topped the 2004 rankings with 53 companies. See "Fortune 500 Largest U.S. Corporations," in *Fortune*, April 5, 2004, B-1– B-13, F-33, F-39 and F-42; and "5 Hundred Ranked Within States," *Fortune*, April 18, 2005, F-1– F-24, F-35, F-41 and F-44. For the 2006–2008 lists, see the data online at http://money.cnn.com/magazines/fortune/fortune500/2006/index.html, http://money. cnn.com/magazines/fortune/fortune500/2007/index.html and http://money.cnn.com/ magazines/fortune/fortune500/2008/index.html, accessed July 25, 2007 and May 27, 2008.

8. See Chet Currier, "California Now U.S. Hub for Mutual Funds," Associated Press, in the *Oakland Tribune*, February 21, 2006, B1, 2.

9. For 2004–2006, the top three states by value of final agricultural output were California, Texas and Iowa, in that order. See U.S. Department of Agriculture, Economic Research Service, State Fact Sheets, http://www.ers.usda.gov/StateFacts/. The 2002 Census of Agriculture reports that the country's top five counties in value of agricultural

production are in California; see the data online at http://www.nass.usda.gov/Census_of
_Agriculture/.

The California Department of Food and Agriculture (CDFA) reports that for 2005 nine California counties rank among the nation's top ten, with first-ranked Fresno County's output estimated at $4.64 billion. See CDFA, *California Agriculture Highlights 2006* (Sacramento: CDFA, 2007, accessed July 8, 2007), http://www.cdfa.ca.gov/ Publications.html.

For estimates of California's 2006 agricultural exports, see the documents available from the University of California Agricultural Issues Center, including Omid Rowhani and Daniel A. Sumner, "California's International Agricultural Exports in 2006," *AIC Issues Brief*, no. 32, December 2007, http://aic.ucdavis.edu/pub/briefs/brief32.pdf, and Table 2, California Share of U.S. Exports, 2005–2006, http://aic.ucdavis.edu/pub/ exports.html. Data in the latter document point to no less than eighteen export commodities for which California supplied between 90 and 100 percent.

California is the leading dairy producer in the United States and the second-largest cotton grower. On California's dairy industry, see CDFA, *California Dairy Statistics and Trends 2006* (Sacramento: CDFA, 2007), 6–10; on California's cotton growing industry, see the Web pages of the California Cotton Ginners and Growers Associations at http:// ww.ccgga.org, particularly www.//ccgga.org/cotton_information/.

10. Scott Duke Harris, "How Globalization Strengthens the Tech Economy," *San Jose Mercury News*, November 26, 2007.

11. Data on values of state and national exports of some categories of products, using the North American Industry Classification System (NAICS) and other classification systems, are available from TradeStats Express™, U.S. Department of Commerce, International Trade Administration and Office of Trade and Industry Information, Manufacturing and Services, at http://tse.export.gov.

12. For April 2008, the top five Internet search engines (by number of searches from the United States) were Google, Yahoo! Search, MSN/Windows Live Search, AOL Search and Ask.com Search, in that order. See "Nielsen Online Announces April U.S. Search Share Rankings," May 19, 2008, www.netratings.com/press.jsp (accessed May 29, 2008). Meanwhile, Wikipedia relocated from Florida to San Francisco early in 2008, and Palo Alto's Facebook, founded in 2004, ranked second worldwide among online social networks with 73.5 million visitors, individuals fifteen years or older, in September 2007. See the data from comScore World Metrix in "Social Networks Go Global," *Wall Street Journal*, November 1, 2007, B3.

13. On biomedical firms, see Kevin Starr, *Coast of Dreams: California on the Edge, 1990–2003* (New York: Knopf, 2004), 279. According to Starr, the San Francisco Bay Area has the largest number of biotech firms in the country, San Diego is fourth and Los Angeles/Orange County ranks sixth.

According to the California Healthcare Institute, as of 2006, California had 2,700 biomedical companies, with $72.8 billion in revenues and 267,600 employees. The state saw $3.2 billion in venture capital investment in biotechnology, medical devices and related equipment for 2006, a value more than three times that of runner-up Massachusetts. See

California Healthcare Institute and PriceWaterhouseCoopers, *California's Biomedical Industry, 2008 Report*, January 2008, 7, 10, 24–26.

14. The International Association of Nanotechnology, with headquarters in San Jose, has been at the forefront of such endeavors, which include the California Nanotechnology Initiative, the California Institute of Nanotechnology and Innovation California. See www.ianano.org. The Northern California Nanotechnology Initiative, in Menlo Park, and the California Nanosystems Institute, based jointly at UCLA and UCSB, also are major entities. See www.ncnano.org/, www.cnsi.ucla.edu/ and www.cnsi.ucsb.edu/. On "clean technology" ventures, see, for example, *California Green Innovation Index*, 2008 Inaugural Issue (Palo Alto: Next 10, 2007). See also Harris, "Tech Economy."

15. Toward the end of the 1990s and into the twenty-first century, studies provided various estimates of the Los Angeles studios' collective global market share. Perhaps the most frequently quoted figure is 85 percent, a United Nations Education, Scientific and Cultural Organization (UNESCO) estimate relying on data from the 1980s and 1990s. See *A Survey on National Cinematography* (Paris: UNESCO Culture Sector, Division of Creativity, Cultural Industries and Copyright, March 2000), 18. Another datum often mentioned is contained in a September 12, 2000, report by ABN Amro, an international bank based in Holland, which concludes that U.S. studios supply 75 percent of nondomestic markets. One political scientist has stated Hollywood's share of global film markets at 80 percent and television markets at 70 percent. See Kerry Chase, "Globalization Versus Localization: Cultural Protection and Trade Conflict in the World Entertainment Industry," draft (Los Angeles: International Studies Association, March 2000), 12. Toby Miller and others at the British Film Institute find that Hollywood's share of global film markets in the early twenty-first century is twice the size of its 1990 take; see Toby Miller, et al., *Global Hollywood 2* (London: British Film Institute, 2005), 10. Writing in 2005, one economist estimates the U.S. control—understood as the control of the major Hollywood studios—of the global motion picture market at 83 percent. David Waterman, *Hollywood's Road to Riches* (Cambridge, MA: Harvard University Press, 2005), 6, 326. Waterman writes further (167) that Hollywood's fare predominates in international trade of television shows, though the gains here are less impressive than those from movies.

Hollywood's share of most individual film markets outside the United States has been estimated at 60 to 90 percent. See Priyanka Khanna, "Hollywood Studios Have Mixed Record in India," Indo-Asian News Service, January 30, 2005, www.bollywood.com/content/hollywood-studios-have-mixed-record-india (accessed August 28, 2008).

16. The Motion Picture Association of America (MPAA) reports that, for 2005, the U.S. enjoyed a positive trade balance of $9.5 billion in motion picture and television products. See the association's report, *The Economic Impact of the Motion Picture & Television Production Industry on the United States*, 2006, 2, 5, 10. See also Chase, "Globalization Versus Localization," 13, and Waterman, *Road to Riches*, 167, 359. Waterman suggests that total U.S. exports of audiovisual products contributed to a trade surplus in this category of some $14 billion for 2000; U.S. exports of films and tape rentals alone

amounted to over $9.3 billion in 2001, with U.S. films taking more than half the market share in France, more than 60 percent in Japan and Italy, and more than 75 percent in the United Kingdom, Germany and Spain. See Allen J. Scott, *On Hollywood: The Place, The Industry* (Princeton, NJ: Princeton University Press, 2005), 152, 160, passim.

17. National Science Foundation, Division of Science Resources Statistics, "*Survey of Research and Development Expenditures at Universities and Colleges*," FY 2006, Table 27, www.nsf.gov. For 2006, Johns Hopkins University was ranked first; UC Los Angeles was third, UC San Francisco fifth, UC San Diego seventh and Stanford University eighth. UC Davis ranked sixteenth, and UC Berkeley nineteenth. The University of Southern California came in thirtieth, and the California Institute of Technology sixty-fifth, out of a total of 640 institutions.

18. The ten are Stanford, California Institute of Technology, the University of Southern California and the campuses of the University of California at Berkeley, San Diego, Los Angeles, San Francisco, Santa Barbara, Davis and Irvine. Stanford, Berkeley and Cal Tech are listed among the top six. See Institute of Higher Education, Shanghai Jiao Tong University, "Academic Ranking of World Universities," 2007, http://ed.sjtu.edu.cn.

19. Patents issued to Californians in 2007 numbered 22,601, to Texans 6,228, and to New Yorkers 6,025. See U.S. Patent Office, "Patent Counts by Country/State and Year; All Patents, All Types; January 1, 1977–December 31, 2007," March 2008, www.uspto.gov.

20. See California Business, Transportation and Housing Agency, *Toward a California Trade and Investment Strategy: Potential Roles for the State in Global Market Development* (Sacramento, October 1, 2007), 76.

21. For detailed information on Nobel laureates in California and elsewhere, see http://nobelprize.org.

22. For 2007 data on wealth, see Matthew Miller, "The 400 Richest Americans," September 20, 2007, www.forbes.com/2007/09/19/richest-americans-forbes-lists-richlist07-cx_mm_0920rich_land.html (accessed September 20, 2007). For 1982, see "The Forbes Four Hundred," *Forbes*, September 13, 1982, 99–186, esp. 176–86.

23. For data on foundations, see the Foundation Center, "Top 100 U.S. Foundations by Asset Size," September 11, 2008, http://foundationcenter.org/findfunders/statistics/ (accessed October 15, 2008).

24. See Philip Matier and Andrew Ross, "State a Gold Mine for Presidential Candidates," *San Francisco Chronicle*, June 4, 2008.

25. See Deborah Reed, Melissa Glenn-Haber and Lawrence Mamersh, *The Distribution of Income in California* (San Francisco: PPIC, 1996); Deborah Reed, *California's Rising Income Inequality: Causes and Concerns* (San Francisco: PPIC, 1996); and Deborah Reed, "Recent Trends in Income and Poverty" in *California Counts: Population Trends and Profiles*, ed. Hans G. Johnson (San Francisco: PPIC, February 2004).

26. Several calculations and estimates have been made of California's homeless populations. The National Alliance to End Homelessness estimated 170,270 homeless Californians for January 2005, almost three times the figures for New York (61,094) and

Florida (60,867), with California very near the top in per capita terms. See National Alliance to End Homelessness, *Homelessness Counts*, January 2007, 13–14, www.endhomelessness.org. In the late 1990s, the California Department of Housing and Community Development produced an estimate, for 1996–1997, of 361,000 homeless persons at a given point in time. See California Department of Housing and Community Development, *The State of California's Housing Markets, 1990–1997, Statewide Housing Plan Update, Phase II*, January 1999, 121, www.hcd.ca.gov/hpd/hrc/plan/shp/ (accessed July 10, 2007). The Los Angeles Homeless Services Authority (LAHSA) has offered a point-in-time estimate of 195,637 homeless Californians; see LAHSA, "The Los Angeles Homeless Services Authority Releases a Groundbreaking Report on the Homeless Population in Los Angeles County," press release, January 12, 2006. See also LAHSA, *2005 Greater Los Angeles Homeless Count*, January 12, 2006, www.lahsa.org.

The total of those who experience homelessness over the course of a calendar year is much higher—anywhere from three to six times as high as time-point estimates, according to the Urban Institute. California's over-the-year totals have been estimated to range from 1 million to 2 million. See Lisa K. Foster and Patricia Snowdon, *Addressing Long Term Homelessness: Permanent Supportive Housing* (Sacramento: California Research Bureau, August 2003), 16; and the California Governor's Office of Planning and Research, *A Summary Report on California's Programs to Address Homelessness*, March 2002, 7–8.

27. Los Angeles ranked third, San Francisco fourth, San Diego seventeenth, San Jose twenty-ninth, Palo Alto thirty-first and Sacramento thirty-eighth among all U.S. cities. See Peter J. Taylor and Robert E. Lang, "U.S. Cities in the 'World City Network' " (Washington, DC: Brookings Institution, 2005).

28. See the data posted by the American Association of Port Authorities, "World Port Ranking—2006," www.aapa-ports.org (accessed May 29, 2008). Los Angeles ranks tenth and Long Beach twelfth in total TEUs processed; Singapore, Hong Kong, Shanghai, Shenzhen and Busan, in that order, are the top five ports, followed by Kaohsiung, Rotterdam, Dubai and Hamburg, for ranks six through nine. The Port of Oakland ranks thirty-ninth internationally and fourth in the United States, behind New York-New Jersey.

29. For all foreign waterborne trade, see the data from the Census Bureau's Foreign Trade Division, and for foreign container trade, see data from the Port Import Export Reporting Service (PIERS). Both sets are available at the Web site of the U.S. Department of Transportation, Maritime Administration, www.marad.dot.gov/MARAD _statistics/index.html (accessed May 28, 2008). For an analysis, see Haveman, Jennings and Shatz, *California and the Global Economy*, iii, 23, 25.

30. Data on cargo volumes and passengers handled at the world's airports are available at the Web site of the Airports Council International, www.airports.org (accessed May 29, 2008). Preliminary data for 2007 put LAX again in fifth place for passenger totals and twelfth in cargo handling.

31. Data on the value of total exports by state are available from the World Institute for Strategic Economic Research, wisertrade.org.

32. See Jack Kyser, et al., *2008–2009 Economic Forecast & Industry Outlook for California & Southern California, Including the National and International Setting* (Los Angeles: Los Angeles County Economic Development Corporation, February 2008), 15.

33. See the *Engineering News-Record* at www.enr.construction.com/people/topLists/topDesignBuild/topdb_ 1-50.asp (accessed May 29, 2008). Parsons has a presence in more than fifteen countries; Bechtel and Jacobs have offices in more than twenty countries. See also the respective company Web sites: www.jacobs.com, www.bechtel.com and www.parsons.com.

34. For enrollment figures, see the annual *Open Doors* reports put out by the Institute of International Education, New York, http://opendoors.iienetwork.org/. For contributions to the state economy, see the NAFSA: Association of International Educators' "Economic Impact Statements" for California for recent years, available via www.nafsa.org.

In the 2001–2002 academic year, the University of Southern California (USC) surpassed New York University as the leading host institution in the country for foreign students. USC has maintained its first-place rank ever since, and it has increased its enrollments of international graduate and undergraduate students almost every year since 1997, even as national enrollment of foreign students has fallen in the post-9/11 environment. According to the USC Factbook, the university had 1,528 undergraduate and 4,109 graduate international students in the fall 2006 term, making up 9.1 percent and 24.7 percent of the university's undergraduate and graduate student bodies, respectively. See www.usc.edu/about/ataglance/student_facts_200607.html. See also, for various academic years, the *International Student Enrollment Report*, published by the Office of International Services, Division of Student Affairs, USC, downloadable from www.usc.edu/student-affairs/OIS/Service/pdfs.

Significantly, for the 2005–2006 academic year, 22,683 students who were enrolled for the fall term in a California degree-granting institution studied abroad, a figure that, while highest in absolute numbers, was less than 1 percent of all such California students at that time, well below the mean of 1.3 percent for all states and the District of Columbia. See NAFSA, "Study Abroad Participation by State, 2005-2006 Academic Year," www.nafsa.org.

35. The Internet Movie Database, www.imdb.com, maintains rankings of films according to gross box office receipts. As of summer 2007, the site lists 303 films that appeared from 1996 through mid-July 2007 in one or more of its All-Time USA, All-Time Non-USA and All-Time Worldwide Box Office rankings. Of these 303 movies, 170, or 56 percent, involved in some way at least one production company based in the Los Angeles area and scored higher foreign than domestic gross box office receipts. Additional data on international box office receipts can be found at www.hollywoodreporter.com. Box office rankings of U.S. films with adjustments for inflation may be found at www.filmsite.org. The same, similar or related data can be obtained via Movieweb.com, Boxofficereport.com, The-Movie-Times.com and Boxoficemojo.com.

David Waterman suggests similarly that the majority of the studios' movie income is generated in U.S. markets but also points to their great international success: "In fact,

American films now earn more than half the box office in nearly all major markets of the world, and the U.S. share routinely exceeds 80 percent in several major countries, including Germany and Britain." See Waterman, *Road to Riches*, 3, 5.

36. Figures on international sales for specific Silicon Valley companies such as Intel and Applied Materials, each of which reported more than three-fourths of net sales as international for 2004–2007, are available on their Web sites or in SEC 10-k filings. See also the Bay Area Economic Forum's *International Trade and the Bay Area Economy: Regional Interests and Global Outlook, 2005–2006*, July 2005, 29–33. In recent years, several companies, including Hewlett Packard and Cisco Systems, highlighted a rapid growth of exports to emerging markets, especially the BRIC countries (Brazil, Russia, India and China). See Harris, "Tech Economy," and reports of the Semiconductor Industry Association, available at www.sia-online.org.

37. For a parallel discussion of California's international diversity, its origins and effects, see Starr, *Coast of Dreams*, 141–177. See also Peter Schrag, *California: America's High Stakes Experiment* (Berkeley: University of California Press, 2006).

38. Teresa Watanabe, "California is Leading Nation in Diversity," *Los Angeles Times*, May 17, 2007, B2. This article draws on July 2006 population estimates by the U.S. Census Bureau.

39. Fortuny, Capps and Passel, relying on data from the March 2004 supplement to the Current Population Survey, compute 7.3 million authorized immigrants in California and 25 million in the United States. See Karina Fortuny, Randy Capps and Jeffrey S. Passel, *The Characteristics of Unauthorized Immigrants in California, Los Angeles County, and the United States* (Washington, DC: The Urban Institute, March 2007), 45.

40. See Michael Hoefer, Nancy Rytina and Christopher Campbell, "Estimates of the Unauthorized Immigrant Population Residing in the United States: January 2006," Population Estimates, U.S. Department of Homeland Security, Office of Immigration Statistics, August 2007, 4.

41. These rankings apply to U.S. cities with populations of 100,000 or higher, as of 2006. See Table 1: Annual Estimates of the Population for Incorporated Places over 100,000, Ranked by July 1, 2006 Population: April 1, 2000 to July 1, 2006 (SUB-EST2006-01), Population Division, U.S. Census Bureau, June 28, 2007, via www.census.gov; and GCT0501: Percent of People Who Are Foreign Born: 2006, 2006 American Community Survey, 2006 Puerto Rico Community Survey, www.census.gov/acs/www/ and http://factfinder.census.gov. The American Community Survey data do not include populations "living in institutions, college dormitories and other group quarters."

42. See PPIC, "Just the Facts: Immigrants in California," June 2008, www.ppic.org. Data taken from decennial censuses.

43. For the projection of the foreign-born fraction of California's population in 2030, see Dowell Myers, John Pitkin and Julie Park, *California Demographic Futures: Projections to 2030, by Immigrant Generations, Nativity and Time, Arrival in U.S.* (Los Angeles: School of Policy, Planning and Development, University of Southern California, January 2005). For an informative report on the increasing numbers of foreign-

born persons residing outside California, see Robin Fields, "A Dispersing of New Minorities to New Places," *Los Angeles Times*, August 15, 2006.

The proportions of recently arrived (in the ten-year period preceding the decennial census) foreign-born individuals to the United States living in California have declined from the 1990 figure of 37.6 percent to 24.8 percent for 2000 and 20.8 percent for 2005. See Table P036: Year of Entry, in *Census 1990 summary tape file 3*; Table P22: Year of Entry for the Foreign-Born Population, in *Census 2000 summary tape file 3*; and Table C05005: Year of Entry by Citizenship Status in the United States, in the 2005 American Community Survey, all available via www.census.gov.

In their counts and estimates, the decennial census and the American Community Survey make no distinctions regarding authorization status of the foreign-born. During the 1990s, some 32 percent of the documented international immigrants to the United States indicated their intended residence as California; between 10 and 19 percent of the national total stated the Los Angeles-Long Beach-Santa Ana Core-Based Statistical Area of Residence. See, among other sources, U.S. Department of Homeland Security, "Table 13, Immigrants Admitted by State of Intended Residence: Fiscal Years 1988-2002," in *2002 Yearbook of Immigration Statistics* (Washington, DC: DHS, Office of Immigration Statistics) www.dhs.gov/ximgtn/statistics/publications/YrBko2Im.shtm; and U.S. Department of Homeland Security, "Persons Becoming Legal Permanent Residents (LPRs) by Core-Based Statistical Area of Residence (CBSA): 1990 to 1999," in *Mapping Immigration: Legal Permanent Residents* (Washington, DC: DHS, Office of Immigration Statistics), www.dhs.gov/ximgtn/statistics/data/lprmaps.shtm.

For the period 2000–2004, California was still the intended residence of some 25–27 percent of authorized immigrants. See U.S. Department of Homeland Security, Office of Immigration Statistics, *2005 Yearbook of Immigration Statistics* (Washington, DC: DHS, November 2006), 16. For the years 2002–2004, California provided five of the ten most frequently mentioned metropolitan areas. See Nancy F. Rytina, "U.S. Legal Permanent Residents: 2004," in *Annual Flow Report* (Washington, DC: DHS, Office of Immigration Statistics, June 2005), 5. For 2005 and 2006, California's share declined, with about 21 percent of the flow of legal permanent residents locating their homes in the state. See Kelly Jeffreys, "U.S. Legal Permanent Residents: 2006," in *Annual Flow Report* (Washington, DC: DHS, Office of Immigration Statistics, March 2007), 4. Even with this reduction, California remains the most frequently named state of intended residence, substantially ahead of runners-up New York and Florida (14.2 and 12.3 percent, respectively, for 2006).

Moreover, for the years 2003–2004, California was home to over 28 percent of the estimated total of 11.55 million legal permanent residents in the United States, more than twice the percentage of runner-up New York (with about 13 percent) and three times that of third-ranking Texas (with about 9.5 percent). See Nancy F. Rytina, "Estimates of the Legal Permanent Resident Population and Population Eligible to Naturalize in 2003" in *Population Estimates* (Washington, DC: DHS, Office of Immigration Statistics), January 2005, 5; and Nancy F. Rytina, "Estimates of the Legal Permanent Resident Population and Population Eligible to Naturalize in 2004," in *Population Estimates* (Washington, DC: DHS, Office of Immigration Statistics, February 2006), 5.

44. See the data from Census 2000, "Summary File 3, PCT19," on numbers and places of birth of foreign-born persons in each state, available via www.census.gov. See also the 2006 American Community Survey, whose data are accessible via www.census.gov/acs/www/ or http://factfinder.census.gov.

45. In addition to the data available from the Census Bureau mentioned in the previous note, see the estimates on countries of origin and destination for 2000 stored in the Global Migrant Origin Database, maintained by the Development Research Centre on Migration, Globalisation and Poverty, University of Sussex, accessible at www.migrationdrc.org/research/typesofmigration/global_migrant_origin_database.html. The present study makes use of Version 1.

46. The Mexican Instituto Nacional de Estadística, Geografía e Informática (INEGI) counts the population of the city of Zacatecas at 122,889, the municipality at 132,035, for 2005. Data can be downloaded from www.inegi.gob.mx/est/contenidos/espanol/sistemas/conteo2005/localidad/iter/; the home page can be reached via www.inegi.gob.mx. *La Opinión* reported in late 2003 an estimate of over 200,000 Zacatecanos in Los Angeles; Lucero Amador, "Zacatecas en Los Angeles," *La Opinión*, December 31, 2003. Cf. Carol Zabin and Luis Escala Rabadan, "Mexican Hometown Associations and Mexican Political Empowerment in Los Angeles" (Washington, DC: The Aspen Institute, Nonprofit Sector Research Fund, Working Paper Series, Winter 1998), 9.

47. See the 2006 American Community Survey, www.census.gov/acs/www/ or http://factfinder.census.gov.

48. For the 2006–2007 school year, the non-Hispanic white enrollment at L.A. Unified was estimated at not quite 9 percent. For San Diego Unified in the same period, non-Hispanic whites constituted an estimated 25.5 percent of enrollment. Education Data Partnership, www.ed-data.k12.ca.us/ (accessed November 10, 2007).

See Michael Fix, et al., *Los Angeles on the Leading Edge: Immigrant Integration Indicators and Their Policy Implications* (Washington, DC: Migration Policy Institute, April 2008), 4.

49. The proportion of Californians speaking languages other than English at home was computed at 39.5 percent by Census 2000; it was estimated at 42.3 percent by the 2005 American Community Survey (and at 19.4 percent for the nation); and at 42.5 percent for the state and 19.7 percent for the country by the 2006 survey. See Census 2000, "Summary File 3, QT-P16," available at www.census.gov, and the ACS data at www.census.gov/acs/www/ or http://factfinder.census.gov.

50. See U.S. Department of Commerce, Bureau of the Census, *2002 Survey of Business Owners*, www.census.gov/csd/sbo.

51. See Vivek Wadhwa, et al., *America's New Immigrant Entrepreneurs* (Durham, NC: Master of Engineering Management Program, Duke University; Berkeley: School of Information, University of California, January 4, 2007), 4.

52. See AnnaLee Saxenian, *Silicon Valley's New Immigrant Entrepreneurs* (San Francisco: PPIC, April 1999), 23. See also AnnaLee Saxenian, *The New Argonauts* (Cambridge, MA: Harvard University Press), 2006.

53. See Hans P. Johnson and Deborah Reed's study, "Can California Import Enough College Graduates to Meet Workforce Needs?" *California Counts*, 8, no. 4 (May 2007).

54. California has reduced its rate of increases in emissions, but overall emissions continue to rise. See Gerry Bemis and Jennifer Allen, *Inventory of California Greenhouse Gas Emissions and Sinks: 1990 to 2004 Staff Final Report Update* (Transportation Technology Office, Fuels and Transportation Division, California Energy Commission, December 2006), 1.

Per capita, for 2004, according to U.S. Department of Energy data and Census Bureau population estimates, California's carbon dioxide emissions are at nearly 11 metric tons, less than any other state but Rhode Island. See emissions estimates from the Department of Energy at www.eia.doe.gov/environment.html and population estimates at www.census.gov/popest/datasets.html. See also Seth Borenstein, "Blame Coal; Texas Leads Carbon Emissions," Associated Press, *San Francisco Chronicle*, June 2, 2007.

UC Berkeley researchers estimate the state could profit by some $60 billion and create 20,000 jobs over the longer term through policies that encourage further emissions reductions. See the California Climate Change Center, *Managing Greenhouse Gas Emissions in California* (Berkeley: University of California, January 2006), http://calclimate.berkeley.edu/.

55. For effects overseas caused by the U.S. subprime mortgage downward spiral, see, for example, "Woes Know No Border; IKB's Hit Worsens in Germany; a Loss in Norway," *Wall Street Journal*, November 29, 2007, C2. For the third quarter of 2007, some 34 percent of all U.S. subprime adjustable rate mortgages that began foreclosure procedures were in California and Florida; see Jeannine Aversa, "Delinquent Payments Skyrocket; 3rd Quarter Foreclosures at an All-Time High Level," Associated Press, *San Francisco Chronicle*, December 7, 2007, D1, D6.

56. Member nations of UNESCO in 2005 approved (by a vote of 148–2, with the United States and Israel in opposition) a Convention on the Protection and Promotion of Diversity of Cultural Expressions. The convention states that nations may "maintain, adopt and implement policies and measures that they deem appropriate for the protection and promotion of the diversity of cultural expressions on their territory." Hollywood was a key target of this measure. See Molly Moore, "U.N. Body Endorses Cultural Protection; U.S. Objections Are Turned Aside," *Washington Post*, October 21, 2005, A14; Alan Riding, "Entr'acte: Cultural Imperialism or the Free Flow of Ideas," *International Herald Tribune*, February 3, 2005; and Peter Ford, "Treaty Targets Hollywood Homogenization of Culture," *Seattle Times*, October 20, 2005.

57. As of March 31, 2008, the CalPERS investment portfolio was worth $240.9 billion, of which $48 billion was in international equities. See CalPERS, Facts at a Glance, March 31, 2008, www.calpers.ca.gov (accessed May 29, 2008).

58. The Capital Group's American Funds alone were reported to manage 13.4 percent, or $1.1 trillion, of the $8.2 trillion total in stock and bond funds in 2007, more than Vanguard or Fidelity, the country's second- and third-largest money management firms. See Geraldine Fabrikant, "Fidelity, Thy Name is Ned," *New York Times*, July 29, 2007.

59. These figures are for direct investment by nonbank majority-owned U.S. affiliates. For all nonbank affiliates, the estimated value of "gross property, plant and equipment" is given at $123.5 billion. See Bureau of Economic Analysis, International Economic Accounts, "Foreign Direct Investment in the U.S.: Financial and Operating Data for U.S. Affiliates of Foreign Multinational Companies," www.bea.gov/international/di1fdiop. htm. California leads all other states in foreign investment and the number employed in foreign-owned firms, but these figures remain below the peak levels achieved in 1999–2000.

60. The top sources of international visitors to California are Canada, Mexico, the United Kingdom, Japan, Australia, Germany, South Korea and Taiwan; tourism from China and India is rising. For 2007 figures, see Dean Runyon Associates, *California Travel Impacts by County: 2007 Preliminary State Estimates*, prepared for the California Travel and Tourism Commission, March 2008, 4. For California's share of the U.S. market for overseas tourism, see the data in "Historical Profiles of Overseas Visitors to U.S. States and Territories," http://tinet.ita.doc.gov/outreachpages/inbound_historic_visitation _2007.html; and *Overseas Visitation Estimates for U.S. States, Cities and Census Regions: 2007*, at http://tinet.ita.doc.gov/outreachpages/inbound.general_information.inbound _overview.html, both from U.S. Department of Commerce, International Travel Administration, Office of Travel and Tourism Industries, accessed May 30, 2008.

61. See Deborah Vrana and Ronald D. White, "Weak Dollar Has a Silver Lining for L.A. Tourism," *Los Angeles Times*, December 17, 2004, A-1. On projections of major Chinese tourism abroad, see, for example, Samantha Gross, "U.S. Businesses Target Chinese Tourist Boom," *Oakland Tribune*, June 20, 2007.

62. See "Vacations Mean Business, Port Says," *Los Angeles Times*, April 5, 2007.

63. See Jon D. Haveman, Howard J. Shatz and Ernesto Vilchis, *California and the World Economy: Exports, Foreign Direct Investment and U.S. Trade Policy* (San Francisco: PPIC, Occasional Papers, December 2002), 3. The authors report that from 1990 to 1997, growth in goods exports from the other U.S. states averaged 8.1 percent, and that from 1997 to 2001, California's 1.9 percent growth rate was quite close to the 1.5 percent rate for the other 49 states. From 2001 to 2006, goods exports from California grew in value from $107 to $128 billion, representing an increase of nearly 20 percent and an annual average growth rate of slightly over 4 percent. Data on which these figures are based can be downloaded from the World Institute for Strategic Economic Research, www. wisertrade.org.

In their paper, Haveman, Shatz and Vilchis discussed whether Texas's leadership in value of merchandise exports would continue. As of May 2008, Texas has held on to its first-place ranking, with an average annual growth rate of more than 10 percent from 2001 to 2007.

64. See, for example, Ross C. DeVol, *The Asian Crisis Tsunami: Trade and Other Impacts on California and the United States*, policy brief (Santa Monica, CA: Milken Institute, September 1998). DeVol projected that the Asian financial crisis of 1998–1999 would slow California growth by twice as much as it would affect the U.S. average.

65. See Jon D. Haveman and David Hummels, *California's Global Gateways: Trends and Issues* (San Francisco: PPIC, 2004). See also "A Contentious Cargo Plan," *Los Angeles Times*, January 19, 2007, for a report on proposals to respond to the fact that the Hobart rail yard serving Los Angeles has reached its full capacity of 1.5 million 40-foot cargo containers.

66. The Census Bureau counted California's foreign-born population at 1.3 million in 1960; by 2000 the figure hit 8.8 million. See U.S. Department of Commerce, Bureau of the Census, *Profile of the Foreign-Born Population in the United States*, December 2001, 14. Virtually all of California's population growth in the past decade is attributable either directly to recent international immigration or to the fertility of recent immigrants; 45 percent of the births in California in the late 1990s were to foreign-born women, and more than half the babies born in California since late 2001 have been Latino. See California Department of Health Services, Vital Statistics Section, "California Birth Public Use Tape"; and David E. Hayes-Bautista, *La Nueva California: Latinos in the Golden State* (Berkeley: University of California Press, 2004), xv and passim.

67. See "Orange Empires," *Pacific Historical Review*, Special Issue, vol. 68, no. 2 (May 1999) for an interesting comparative discussion of Los Angeles and Miami as the national frontiers. Compare, also, two books by journalist David Rieff: *Los Angeles: Capital of the Third World* (New York: Simon and Schuster, 1991) and *Going to Miami: Exiles, Tourists, and Refugees in the New America* (New York: Simon & Schuster, 1993).

68. See Jon D. Haveman, *California's Vested Interest in U.S. Trade Liberalization Initiatives* (San Francisco: PPIC, 2001).

69. The medical community in California has mobilized recently, for instance, to confront Chagas' disease, a parasitic infection that can lead to chronic heart trouble, and which has been observed particularly among the Latin American immigrant community. See "Olive View Medical Center Named Center of Excellence for Chagas' Patients," *The Public's Health*, vol. 7, no. 9 (October 2007), 1, and "Chagas' Disease Locally," in *The Public's Health*, vol. 7, no. 9 (October 2007), 1, 3. See also Mary Engel, "L.A. Clinic the First to Treat Chagas Disease," *Los Angeles Times*, November 5, 2007.

70. The U.S. Environmental Protection Agency estimates, for example, that on certain days nearly 25 percent of the particulate matter in the skies above Los Angeles can be traced to China, and some experts predict that China could eventually account for one-third of all of California's air pollution. See Terence Chea, "China's Growing Pollution Reaches U.S.," Associated Press, July 28, 2006.

71. See Robert Lee Hutz, "Asian Air Pollution Affecting Weather," *Los Angeles Times*, March 6, 2007.

72. In the annual volumes of *California Policy Choices*, published from 1984 through 1993 by the School of Public Administration at the University of Southern California, and since 1997 by the School of Public Policy and Social Research at the University of California, Los Angeles, only 3 of the more than 120 articles dealt with international issues, and only a few others treat California's external relations in even a cursory way.

The Public Policy Institute of California, the state's leading think tank, undertook in 1999 a "Global California" initiative, which originally commissioned this monograph;

from 2001 until 2006, a flow of relevant reports was published by PPIC, but the research program was phased out in 2007.

73. For a provocative analysis of the causes and consequences of New York's historic but waning domination of American foreign policy formulation, see James R. Kurth, "Between Europe and America: The New York Foreign Policy State," in *Capital of the American Century: The National and International Influence of New York City*, ed. Martin Shefter (New York: Russell Sage Foundation), 1993.

74. The most important Supreme Court decisions are *Crosby v. National Foreign Trade Council* 530 U.S. 363 (2000), holding that a Massachusetts statute which prohibited (on human rights grounds) the state's government agencies from contracting with firms that do business with Burma was unconstitutional because it was preempted by a 1986 federal statute imposing sanctions on Burma; and *American Insurance Association et al. v. Garimendi, Insurance Commissioner, State of California* 53905396 (2003), which held that California's Holocaust Victims Insurance Relief Act of 1999, requiring insurers doing business in California to disclose information about all policies held in Europe between 1920 and 1945 by a company or anyone related to it, was unconstitutional because it interfered with the president's conduct of the nation's foreign policy. In *National Foreign Trade Council v. Giannoulias*, decided in February 2007, the U.S. District Court for the Northern District of Illinois held unconstitutional the Illinois Sudan Act, a statute that prohibited investing state funds in commercial instruments of Sudan and depositing state funds into any financial institution that did not certify that it had implemented policies requiring loan applicants to certify that they did not own or control Sudan-related property or engage in certain Sudan-related transactions. For a discussion of the Crosby case, predicting that it will not resolve debates about how the principles of federalism should apply in the realm of foreign relations, see Peter J. Spiro, "U.S. Supreme Court Knocks Down State Burma Law," *ASIL Insights*, June 2000, www.asil.org/insights/insigh46.htm. For a thoughtful exploration of the implications of the Massachusetts "Burma Law" for various international relations issues, practical, legal and theoretical, see Terence Guay, "Local Government and Global Politics: The Implications of Massachusetts' 'Burma Law,'" *Political Science Quarterly*, 115 (Fall 2000), 353–77. For an informative review, see Jeanne J. Grimmett, "State and Local Economic Sanctions: Constitutional Issues," CRS Report for Congress (Washington, DC: Congressional Research Service, April 2, 2007).

75. An interesting similar argument about the Midwestern United States is made in Richard C. Longworth, *Caught in the Middle: America's Heartland in the Age of Globalism* (New York: Bloomsbury USA), 2008. Longworth explicitly notes that California is better prepared than the Midwest to respond creatively to the challenges of globalization, but many of his analyses and recommendations regarding the Midwest are relevant to California's needs. See also Charles Madigan, ed., *Global Chicago* (Urbana and Chicago: University of Illinois Press, 2004); and an earlier study on New York, Margaret Crahan and Alberto Vourvoulias-Bush, eds., *The City and the World: New York's Global Future* (New York: Council on Foreign Relations), 1997.

76. Perhaps the first suggestion that California should develop its own foreign policy, briefly set forth and without much consideration of the practical difficulties, was an essay by veteran international correspondent James Goldsborough, then with the *San Jose Mercury News*, on "California's Foreign Policy," published in *Foreign Affairs* in Spring 1993. In a 2001 unpublished essay, "Should California Have a Foreign Policy?" international lawyer Greyson Bryan argued that California can and should pursue its own foreign policy within a zone of permissible state behavior allowed by court decisions. (Manuscript consulted and cited with author's permission.) For a detailed argument in the same vein, see Robert Collier, *California on the Global High Road: State Trade and Investment Strategy for the 21ˢᵗ Century* (Berkeley: Institute of Governmental Studies, University of California, May 20, 1999).

A parallel argument, focused on municipal initiatives, was advanced by Michael H. Shuman in "Dateline Main Street: Local Foreign Policies," *Foreign Policy*, Winter 1986–1987, 154–74, and in a 1995 unpublished book-length manuscript, "Local Rights and Global Wrongs: The Legality of Municipal Foreign Policy," consulted with the author's permission in October 2005.

For a defense of the judicial tendency to limit the international policy scope for states and municipalities, see Brannon P. Denning and Jack H. McCall, "State's Rights and Foreign Policy: Some Things Should Be Left to Washington," *Foreign Affairs*, 79, no. 1 (January–February 2000), 9–14. See also Peter J. Spiro, "Taking Foreign Policy Away from the Feds," *Washington Quarterly*, Winter 1988, 191–203, for a further argument against state and local intrusion into the foreign policy arena.

Chapter 2

1. Gerald D. Nash, "Stages of California's Economic Growth, 1870–1970: An Interpretation," in *Essays and Assays: California's History Reappraised,* ed. George H. Knoles (San Francisco: California Historical Society in cooperation with the Ward Ritchie Press, 1973). Cf. Paul W. Rhode, *The Evolution of California Manufacturing* (San Francisco: PPIC, 2001); and Paul W. Rhode, "The Nash Thesis Revisited: An Economic Historian's View," *Pacific Historical Review*, 1994, 363–92.

2. For an interesting parallel discussion, see Richard A. Walker, "At the Crossroads: Defining California Through the Global Economy," in *A Companion to California History*, eds. William Deverell and David Igler (London: Blackwell Publishing, 2008).

3. Hayes-Bautista, *La Nueva California*, 16 (see note 14).

4. U.S. Treasury Secretary Robert Walker, for example, declared in 1848 that "by our recent acquisitions in the Pacific, Asia has suddenly become our neighbor, with a placid intervening ocean inviting our steamships upon the track of a commerce greater than that of all Europe combined." See Walter LaFeber, *The Clash: A History of U.S.-Japan Relations* (New York: W.W. Norton, 1997), 11. President Abraham Lincoln's Secretary of State, William Seward, declared after the purchase of Alaska, that "henceforth, European commerce, European politics and European activities, although becoming

certainly more intimate, will nevertheless sink in importance, while the Pacific Ocean, its shores, its islands, and the vast regions beyond, will become the chief center of events in the world's great hereafter," as quoted in Starr, *Coast of Dreams*, 290 (see Chap. 1, note 13).

5. J. Alan Greb, "Opening a New Frontier: San Francisco, Los Angeles and the Panama Canal, 1900–1914," *Pacific Historical Review*, 47, no. 3 (1978): 405–24.

6. See, for example, Kevin Starr's discussion of the Pacific Rim concept and nineteenth and early-twentieth century discourse on California's potential role in the Asia-Pacific Basin in Starr, *Coast of Dreams*, 290–92.

7. David J. St. Clair, "New Almaden and California Quicksilver in the Pacific Rim Economy," *California History*, 53, no. 4 (Winter 1994–1995), 294.

8. See David St. Clair, "California Quicksilver in the Pacific Rim Economy, 1850–1890," in *Studies in the Economic History of the Pacific Rim*, eds. A.J.H. Latham, Dennis O'Flynn and Sally Miller (London: Routledge, 1998); and David St. Clair, "The Gold Rush and the Beginnings of California Industry," *California History*, 77, no. 4 (Winter 1998–1999) 185–208.

9. Walker, "Defining California," 77.

10. Lynn Bailey, *Supplying the Mining World: The Mining Equipment Manufacturing of San Francisco, 1850–1900* (Tucson, AZ: Westernlore Press, 1996), viii.

11. The estimate of California's population as of 1850 at 165,000 and the statement that one-fourth of that population was foreign-born comes from Carey McWilliams, *The Great Exception*, rev. ed. (1949; repr. Berkeley: University of California Press, 1999), 66–67.

A U.S. Census Bureau report provides different, lower numbers (a population in 1850 of only 92,597 persons), but states that 23.5 percent were foreign-born. See Campbell J. Gibson and Emily Lennon, "Historical Statistics on the Foreign-Born Population of the United States, 1850–1990," Working Paper 29 (Washington, DC: U.S. Census Bureau, Population Division, February 1991), Table 13.

12. See Alexander Saxton, *The Indispensable Enemy: Labor and the Anti-Chinese Movement in California* (Berkeley: University of California Press, 1971).

13. See Roger Daniels, *The Politics of Prejudice: The Anti-Japanese Movement in California and the Struggle for Japanese Exclusion* (Berkeley: University of California Press, 1992).

14. See José Hernández, "Foreign Migration and California," in *California's Twenty Million*, eds. Kingsley David and Frederick G. Styles (Berkeley: University of California Press, 1971), 62. See also Walker, "Defining California," 79.

15. The precise share of newcomers to California from 1890 to 1920 who came from foreign countries was 28.7 percent, according to calculations by Mark Frame from the decennial censuses for 1890 through 1920. Interestingly, Paul Rhode suggests that by restricting low-wage Asian immigrants and attracting U.S.-born and -educated migrants from the American Midwest, California put itself on a path to base its economic comparative advantage on educated human resources and relatively high wages, thus privileging high-value-added sectors. See Rhode, *California Manufacturing*, 79–80.

16. Hayes-Bautista, *La Nueva California*, 16.

17. See Wallin Carlson, "A History of the San Francisco Mining Exchange," master's thesis, Department of Economics, University of California, Berkeley, cited in Walker, "Defining California," 78.

18. McWilliams, *Great Exception*, 58.

19. The Stevenson quote is in R. A. Burchell, *The San Francisco Irish, 1948–1880* (Berkeley: University of California Press, 1980), 180.

20. McWilliams, *Great Exception*, 41. A similar point is made by University of California President Benjamin Ide Wheeler in "A Forecast for the Pacific Coast," *The Outlook*, September 23, 1911, 67–74.

21. See Rodman W. Paul, "The Wheat Trade Between California and the United Kingdom," *Mississippi Valley Historical Review*, 45 (December 1958), 391–412.

22. Rodman W. Paul, "The Beginning of Agriculture in California: Innovation vs. Continuity," in Knoles, *Essays and Assays*, 32.

23. McWilliams, *Great Exception*, 113–14; and Alan L. Olmstead and Paul W. Rhode, "An Overview of the History of California Agriculture," in *California Agriculture: Issues and Challenges*, ed. Jerome B. Siebert (Berkeley: University of California, Giannini Foundation, Division of Agriculture and Natural Resources, 1997), 7–8.

24. Jose Morillo Ortiz, Alan L. Olmstead and Paul W. Rhode point out that agriculture histories of California and other regions are "quite provincial, seldom asking how the transformation of frontier areas affected global economic conditions" or putting regional agricultural history within a comparative and global context. See Jose Morillo Ortiz, Alan L. Olmstead and Paul W. Rhode, " 'Horn of Plenty': The Globalization of Mediterranean Horticulture and the Economic Development of Southern Europe, 1880–1930," *Journal of Economic History*, 59, no. 2 (June 1999), 316–52.

25. Gary Brechin, *Imperial San Francisco: Urban Power, Earthly Ruin* (Berkeley: University of California Press, 1999), 127–28, 162.

26. Rhode, *California Manufacturing*, 13.

27. Joel Kotkin and Paul Grabowicz, *California Inc.* (New York: Rawson, Wade, 1982), 30.

28. Roger W. Lotchin, *Fortress California: From Warfare to Welfare* (New York: Oxford University Press, 1992).

29. Earl Pomeroy, *The Pacific Slope: A History of California, Oregon, Washington, Idaho, Utah and Nevada* (New York: Alfred A. Knopf, 1965), 261.

30. The statement that the United States supplied 60 percent of Japan's energy in the late 1930s is from LaFeber, *The Clash*, 200.

31. See Eleanor Donoghue and Ewing Haas, associate eds., *California Blue Book* (Sacramento, CA: George H. Moore State Printer, 1942), 354.

32. See Izumi Hirobe, *Japanese Pride, American Prejudice: Modifying the Exclusion Clause of the 1924 Immigration Act* (Stanford, CA: Stanford University Press, 2001), 58–59, 161–62, 215, passim. See also A. T. Hubbard, ed., *Foreign Traders of San Francisco Bay* (San Francisco: FFG Harper, 1926).

33. See Henry F. Grady, "Tariff and Trade: the New American Schedule in Relation to Pacific Commerce," *Pacific Affairs*, 3, no. 8 (August, 1930), 734. Benjamin Park Avery,

Asa Burlingame, and others pushed for closer relationships with China and for a Pacific orientation. See Starr, *Coast of Dreams*, 290.

34. See Steven Erie, *Globalizing L.A.: Trade, Infrastructure and Regional Development* (Stanford, CA: Stanford University Press, 2004), passim. Celebrating Von Kleinsmid's inauguration as the president of the University of Southern California in 1922, USC hosted academic delegates from a Pan American Congress and awarded them honorary degrees, and Von Kleinsmid's inaugural address stressed the intense internationalism of Los Angeles. See Kevin Starr, speech to the Los Angeles World Affairs Council, May 5, 2003, http://www.lawac.org/speech/pre%20sept%2004%20speeches/starr%202003.htm.

35. Kevin Starr, *Embattled Dreams: California in War and Peace, 1940–1950* (New York: Oxford University Press, 2002), 26.

36. LaFeber, *The Clash*, 89.

37. Ibid., 105.

38. See Hirobe, *Japanese Pride*, 6–9.

39. See Mae M. Ngai, "The Architecture of Race in American Immigration Law: A Reexamination of the Immigration Act of 1924," *The Journal of American History*, June 1990, 90. For the forced repatriation of Mexicans in the 1930s, see Francisco E. Balderrama, *Decade of Betrayal: Mexican Repatriation in the 1930s* (Albuquerque: University of New Mexico Press, 1995). Cf. Abraham Hoffman, *Unwanted Mexican Americans in the Great Depression: Repatriation Pressures, 1929–1939* (Tuscon: University of Arizona Press, 1974).

40. Alan L. Olmstead and Paul W. Rhode, "The Evolution of California Agriculture, 1850–2000," in *California Agriculture; Dimensions and Issues*, ed. Jerry Siebert (Davis: Giannini Foundation for Agricultural Economics, University of California, 2004), 1–28, passim, esp. 7, 16, 20–29.

41. Starr, *Embattled Dreams*, 133.

42. Ibid., x.

43. Timothy M. Chambless, "Pro-Defense, Pro-Growth, and Anti-Communism: Cold War Politics in the American West," in *The Cold War and the American West*, ed. Kevin Fernlund, 7th ed. (Albuquerque: University of New Mexico Press, 1998), 102.

44. James J. Rawls and Walton Bean, *California: An Interpretive History* (Boston, MA: McGraw Hill, 1998), 270, 346–49; Gerald Nash, *The American West Transformed: The Impact of the Second World War* (Bloomington: Indiana University Press), 25; and James C. Clayton, *The Economic Impact of the Cold War: Sources and Readings* (New York: Harcourt, Brace and World, 1970), 31.

45. Paul Rhode, "After the War Boom: Reconversion on the Pacific Coast, 1943–1949," in *History Matters: Essays on Economic Growth, Technology and Demographic Change*, eds. W. Sundstrom, T. Guinnane, and W. Whetley (Stanford, CA: Stanford University Press, 2004), 187–220.

46. The expulsion of Mexicans from California in the 1930s has not received the attention it deserves. See Steve Lawrence, "CA Lawmaker Trying Again to Address 1930s Deportations," *San Luis Obispo Tribune*, May 15, 2005.

47. See Nash, *American West Transformed*, and Rhode, "After the War Boom."

48. Starr, *Embattled Dreams*, 154.

49. See Board of Harbor Commission, Los Angeles, *Annual Report*, Fiscal Year 1935–1936, 19.

50. Between the two world wars, those who developed Los Angeles spoke of it as the last major English-speaking city. They allowed only Caucasians to work on the aqueduct and live in various areas, and they established elite clubs, from which blacks, Jews and other minorities were excluded. See Kevin Starr, speech before the Los Angeles World Affairs Council.

51. Schrag, *High Stakes Experiment*, 24 (see Chap. 1, note 37).

52. I have found it difficult to find dispositive data, but experts on California's economic history I have consulted concur with this statement.

53. See James C. Williams, *Energy and the Making of Modern California* (Akron, OH: University of Akron Press, 1997), 349–50.

54. McWilliams, *Great Exception*, 346–66, passim.

55. Hayes-Bautista, *La Nueva California*, 15. See also William Deverell, *Whitewashed Adobe: The Rise of Los Angeles and Remaking of Its Mexican Past* (Berkeley: University of California Press, 2003); Deverell argues that Los Angeles "came of age by cutting ties with Mexican places and people" in the nineteenth and early twentieth centuries.

56. Figures in this paragraph come from James L. Clayton, "Defense Spending: Key to California's Growth," *Western Political Quarterly*, 15 (1962), 280–93.

57. James R. Carroll, "Perspective from Washington," *California Journal*, 16, no. 6 (1985), 260.

58. Peter A. Morrison, "The Role of Migration in California's Growth," in *California's Twenty Million*, eds. Kingsley Davis and Frederick Styles (Berkeley: Institute of International Studies, University of California, Berkeley, 1971).

59. In the twenty-first century, according to U.S. Census figures, the gap between California's population and that of Texas has begun to close slowly, from a 13.02 million gap in 2000 to 12.65 million in 2007. See U.S. Census Bureau, Census 2000 and 2007 Population Estimates at www.census.gov (accessed June 8, 2008).

60. Stephen Schlesinger, *Act of Creation: The Founding of the United Nations* (Boulder, CO: Westview, 2003).

61. Kotkin and Grabowicz, *California Inc.*, 233.

62. Williams, *Making of Modern California*, 273.

63. Julian B. Heron Jr. and Pamela D. Walther, "Pacific Rim as a Future Market for U.S. Agricultural Trade," in *UC Davis Law Review* 23, no. 3 (1990); 525–49.

64. Everett B. Clary, *History of the Law Firm of O'Melveny and Myers, LLP, 1965–1990 and Beyond*, vol. 3 (Los Angeles, 2001, privately printed, available in Los Angeles Public Library).

65. The Hoover Institution on War, Revolution and Peace was established in 1919 on the Stanford campus, without being part of the university, and for many decades was mainly a library and historical research facility. In recent years it has become more integrated with the university and has taken up extensive research and publication on contemporary policy issues.

66. Stephen Schwartz argues that California has all along played a major role in shaping American cultural, social and political history. See Stephen Schwartz, *From West to East: California and the Making of the American Mind* (New York: The Free Press, 1998).

67. California State Department of Finance, Demographic Research Unit, "Current Population Survey Report," March 2001.

68. See Elias Lopez, "Major Demographic Shifts Occurring in California," presented to the Annual Meeting of the Council of State Governments–West, July 16, 1999, published in *CRB Notes*, 6, no. 5 (October 1999).

69. See California Department of Finance, Demographic Research Unit, *They Moved and Went Where: California's Migration Flow, 1995–2000* (Sacramento: California Department of Finance, June 2007), 1, 26; and California Department of Finance, *Race/Ethnic Population Estimates: Components of Change for California Counties, April 1990 to April 2000* (Sacramento: California Department of Finance, August 2005).

70. For an excellent analysis of recent immigration data, see Dowell Myers, John Pitkin and Julie Park, *California's Immigrants Turn the Corner*, Urban Policy Brief (Los Angeles: University of Southern California, 2004).

71. Some of the data in this paragraph is from the decennial censuses, some from the reports of the Demographic Research Unit of the California Department of Finance, and some from Kevin F. McCarthy and George Vernez, *Immigration in a Changing Economy: California's Experience* (Santa Monica, CA: RAND, 1997), esp. Figure 2:1, 17. McCarthy and Vernez also point out that the composition of immigration within regions has been changing, with a smaller share of Latin American immigrants coming from Mexico and many more from Central America, and with rising numbers of Asian immigrants from Indochina and South Asia.

72. See Ashok Deo Bardhan and David K. Howe, *Globalization and Restructuring During Downturns: A Case Study of California* (Berkeley: Fisher Center for Real Estate and Urban Economics, University of California, 1999).

73. William A. V. Clark, *The California Cauldron: Immigration and the Fortunes of Local Communities* (New York: Guilford, 1998); McCarthy and Vernez, *Immigration in a Changing Economy*; and Dowell Myers, *The Changing Immigrants of Southern California*, Research Report LCRI-95-04R (Los Angeles: University of Southern California, 1995).

For an excellent recent analysis of the impact of immigration on Los Angeles, see Fix et al., *Los Angeles on the Leading Edge* (see Chap. 1, note 49).

74. Lydia Chavez, *The Color Bind: California's Battle to End Affirmative Action* (Berkeley: University of California Press, 1998).

75. See "International Trade Activity in Southern California Will Rise to Record Level in 2005, but Industry Faces Major Challenges," in *International Trade Trends and Impacts*, Los Angeles: Los Angeles County Economic Development Corporation (May 4, 2005).

76. Everett B. Clary, *History of the Law Firm*, vol. 4.

77. Center for the Continuing Study of the California Economy, *California Economic Growth—2002 Edition* (Palo Alto, 2002).

78. These data are from New American Media, a San Francisco-based clearing house, as reported by Ruben Martinez in the *Los Angeles Times*. See Ruben Martinez, "Rereading L.A.," *Los Angeles Times*, April 15, 2007.

79. Williams, *Making of Modern California*.

80. See, for example, David W. Lyon, *Global California: The Connection to Asia* (San Francisco: PPIC, Occasional Papers, 2003); Bay Area Economic Forum, *Ties That Bind: The San Francisco Bay Area's Economic Links to Greater China* (San Francisco: Bay Area Economic Forum, November 2006); and Bay Area Economic Forum, *Shared Values, Shared Vision: California's Economic Ties with Canada* (San Francisco: Bay Area Economic Forum, March 2007).

81. See Jock O'Connell, "State Government Ventures Abroad," *The Golden State Report*, January 1990.

82. See Leo McCarthy, "An International Trade Policy for California," (presentation to the California State World Trade Commission, September 26, 1986).

83. See Douglas Smurr, "California Adrift Internationally: Resetting Course for the 21st Century," unpublished manuscript in the author's possession (master's thesis, Fletcher School of Law and Diplomacy, Tufts University, July 20, 2005), 13, 32.

84. See "Special Report: California State Government and the Global Economy," *The CalTrade Report* (February 16, 2004), available at www.caltradereportcom.

85. See California State Assembly, *Pride and Prejudice* (booklet), 1985; and Dick Damm, Senate Office of Research, *Universal Dignity and Freedom; Senate Stands Up for Human Rights*, written for the California State Senate, September 1985. The former notes the address to the assembly in 1985 by eventual Nobel Laureate Desmond Tutu; the latter document offers, among others, the following observation: "Above all, international human rights issues have been embraced by the Senate through the theme of universal dignity and freedom. The consistent thread, California as a fair, compassioned (*sic*) competitor in an often unjust, callous world, runs throughout the policies and actions of the Senate." (1–2)

86. See www.senate.ca.gov/soir, www.sen.ca.gov/cirf, and www.cjsp.ca.gov/. From 1999 through 2006, these institutions have been involved with the reception and programming of over 5,100 visitors, whose numbers increased from 373 in 1999 to 748 in 2006. They also are active regarding—as examples of two additional internationally oriented programs—the California International Fellowship Program and the California-Brazil Partnership. For more information on these, see http://sinet2.sen.ca.gov/soir/Brazil/ and www.sen.ca.gov/cirf/projects.html.

87. See, for example, California Senate Select Committee on California's Role in the World Trade Organization public hearings, "The Need for Legislative Oversight in the Global Economy," State Capitol, Sacramento, August 23, 2000; California Senate Committee on Banking, Commerce and International Trade and the Senate Select Committee on International Trade Policy and State Legislation, "A Joint Informational Hearing on International Trade Agreements and the Role of the State," transcript, State Capitol, Sacramento, May 16, 2001; Senate Select Committee on International Trade Policy and State Legislation, cosponsored by the National League of Cities and the League of

California Cities, "A Town Hall Meeting on the Impact of International Trade Agreements on Local, State and Federal Lawmaking Authority," held at the National Council of Jewish Women, West Hollywood, December 10, 2001; California Senate Select Committee on International Trade Policy and State Legislation, "An Informational Hearing on Offshoring California's Democracy and Capital: NAFTA, CAFTA and the Tradeoffs of Free Trade," Santa Clara County Board Chambers, San Jose, October 13, 2004; California Senate Subcommittee on International Trade Policy and State Legislation, "An International Hearing on the World Trade Organization and California: Will New WTO Rules Erode California's Public Health and Environmental Standards?" State Capitol, Sacramento, January 23, 2006.

88. See Robert Hertzberg, "Global California" (unpublished draft manuscript in the author's possession, dated September 20, 2002).

89. See Starr, *Coast of Dreams*, 292.

90. See ibid., 299, and Abraham F. Lowenthal and Katrina Burgess, eds., *The California-Mexico Connection* (Stanford, CA: Stanford University Press, 1993).

91. James O. Goldsborough, "California's Foreign Policy," *Foreign Affairs*, 72, no. 2 (Spring 1993), 88–96.

92. The increased coverage of Mexico by the *Los Angeles Times* is evident, for example, in the more detailed coverage of Mexican election campaigns over the years. I am indebted to Mark Frame for a detailed memorandum on this point.

93. See "Through New Initiative, University Amplifies Focus on Global Problem Solving," *Stanford Reports*, May 4, 2005.

94. See Sergio Muñoz, "California Could Use a Foreign Policy," *Los Angeles Times*, May 28, 1993. The present author was the founding president of the Pacific Council from 1995 through mid-2005 and is now president emeritus and senior fellow of the Pacific Council.

A study of more than 100 California-based institutions focusing on international affairs in 2001, prepared by Mark Frame for this project, shows that more than 70 percent of these were established after 1970, and more than half of these in the 1980s alone. See Mark Frame, "Selected International Organizations and Policy Institutions by Decade of Founding or Incorporation" (unpublished memorandum in the author's possession, January 2001).

95. See www.pacificcouncil.org for information on these studies and other publications.

96. The California Council for International Trade merged in 2007 with the California Chamber of Commerce International Trade Committee to become the California Chamber Council for International Trade. See www.calchamber.com.

97. For a suggestion that a global mindset is beginning to gain ground in California, and that the Pacific Council on International Policy is contributing to that development, see Tom Plate, "The West Coast Outlook," *Seattle Times*, August 3, 2005.

A more skeptical view, arguing that California does not have a distinct perspective on international policy and does not yet generate the kind of independent thinking that could significantly influence the current debate about the world role of the United

States, is offered by Evaki A. Thanassopoulo in "Does California See the World Differently?" (unpublished manuscript prepared for the Pacific Council on International Policy, July 2000; copy in author's possession).

98. See Douglas Smurr, "California Adrift," for a well-informed account of the implosion of California's international programs in 2003, together with a broad-gauged proposal for revitalizing them on a new basis.

For the critique of the California Technology, Trade and Commerce Agency, see Kimberly Kindy, "Trade Secrets," *Orange County Register*, May 25, 2003. For a well-informed and balanced perspective, see Jock O'Connell, "State's Mini-Embassies Are Out to Lunch," *Sacramento Bee*, May 9, 1999. The author's own headline, more faithful to the text than what the newspaper used, was "California's Foreign Trade Offices at a Crossroads," available at http://jockoconnell.tripod.com/. See also Jock O'Connell, "Foreign Trade Offices and More Politics than Business," *Los Angeles Times*, March 12, 2000; and Robert Collier, "Local Politics Goes Global; California to Open Trade Office in Armenia," *San Francisco Chronicle*, October 14, 2002.

99. See California Business, Transportation and Housing Agency, *Trade and Investment Strategy*, 9 (see Chap. 1, note 20). The statement that California became the only state without a formal international trade and investment promotion program is based on a working paper prepared by Jerry Levine, Mentor International, "California's Global Initiatives: Learning from other States and other Countries" (June 24, 2007).

Chapter 3

1. In preparing this chapter, I have been aided by the discussions of the Pacific Council's project on "Mapping Globalization's Impact on the America West," and by the papers prepared for that project. See Gregory F. Treverton, *A Tale of Five Regions: Meeting the Challenges of Globalization in the U.S. West* (Los Angeles: Pacific Council on International Policy, July 2003) and the papers summarized in that essay (and cited below) by Richard Feinberg and Gretchen Schuck on San Diego, Sarah L. Bachman on the San Francisco Bay Area, Georges Vernez on immigration and Los Angeles and Steven Erie on Southern California's Trade Infrastructure.

2. A new emphasis on regionalism has emerged in California in recent years, as analysts and policymakers seek to disaggregate the vast state in order to focus on concrete issues such as land use, environmental protection and transportation at the level where they can be most coherently addressed. See California Center for Regional Leadership, *The State of California's Regions, 2001* (San Francisco, April 2001). Michael Dardia and Sherman Luk argue that businesses made investment decisions in California on a regional basis, not on statewide considerations. See Michael Dardia and Sherman Luk, *Rethinking the California Business Climate* (San Francisco: Public Policy Institute of California, 1999).

Definitions of California's regions vary at different levels of aggregation, depending on the purpose of the regional breakdown. In a recent demographic analysis, Hans

Johnson of the Public Policy Institute of California (PPIC), distinguishes nine regions: Far North, Sacramento Metro, Sierras, San Francisco Bay Area, San Joaquin Valley, Central Coast, Inland Empire, South Coast and San Diego. See Hans P. Johnson, "A State of Diversity: Demographic Trends in California's Regions," in *California Counts: Population Trends and Profiles*, 3, no. 5 (May 2002).

In his analysis of public opinion, Mark Baldassare of PPIC focuses on four regions—Los Angeles, the San Francisco Bay Area, the Central Valley and Orange County and the Inland Empire combined—which account for 80 percent of California's population. See Mark Baldassare, *California in the New Millennium: The Changing Social and Political Landscape* (Berkeley: University of California Press, 2000), esp. chapter 5, 136–80. This chapter uses Baldessare's emphasis, plus San Diego, thus accounting for about 90 percent of the state's population.

For a general introduction to the growing relevance of regionalism, see Neal Peirce, Curtis Johnson, and John Stuart Hall, *Citistates: How Urban America Can Prosper in a Competitive World* (Arlington, VA: Seven Locks Press, 1993). See also Manuel Pastor Jr., et al., *Growing Together: Linking Regional and Community Development in a Changing Economy* (Minneapolis: University of Minnesota Press, 1997).

3. See U.S. Department of State, List of Foreign Consular Offices in the United States as of August 1, 2007, available at www.state.gov (accessed June 11, 2008).

4. Rieff, *Capital of the Third World* (see Chap. 1, note 68). Michael Parks, then an editor at the *Los Angeles Times*, began referring to Los Angeles as the prospective "capital of the 21st century" in the mid-1990s; others adopted the phrase, including L.A. Mayor Richard Riordan. The reference to Venice is by current Los Angeles Mayor Antonio Villaraigosa, as quoted in Matthew Garrahanin, "El Salvador and LA Fight Gang Crime," *Financial Times*, May 2, 2007, 7. For a recent affirmation of L.A.'s Pacific Rim destiny by a member of the Los Angeles City Council, see Eric Garcetti, "Our Pacific Destiny," available from the City of Los Angeles Web site, www.ci.la.ca.us/council/cd13/oped/ND11141.pdf. President Steven Sample of the University of Southern California has also been sounding this theme.

5. See U.S. Census Bureau, Population Estimates Program, 2006 Population Estimates, http://factfinder.census.gov. See also Ping Chang, *State of the Region: 2006; Measuring Regional Progress* (Los Angeles: Southern California Association of Governments, December 14, 2006), 19, www.scag.ca.gov/sotr/ (accessed August 31, 2007). The Southern California Association of Governments covers the five mentioned counties together with Imperial County and reports a regional population increase of some 220,000 for 2005 alone. Entering 2006, the region's estimated 18.2 million residents constituted a population equal approximately to half of California's total, more than any state but Texas, New York and California as a whole.

6. Census 2000 data show 40.9 percent of the residents of the city of Los Angeles as foreign-born; the figure is 36.2 percent for the county. The 2006 American Community Survey estimates the foreign-born of the city of Los Angeles at 39.9 percent; the figure for the county is 35.4 percent. The American Community Survey samples only households. See http://factfinder.census.gov, and www.census.gov (accessed September 17, 2007).

7. This discussion draws on Georges Vernez, *The New Melting Pot: Changing Faces of International Migration and Policy Implications for Southern California* (Los Angeles: Pacific Council on International Policy, October 2003). See also Roger Waldinger and Mehdi Bozorgmehr, eds., *Ethnic Los Angeles* (New York: Russell Sage Foundation, 1996); and Asian Pacific American Legal Center of Southern California, *The Diverse Face of Asians and Pacific Islanders in Los Angeles County* (Los Angeles: Asian Pacific American Legal Center, 2004).

8. The 2006 American Community Survey estimates the city of Los Angeles's Mexican Latinos at 1,276,870 and the county's total at 3,628,997. The survey's 2005 estimates were 1,254,396 for the city and 3,571,258 for the county. See http://factfinder.census.gov (accessed September 19–21, 2007). The government of Mexico's Instituto Nacional de Estadística Geografía e Informática (INEGI) reports, for 2005, the six most populous Mexican cities as Ciudad de México (8,463,906), Ecatepec (1,687,549), Guadalajara (1,600,894), Puebla (1,399,519), Ciudad Juárez (1,301,452) and Tijuana (1,286,127). These data can be found at the INEGI Web site, www.inegi.gob.mx, as well as at the helpful site of City Population, www.citypopulation.de, particularly www.citypopulation.de/Mexico-Cities.html.

9. Vernez, *New Melting Pot*, 6, indicates ten countries: Armenia, China, El Salvador, Guatemala, India, Japan, Korea, Mexico, Philippines and Vietnam. The eleventh is Iran, the place of birth for 106,205 persons in Los Angeles County alone and the country of "first ancestry reported" of some 119,000 in the five-county region, as of the middle part of this decade (2000–2010). See the data of the 2006 American Community Survey online at http://factfinder.census.gov. The survey data show further that Los Angeles County is home to over 100,000 persons who report their first ancestry as English, German, Irish, Italian or Russian.

10. The 2006 American Community Survey estimates 202,371 persons of Korean extraction; 267,052 foreign-born Salvadorans; 163,449 persons reporting Armenian as their first ancestry; 24,407 foreign-born Cambodians; 295,888 ethnic Filipinos; 160,152 foreign-born Guatemalans; and 22,511 foreign-born Thais. See http://factfinder.census.gov. The Web site of the City of Los Angeles claims that thirty nationalities have their largest population outside their home country in Los Angeles, but the Office of the Mayor could not provide a specific source for this statement. Information was accessed at www.lacity.org/mayor on May 7, 2008, and verified in telephone communication between the author's assistant, Melissa Lockhart, and the Mayor's Office. The Mayor's Web site is constantly reviewed and updated, and this exact data is no longer available online.

11. Asia Pacific American Legal Center of Southern California, *Diverse Face*, 6.

12. "Parade Marks Sikh Holiday," *Los Angeles Times*, April 9, 2007.

13. See Mark Baldassare, ed., *The Los Angeles Riots: Lessons for the Urban Future* (Boulder, CO: Westview Press, 1994); Jeffrey Toobin, *The Run of His Life: The People vs. OJ Simpson* (New York: Random House, 1996); Jack Miles, "Blacks vs. Browns," *The Atlantic Monthly*, October 1992, 41–68; and Edward Chang and Jeannette Diaz-Veizades, *Ethnic Peace in the American City: Building Community in Los Angeles and Beyond* (New York: New York University Press, 1999).

14. See Edward T. Chang and Russell C. Leong, eds., *Los Angeles: Struggles Toward Multiethnic Community: Asian American, African American and Latino Perspectives* (Seattle: University of Washington Press, 1994). See also Tomas Rivera Policy Institute, *Beyond the Racial Divide: Perceptions of Minority Residents on Coalition Building in South Los Angeles* (Los Angeles: Tomas Rivera Policy Institute, University of Southern California April 2007). Cf. John Mitchell, "Racial Strife Plays Out in Linwood Politics," *Los Angeles Times*, June 5, 2007.

15. Joel Kotkin, *The New Geography: How the Digital Revolution is Reshaping the American Landscape* (New York: Random House, 2000). According to Kotkin and Jack Kyser, nearly one-third of Los Angeles County businesses in the early 1990s were minority-owned, and Los Angeles ranked first among the nation's ten largest metropolitan areas in the percentage of people working in firms with less than one hundred employees and annual sales under $5 million. See Joel Kotkin and Jack Kyser, *Recapturing the Dream: A Winning Strategy for the L.A. Region* (Los Angeles: Los Angeles County Economic Development Corporation [LAEDC], January 2005).

On the role of immigrants in driving the labor movement in the Los Angeles region, see Ruth Milkman, *L.A. Story: Immigrant Workers and the Future of the U.S. Labor Movement* (New York: Russell Sage Foundation, 2006), 116–17, 122–23, 137–40, 170–84. Milkman suggests that Los Angeles's immigrant workers, tied closely within nurturing social networks, shaped by previous experiences of labor or political struggle in their native countries and confronted with disdain and hostility in a foreign land, have been easier and more eager to organize than native-born Californians. She emphasizes also that immigrants and the organizations they constitute have furnished leadership or leadership development. Some activists in the Los Angeles organizing drives of the 1990s first gained experience with the United Farm Workers Union in the 1960s and 1970s. Salvadoran immigrants were among the leaders of the Justice for Janitors campaign of 1990; Mexicans from El Maguey (Guanajuato) were at the forefront of the successful drywall hangers' mobilization in 1992; and immigrants also organized the failed effort in the mid-1990s to increase the pay and reclassify, from independent contractor to trucking firm employee, the employment status of freight truckers working the ports of Los Angeles and Long Beach.

More recently, the Los Angeles County Federation of Labor, led by Maria Elena Durazo, a daughter of Mexican immigrants, became in July 2007 the first U.S. labor organization to cement formal ties with a sister organization in China, the Shanghai Municipal Trade Union Council. See Aurelio Rojas, "Los Angeles Labor Federation Reaches Agreement with Shanghai Counterpart," McClatchy Newspapers, July 5, 2007, www.mcclatchydc.com/economics/story/17637.html (accessed September 8, 2007).

16. See the Web site of the Literacy Network of Greater Los Angeles, www.literacynetwork.org/8_employers.html (accessed August 11, 2007), which states that "Los Angeles has the highest percentage of undereducated adults of any major metropolitan area in the U.S., with 53 percent of all working-age adults in L.A. (3.8 million people) who can't read well enough to use a bus schedule or complete a job application." See also www.literacynetwork.org/1_about.html (accessed August 28, 2008),

where the claim is made that "four out of five children read below grade level and nearly half of the adult population in Los Angeles County reads below the national average as defined by the National Institute for Literacy." See also the report of the Literacy Network of Greater Los Angeles and United Way of Greater Los Angeles, *Literacy@Work: the L.A. Workforce Literacy Project* (Los Angeles: Literacy Network of Greater Los Angeles and United Way of Greater Los Angeles, September 2004), summary, 4, www.unitedwayla.org/getinformed/rr/socialreports/Pages/LiteracyReport.aspx, August 11, 2007. Some of the data in this report go back to 2000.

17. The percentages are taken or computed from census data for the various years. For 1970, I use the figures of 7,042,000 for the total county population and 1,051,409 for the Spanish origin population reported in U.S. Census Bureau, *State and Metropolitan Area Data Book 1979: A Statistical Supplement: Regions, Divisions, States, Metropolitan Areas* (Washington DC: U.S. Government Printing Office, 1980), 294, 296–97. Census 1980 counted the county's Latino population at 2,066,103; see U.S. Census Bureau, *1980 Census of Population, Volume 1, Characteristics of the Population, Chapter B, General Population Characteristics, Part 6, California*, July 1982, Table 16. Census 1990 counted the county's Latino population at 3,351,242; see *Summary Tape File 1, P008, Persons of Hispanic Origin*. Los Angeles County had a Hispanic population of 4,242,213 in 2000; see *Census 2000, Summary File 1, QT-P9, Hispanic or Latino by Type*. Los Angeles County had a Hispanic population of around 4.6 million in 2004; see "Texas Becomes Nation's Newest 'Majority-Minority' State, Census Bureau Announces," a Census Bureau press release of August 11, 2005, at www.census.gov. The American Community Survey of 2006 estimates the number of Hispanic or Latino residents of the county at 4,706,994, 47.3 percent of the total; see http://factfinder.census.gov (accessed September 17, 2007).

Census 2000 occasioned greater attention to the issue of undercounts, a serious problem in Los Angeles County and in other areas with high concentrations of impoverished or minority residents. According to two researchers, "The undercount rate for Los Angeles County (1.76 percent of the county's adjusted population) is higher than the undercount rate for California (1.48 percent of the state's adjusted population), which is higher than the rate for the nation (1.14 percent)." Paul M. Ong and Doug Houston, *The 2000 Census Undercount in Los Angeles County*, Working Paper 42 (Los Angeles: The Ralph and Goldy Lewis Center for Regional Policy Studies, University of California, December 2002) 4, http://lewis.sppsr.ucla.edu/publications/workingpapers/LACensusUndercount.pdf (accessed August 11, 2007).

18. The 2006 American Community Survey reports 1,288,643 persons of Asian ethnicity alone and 1,372,493 persons of Asian ethnicity alone or in combination with some non-Asian ethnicity. These correspond to 13 percent and 14 percent of the county's total estimated population, respectively. See http://factfinder.census.gov, www.census.gov.

19. The non-Hispanic white percentage is computed from totals estimated for that grouping and for the county reported by the 2006 American Community Survey. The U.S. Census Bureau's *State and Metropolitan Area Data Book 1979* offers no category for non-Hispanic whites but does state totals of 1,051,409 persons of Hispanic origin and 6,006,500 whites for Los Angeles County for 1970. Thus, even if all persons who

declared themselves of Hispanic origin also identified themselves as white (making His-panic whites total 1,051,409 out of the 6,006,500 whites), then non-Hispanic whites, i.e. the remaining 4,955,091 white individuals, would compute to 70 percent of the county's 1970 population.

20. Census 1990 states the total population of Los Angeles County at 8,863,164, an in-crease of 1.82 million over the figure of 7,042,000; whites in 1990 were counted at 5,035,103 and non-Hispanic whites at 3,618,850. Figures for Census 1990 are available via www.census.gov; see also U.S. Census Bureau, *State and Metropolitan Area Data Book 1979*.

21. Xochitl Bada, "Mexican Hometown Associations," *Citizen Action in the Ameri-cas*, no. 5, Interhermispheric Resource Center, March 2003. See also Zabin and Rabadon, *Mexican Hometown Associations* (see Chap. 1, note 47).

22. Other important immigrant-based organizations, such as the William C. Ve-lasquez Institute and its Southwest Voter Registration Project, have important regional headquarters in Los Angeles.

23. Peter Schrag emphasizes the role of ethnic media outlets as "linking Southern California and the global society that this state, above all, is so much a part of." See Pe-ter Schrag "Niche Media Rising to Surface," *Oakland Tribune*, January 26, 2006, M4.

24. See Sandip Roy, "When Iranians Shout, Iran Listens," Pacific News Service, June 19, 2003, www.16beavergroup.org/mtarchive/archives/000269.php.

25. According to the American Community Survey 2006, 61.9 percent of Asian-born persons residing in Los Angeles County were naturalized. See www.census.gov. For the 2001 percentage of Mexican naturalization, see Sarah Margon, *Naturalization in the United States* (Washington, DC: Migration Policy Institute, May 1, 2004), available at www.migrationinformation.org.

26. Details on Latino officeholders in Los Angeles and elsewhere are available from their Web sites, as well as from the National Association of Latino Elected and Ap-pointed Officials (NALEO), www.naleo.org. See, for example, NALEO's *National Direc-tory of Latino Elected Officials* for various years, and NALEO Education Fund, 2008 Primary Election Profiles, California" (accessed June 7, 2008). Additional information is available at the Web site of the Latino Legislative Caucus, http://democrats.assembly.ca.gov/LatinoCaucus/.

Information on voting by Latinos is from the Tomas Rivera Policy Institute. See www.trpi.org. See also Rachel Vranga, "L.A. Region National Capital of Influential Lati-nos," *L.A. Daily News*, August 15, 2005.

27. For example, 82 percent of Latino voters supported Proposition BB, the City of Los Angeles School Bond Initiative in 1997, compared to 76 percent of African Ameri-cans and 67 percent of non-Hispanic white voters. For more on the political and policy impact of immigrants, see Gary M. Segura, Dennis Falcon and Harry Pachon, "Dynam-ics of Latino Partisanship in California: Immigration, Issue Salience, and Their Implica-tions," *Harvard Journal of Hispanic Politics*, 10 (1997), 62–80.

For additional data and perspectives see also Mollyann Brodie, et al., *2002 National Survey of Latinos* (Menlo Park, CA: Kaiser Family Foundation, and Washington, DC: Pew Hispanic Center, 2002), http://pewhispanic.org/reports/report.php?ReportID=15; Washington Post/Kaiser Family Foundation/Harvard University Survey Project, *Race and Ethnicity in 2001: Attitudes, Perceptions, and Experiences* (Menlo Park, CA: Kaiser Family Foundation, August 2001), 30–33, www.kff.org/kaiserpolls/loader.cfm?url=/commonspot/security/getfile.cfm&PageID=13839; and Roberto E. Villarreal and Norma G. Hernandez, "Old and New Agendas: An Introduction," in *Latinos and Political Coalitions: Political Empowerment for the 1990s*, eds. Norma G. Hernandez and Roberto E. Villarreal (New York: Praeger, 1991), xv–xxvi.

28. See Kyser et al., *2008–2009 Economic Forecast*, 18 (see Chap. 1, note 32).

29. These figures are reported in the LAEDC's, *International Trade Trends & Impacts: The Southern California Region*, May 2007, Table 1, 23.

30. Ibid.

31. For the 1972–2000 figures, see Steven P. Erie, *Enhancing Southern California's Global Gateways: Challenges and Opportunities for Trade Infrastructure Development* (Los Angeles: Pacific Council on International Policy, June 2003), 6; for the 2006 figures, see LAEDC, *International Trade Trends & Impacts*.

32. See Erie, *Enhancing Southern California's Global Gateways*, 1. See also Erie, *Globalizing L.A.* (see Chap. 2, note 31).

33. For the figure of 485,100 jobs, see LAEDC, *International Trade Trends & Impacts: The Southern California Region*, May 2007, 5. In LAEDC, *L.A. Stats*, July 2007, 3–6, LAEDC mentions several other industries whose activities have at least indirect ties to global trade: tourism, motion picture and television production, technology, financial services, wholesale trade and logistics and others. For the aforementioned five industries in the five-county Los Angeles region, relying on the metric of average employment levels for 2006, LAEDC reports a total of 1,863,300 jobs, close to four times that directly involved with foreign trade.

34. These data are available from the Web site of the American Association of Port Authorities, www.aapa-ports.org (accessed June 7, 2008). The association assembles its rank lists with data from a variety of sources.

35. LAEDC, *International Trade Trends & Impacts*, 4.

36. See Haveman, Jennings and Shatz, *California and the Global Economy*, 25–26 (see Chap. 1, note 6).

37. See, for 2006 data, the Web site of the Airports Council International, www.airports.org. For the 2003 ranking, see the U.S. Department of Transportation, Bureau of Transportation Statistics (BTS), *America's Freight Transportation Gateways* (Washington, DC: BTS, 2004), 26, passim.

38. The percentages stated are for 2004. See Haveman, Jennings and Shatz, *California and the Global Economy*, 28.

39. See Alan Bowser, "Freight Transportation: Emerging Issues for Southern California," PowerPoint presentation for Southern California Association of Governments delivered at the Goods Movement Planning Workshop, Detroit, July 10–12, 2001, available online at the U.S. Department of Transportation, Federal Highway Administration, Office of Operations, http://ops.fhwa.dot.gov/freight/Detroit/Appendix/Appendix%20D/SCAG.ppt (accessed September 1, 2007).

40. Erie, *Globalizing L.A.*, 16.

41. Ibid.

42. See Jack Weiss, *Preparing Los Angeles for Terrorism: A Ten Point Plan*, report prepared for Los Angeles City Council (October 2002); and Warren Allen II, et al., *Port Security: Recommendations to Improve Emergency Response Capabilities at the Port of Los Angeles and the Port of Long Beach* (Los Angeles: Riordan Institute for Urban Homeland Security and the School of Public Policy and Social Science Research, UCLA, May 16, 2003). See also Erie, *Globalizing L.A.*, 218–24.

43. See Center for Continuing Study of the California Economy, *California Economic Growth, 2002 Edition* (Palo Alto, CA: 2002), 8–84.

44. This section draws in part on Michael Clough, *Can Hollywood Remain the Capital of the Global Entertainment Industry?* (Los Angeles: Pacific Council on International Policy, 2001). See also Joyce Baron, "The Motion Pictures Production Industry: Impact of 'Runaway Production' to Canada" (Los Angeles: UCLA Anderson Forecasts, June 2000).

45. Scott, *On Hollywood*, 152 (see Chap. 1, note 16). Hollywood today relies more than ever on foreign box-office receipts, according to a *New York Times* report. See Laura M. Holson, "More Than Ever, Hollywood Studios Are Relying on the Foreign Box Office," *New York Times*, August 7, 2006, C1. Global spending on film entertainment is projected to grow at an annual rate of 5.3 percent from 2006 through 2010, with the largest increases expected in Asia and in central and eastern Europe. The report notes for instance, that in its first two months, *The Da Vinci Code* grossed $217 million in domestic box-office receipts and $528 million in foreign box-office receipts. I am indebted to Richard Fox, executive vice president of the International Division of Warner Bros., for an illuminating briefing about the growing importance of international markets for Hollywood.

46. On opening day of the 2008 baseball season, for example, ten of the players on the active roster (twenty-five men) and disabled list of the Los Angeles Dodgers and seven of the players for the Los Angeles Angels of Anaheim were from outside the United States. See Major League Baseball, "Opening Day Rosters Feature 239 Players Born Outside the 50 United States," news release, April 2008, www.mlb.com.

47. See Los Angeles Convention and Visitors Bureau, "L.A. Travel Stats 2006: An Overview of Travel and Tourism in L.A. County," www.laincresearch.com/all/LATravelStats06Final.pdf. According to the bureau's statistics, for 2005, 20.4 million domestic overnighters spent some $9.1 billion, or $446 per person, while the $3.8 billion in expenditures by some 4.6 million international visitors averaged $826 per traveler.

48. LAEDC, *The Los Angeles Area Fashion Industry Profile*, December 2003, 1–2, 9. In 2003, LAEDC estimated the industry's output at $24 billion, with some 78,700 employees in Los Angeles and Orange counties. For 2007, LAEDC estimates 110,600 employees in Los Angeles County and the Riverside-San Bernardino region, an increase over earlier years but part of a slight downward trend from at least 2005 and forecast to continue into 2008. See LAEDC's *2007–2008 Economic Forecast and Industry Outlook Mid-Year Update*, July 2007, Table 31, 51.

49. See *Open Doors 2006: Report on International Education Exchange*, International Institute for Education, with data tables online via www.opendoors.iienetwork.org (accessed September 1, 2007).

50. The University of Southern California, with the highest number of foreign students in the country (6,846 in 2004–2005), estimates university revenue of more than $100 million annually from these students. See James Grant, "USC First in International Students," *USC Chronicle*, 25, no. 13 (December 5, 2005), 1. The overall figure of $988 million for the Los Angeles region is for tuition and fees plus living expenses, net of scholarships and fellowships. See NAFSA: Association of International Educators, "The Economic Benefits of International Education to the United States for the 2004–2005 Academic Year: A Statistical Analysis." The California section is available online at www. nafsa.org/_/File/_/eis2005/California.pdf.

51. For a parallel discussion, to which I contributed and on which I have drawn, see Gregory F. Treverton, *Making the Most of Southern California's Global Engagement* (Los Angeles: Pacific Council on International Policy), June 2001. See also Manuel Pastor Jr., *Widening the Winner's Circle from Global Trade in Southern California* (Los Angeles: Pacific Council on International Policy, August 2001).

52. For an extended discussion, see Erie, *Globalizing L.A.*, chapter 8. See also Lawrence D. Bobo, et al., eds., *Prismatic Metropolis: Inequality in Los Angeles* (New York: Russell Sage Foundation, 2000); Charles Jencks, *Heteropolis: Los Angeles, The Riots, and the Strange Beauty of Hetero-Architecture* (London: Ernest & Sohn, 1993); Mike Davis, *City of Quartz: Excavating the Future in Los Angeles* (New York: Vintage Books, 1992); Allen J. Scott and Edward W. Soja, eds., *The City: Los Angeles and Urban Theory at the End of the Twentieth Century* (Berkeley: University of California Press, 1996); and Michael Dear, H. Eric Shockman and Greg Hise, eds., *Rethinking Los Angeles* (Thousand Oaks, CA: Sage Publications, 1996).

53. Treverton, *California's Global Engagement*. See also Manuel Pastor, "Strategies to Expand L.A.'s International Role," *Los Angeles Times*, January 25, 1998, D4.

54. This point is implicit but is never made explicitly in Joel Kotkin and Jack Kyser's *Recapturing the Dream*, a thoughtful set of proposals for how Los Angeles could regain momentum by focusing on professional business services, tourism, financial services, direct international trade, apparel design and branding for firms in international markets, motion picture and TV production, health services and biomedical industry (including a proposal to develop its presence as a major Pacific Rim medical services hub) and higher education for international students. The specific proposals advanced by Kotkin and Kyser rely heavily on building up L.A.'s global advantages, but they are not put together or presented in this way. See Kotkin and Kyser, *Recapturing the Dream*, esp. 5–29 and 5–33. Cf. Kevin Klowden and Perry Wong, *Los Angeles Economic Project* (Santa Monica, CA: Milken Institute, November 2005).

55. The San Francisco Bay Area as discussed in this chapter includes nine counties: Alameda, Contra Costa, Marin, Napa, San Francisco, San Mateo, Santa Clara, Solano and Sonoma. The U.S. Census Bureau computed the total population of these counties at some 6.8 million in 2000 and estimated it at 6.9 million in 2006. Some analysts refer to a Bay Area "super-region" that includes Merced, Monterey, San Benito, San Joaquin, Santa Cruz, Stanislaus and Yolo Counties; this sixteen-county conglomerate's 2000 population was counted at nearly 8.9 million and estimated at

9.3 million in 2006. Still another metric is the San Francisco-Oakland-San Jose Consolidated Metropolitan Statistical Area (CMSA); this area's recorded population of 7,039,362 in 2000 was the nation's fifth largest. In 2006 the estimated total of 7,228,948 residents in the San Jose-San Francisco-Oakland CMSA was likewise fifth largest nationally among all such areas. See U.S. Census Bureau, Census 2000, "Ranking Tables for Metropolitan Areas," Table 3, Metropolitan Areas Ranked by Population, 2000, www.census.gov/population/www/cen2000/phc-t3.html (accessed August 22, 2007); and U.S. Census Bureau, Population Division, Table 1: Annual Estimates of the Population of Combined Statistical Areas: April 1, 2000 to July 1, 2006, www.census.gov/population/www/estimates/CBSA-est2006-annual.html (accessed August 22, 2007). See also S. L. Bachman, *Globalization in the San Francisco Bay Area: Trying to Stay at the Head of the Class* (Los Angeles: Pacific Council on International Policy, 2003). I am indebted to Ms. Bachman's paper for some of the data and analysis in the subsequent pages.

56. The San Francisco World Trade Center Authority was enacted into law in June 1947 and by December of that year was "authorized to issue revenue bonds to finance structures for a centralized trade headquarters." See "Trade Center Heads Named by Warren," *San Francisco Chronicle*, December 11, 1947, 15. Interesting images of the facility envisioned are contained in the prospectus, *San Francisco World Trade Center*, published by the San Francisco World Trade Center Authority in 1951. With the construction of such headquarters not forthcoming, the San Francisco World Trade Center in 1956 moved into offices and began operations in the Ferry Building. See "World Trade Center Opens This Week," *San Francisco Chronicle*, May 23, 1956, 1.

57. See H. W. Kusserow, "S.F. Trade Building Plan Fails; Bonds Rights Eliminated," *San Francisco Examiner*, October 27, 1968, 15.

58. For a fascinating discussion of San Francisco's evolution and the clash between pro-growth and "progressive" groups, see Richard Edward DeLeon, *Left Coast City: Progressive Politics in San Francisco, 1975–1991* (Lawrence: University Press of Kansas, 1992).

59. See Carolyn Said, "Bay Area's Film Image Adds More Dimension," *San Francisco Chronicle*, November 14, 2007, C14.

60. See Progressive Policy Institute's, "New Economy Index" for metro regions, released in April 2001, as cited in Bachman, *Globalization in the San Francisco Bay Area*. Since that date, when San Francisco ranked highest in the country, it has been surpassed by Seattle-Tacoma. See the study by the Pew Internet and American Life Project, *Internet Use by Region in the United States* (Washington, DC: Pew Internet and American Life Project, 2003).

61. See Intel Corporation's *America Unwired 2005*, 8, www.intel.com/pressroom/archive/releases/20050607corp.htm (accessed August 31, 2007). San Francisco subsequently lost its leading position to Seattle, and a major, three-year-long effort by city officials to arrange for free wireless throughout the city ended in failure in August 2007, when Internet service provider Earthlink declined the terms of an agreement it saw as

unprofitable. Robert Selna, "S.F.'s Wi-Fi Plan Fades Away—Provider Bails," *San Francisco Chronicle*, August 30, 2007, A1, A12.

62. These percentages are computed from Census 1980 and American Community Survey 2006 data for the nine-county region. See the Census of Population and Housing, Summary Tape File 3, (Washington, DC: U.S. Dept. of Commerce, Bureau of the Census, 1982). See also the American Community Survey 2006, www.census. gov, http://factfinder.census.gov (accessed September 17, 2007).

63. See the spreadsheet put together by the California Department of Finance, "Legal Immigration to California by County, 1984–2006," at www.dof.ca.gov/HTML/ DEMOGRAP/ReportsPapers/ReportsPapers.asp (accessed June 10, 2008). The department relies on its own data and those from U.S. Citizenship and Immigration Services.

64. These percentages also are computed from Census 1980 and American Community Survey 2006 data for the nine-county region. Because of differences in the reporting of ethnic categories between the two investigations, the data they offer can be difficult to compare directly. The percentages I state here consider, for 1980, the Asian population to include people of Chinese, Filipino, Indian, Japanese, Korean and Vietnamese ethnicity. The 2006 percentages include other Asian ethnicities, and they reflect only that portion (96.5 percent) of the total estimated nine-county population that reported a single ethnic category. See United States Census Bureau, *1980 Census of Population, Volume 1, Characteristics of the Population, Chapter B, General Population Characteristics, Part 6, California*, July 1982, Tables 15 and 16; see also American Community Survey 2006, "Demographic and Housing Estimates," online via www.census.gov and http://factfinder.census.gov (accessed September 19, 2007).

65. See Kevin Starr, *Coast of Dreams*, 391 (see Chap. 1, note 13). See also Andrew Lam, "Hurry, Hurry by the Bay," *Los Angeles Times*, August 26, 2001.

66. The data in this paragraph are primarily drawn from the Bay Area Economic Forum, *International Trade and the Bay Area Economy: Regional Interests and Global Outlook 2003* (San Francisco, January 2003); Bay Area Economic Forum, *Downturn and Recovery: Restoring Prosperity* (San Francisco, January 2004); and Bay Area Economic Forum, *Regional Interests and Global Outlook 2005–2006* (see Chap. 1, note 36). I have drawn, as well, on several other reports from the Bay Area Economic Forum. The forum's 2003 report relies, in part, on the old Census Bureau Exporter Location data series, now defunct; see 18–19. See also page 16 for comparisons of the Bay Area with other exporting areas. The forum's 2005 report excludes exports from Napa, Solano and Sonoma counties, but includes those from San Benito County; see 2, 29. The 9.5 percent figure comes from Bachman, *Globalization in the San Francisco Bay Area*, 12.

67. See the 2007 Annual Report of the Semiconductor Industry Association, *Make It Happen; American Competitiveness: Consensus Should Lead to Action*, 20. See also the association's "Industry Facts and Figures" Web page. Both materials can be found via www.sia-online.org (accessed August 10, 2007).

68. See the Semiconductor Industry Association, "Semiconductor Forecast Summary, 2006-2009," November 2006, www.sia-online.org (accessed June 10, 2008).

69. These figures are from 2007 Form 10-K submissions by each firm to the Securities and Exchange Commission.

70. See NAFSA: Association of International Educators, "The Economic Benefits of International Education to the United States for the 2004–2005 Academic Year: A Statistical Analysis." The California section is available online at www.nafsa.org/_/File/_/eis2005/California.pdf.

71. See www.flysfo.com/about/press/factsheets/SFO.

72. See Paul T. Rosynsky, "New Era Begins in the Port Alliance," *Oakland Tribune*, January 2006, Metro 2, 4; and Paul T. Rosynsky, "More Shippers Turning to Oakland," *Oakland Tribune*, January 24, 2006, 1, 7.

73. See Bay Area Science and Innovation Consortium, *Visas for Higher Education and Scientific Exchanges: Balancing Security and Economic Competitiveness* (San Francisco: Bay Area Economic Forum, April 2005).

74. See AnnaLee Saxenian, *Regional Advantage: Culture and Competition in Silicon Valley and Route 128* (Cambridge MA: Harvard University Press, 1994).

75. The Committee of 100, the most prominent network of Chinese American leaders in the United States, has more members in the Bay Area than anywhere else, for example.

76. See AnnaLee Saxenian, with Yasuyuki Motoyama and Xiaohong Quan, *Local and Global Networks of Immigrant Entrepreneurs in Silicon Valley* (San Francisco: PPIC, 2002). See also Saxenian, *New Immigrant Entrepreneurs*, (see Chap. 1, note 53). For a report on the role of Indian Americans in India's growing economy, see Evelyn Iritani, "Expatriates Play Key Role in India's Economic Rise," *Los Angeles Times*, August 12, 2006.

77. Except for Daniel K. Inouye of Hawaii, elected in 1959, Mineta and Matsui were the first Japanese Americans to serve in Congress. The first Asian American was Dalip Singh Saund, an immigrant from Punjab, who was elected to the House in 1956 from the Twenty-ninth District, then composed of Imperial and Riverside counties. See Tom Patterson, "Triumph and Tragedy of Dalip Saund," *California Historian*, 38, no. 4 (June 1992), 9–13.

78. On the growing importance of the Chinese American community and other Asian Americans for San Francisco's politics, see "Chinatown Awakens to Politics," *San Francisco Chronicle*, October 23, 2003, A1, 17. As of 2003, 18 percent of San Francisco's registered voters were Asian American, up from 13 percent in 1991.

79. See, for example, David Armstrong, "Bay Area, Chinese Businesses Draw Closer," *San Francisco Chronicle*, April 26, 2007, C1, C5. An April 2007 memorandum of understanding between officials from San Francisco's Bay Area Council, a business-oriented, nonprofit policy advocacy firm in operation since 1945, and the China Yangtze Council, tied to Hong Kong's Shui On Group, set, among several other goals, the institution of a venture capital fund to boost Chinese technology start-ups and the improvement of waterborne trade logistics between the ports of Oakland and Shanghai. The understanding was cemented outside government channels and was unique in envisioning a connection of regions as distinct from cities or countries.

See, for another example, Sabine Muscat, "Venture Capitalists Look for Clean Slate in China; Silicon Valley Invests in Environmental Technology," *San Francisco Chronicle*, September 20, 2007, C-1, for a discussion of the growing attention paid by Silicon Valley to demand for environmental technology in China.

For an in-depth discussion of the importance of China to the culture and economy of the Bay Area, see Bay Area Economic Forum, *Ties That Bind* (see Chap. 2, note 77). For a study of Chinese networks in Silicon Valley, see Bernard P. Wong, *The Chinese in Silicon Valley: Globalization, Social Networks, and Ethnic Identity* (Lanham, MD: Rowman and Littlefield, 2006).

80. See Bay Area Economic Forum, *The Future of Bay Area Jobs: The Impact of Offshoring and Other Key Trends* (San Francisco: Bay Area Economic Forum, with Joint Venture: Silicon Valley Network, Stanford Project on Regions of Innovation and Entrepreneurship, and A.T. Kearney, 2004).

81. For a parallel argument, see Sean Randolph, "Bay Area's Future is Tied to the Global Economy," *San Jose Business Journal*, January 9, 2004. Under Mr. Randolph's leadership as its president, the Bay Area Economic Forum, now the Bay Area Council Economic Institute, has been the most consistent promoter of an international vision for the Bay Area.

82. Among other sources, data and analysis in this section draw upon Richard Feinberg and Gretchen Schuck, *San Diego, Baja California and Globalization: Coming from Behind* (Los Angeles: Pacific Council on International Policy, October 2001) and on papers and memoranda prepared at the initiative of the San Diego Dialogue's Forum Fronterizo on *The Global Engagement of San Diego/Baja California*, including its final report (November 2000). See also San Diego Association of Governments, *Creating Prosperity for the San Diego Region* (2000), esp. 30–31.

83. See, for these figures, the Web site of the *Navy Dispatch Newspaper*, www.navydispatch.com/military.htm (accessed August 10, 2007).

84. See first the 2001 report of Feinberg and Schuck, *San Diego*, 5, where Department of Defense (DOD) employment is quoted at approximately 131,000, for "nearly 9 percent" of the local labor force. Navydispatch.com reports, in 2007, upwards of 90,000 naval, 35,000 marine and 22,500 civilian personnel in San Diego County; www.navydispatch.com/military.htm (accessed August 10, 2007). For the period 2004–2006, the labor market increased from 1.49 million to 1.52 million people, according to the California Employment Development Department; see www.labormarketinfo.edd.ca.gov (accessed August 11, 2007). The new counts would indicate that DOD employees constituted 10 percent of the San Diego labor force at about mid-decade.

85. According to a 2007 report by the San Diego Regional Chamber of Commerce, military spending contributes some $18.3 billion, constituting 14.7 percent of gross regional product, annually. See the January 31, 2007, press release of the chamber at www.sdchamber.org/thechamb/releases/07-0131.html (accessed August 11, 2007).

86. See Steven Erie, "Towards a Trade Infrastructure Strategy for the San Diego-Tijuana Region" (briefing paper prepared for the San Diego Dialogue, February 1999), 3.

87. Feinberg and Schuck, *San Diego*, 8–9.

88. Ibid., 6. See also Steven P. Erie, "The Challenge of Developing the Cross-Border Region's Trade Infrastructure," briefing paper, Forum Fronterizo series on the *Global Engagement of San Diego/Baja California*, May 2000, www.sandiegodialogue.org/archives.htm (accessed August 17, 2007).

89. Ethnic Italians and Portuguese manned San Diego's tuna fishing fleet, which harvested in the eastern tropical Pacific and was, in 1980, the world's greatest, comprising 101 boats. See Mark Schoell, "The Marine Mammal Protection Act and its Role in the Decline of San Diego's Tuna Fishing Industry," *The Journal of San Diego History*, 45, no. 1 (Winter 1999), online at www.sandiegohistory.org/journal/99winter/tuna.htm (accessed August 17, 2007).

90. U.S. Patent Office, "United States Patent Grants by State, County and Metropolitan Area (Utility Patents 1991–1999)," Table 1 (Washington, DC: U.S. Patent and Trademark Office, April 2000).

91. In June 2004, San Diego was named by the Milken Institute as the top region in the country for biotechnology, based on its success in nurturing innovation and creating new companies and products.

92. See Feinberg and Schuck, *San Diego*, 8.

93. These figures come from the California State World Trade Commission and are reported in the Center for the Continuing Study of the California Economy (CCSCE), *California Economic Growth 1999* (Palo Alto: CCSCE, 1999), 5–10; and Gus Koehler, *California Trade Policy* (Sacramento: California Research Bureau, November 1999), 7.

94. See Leslie Berestein, "Decline in Border Crossings Crimps Economy: Waits, Security Issues Hitting Tourism Hard," *San Diego Tribune*, March 11, 2008.

95. The data are from the U.S. Department of Transportation, Bureau of Transportation Statistics, Research and Innovative Technology Administration, *Transportation Statistics, Annual Report* (December 2006), 35–38. See also the bureau's data facility at www.bts.gov/programs/international/border_crossing_entry_data/.

96. These percentages are computed or taken from U.S. Census Bureau data on San Diego County in Census 1990, Summary Tape File 1; Census 2000, Summary File 1; a publication of the 1970 Census of Population, *Japanese, Chinese, and Filipinos in the United States*, Tables 11 and 41, pages 50, 169; U.S. Census Bureau, *State and Metropolitan Area Data Book* (Washington, DC: U.S. GPO, 1980), 387, 380–81; the California Department of Finance's *Race/Ethnic Population Estimates: Components of Change for California Counties, July 1970–July 1990* (Sacramento, July 1999); and California Department of Finance, *Population Projections for California and Its Counties 2000–2050* (Sacramento, July 2007). For 2000, the percentages of whites and Asians vary slightly depending on the consideration of these groups alone or in combination with other races. The Census Bureau had yet to develop the categories of Asian and Asian/Pacific Islander as of the 1970 census, but the numbers of those who would have been so designated in San Diego County were relatively low at that time: fewer than 5,000 ethnic Chinese and only 17,052 Filipinos and Japanese were counted. The combined total of Filipinos and Japanese was a mere 1.3 percent of the total population of 1,358,000. The Department of Finance esti-

mates the population of San Diego County at 1,367,000 and estimates a figure of 29,636, for all Asian and Pacific Islander ethnicities for July 1970, constituting 2.17 percent of the total.

97. Harold Brackman and Steven P. Erie, "Paradoxes of Mexican Integration into Southern California," in *U.S.-Mexican Integration: NAFTA at the Grassroots*, ed. John Bailey (Austin, TX: Lyndon B. Johnson School of Public Affairs, 2001), 99–135.

The three Latina lawmakers representing San Diego County as of mid-2008 were Democratic State Senator Denise Moreno Ducheny (Fortieth) and Democratic Assembly members Lori Saldaña (Seventy-sixth) and Mary Salas (Seventy-ninth).

98. See www.sandiegodialogue.org for information on the San Diego Dialogue.

99. James Flanigan, "Sempra Sees LNG as a Liquid Asset," *Los Angeles Times*, December 28, 2003, C1.

100. For further discussion, see the various background papers prepared in 2000 for the San Diego Dialogue's Forum Fronterizo series on *The Global Engagement of San Diego/Baja California* and the forum's final report on that topic, in November 2000. Available at www.sandiegodialogue.org. Unfortunately, the untimely death of the San Diego Dialogue's executive director, Dr. Charles Nathanson; subsequent personnel, organizational and budget issues; and political and fiscal turmoil in San Diego all significantly impeded implementation of the recommendations in this excellent report.

101. I am indebted to Christina Luhn, senior project manager for the Mega-Region project of the San Diego Economic Development Corporation, for information on this initiative.

102. A classic study of Orange County in transition from this period toward greater cosmopolitanism is Karl A. Lamb, *As Orange Goes* (New York: Norton, 1974).

103. This section draws on a number of materials assembled by Mark Frame, especially Rob Kling, Spencer Olin and Mark Poster, eds., *Post-Suburban California: The Transformation of Orange County Since World War II* (Berkeley: University of California Press, 1991); Mark Baldassare, "New Immigrant Opportunities in a Suburban Region," *Community Sociology*, 6 (1986):105–22; *Orange County Community Indicators 2005* (which draws for its data on the Institute for Economic and Environmental Studies at California State University, Fullerton), available at www.ocbc.org/cip.html; "Chapman University Economic Forecast for the United States, California, and Orange County," published annually in the *Economic and Business Review* of the A. Gary Anderson Center for Economic Research, Chapman University; various issues of the *Orange County Register*; the Orange County Web site (www.orangecounty.net); and the Web site of the City of Santa Ana (www.ci.santaana.ca)

104. See the county estimates data in the 2006 Current Population Survey, via www.census.gov (accessed August 10, 2007). Los Angeles County ranks as the most populous in the country, followed by Cook (Illinois), Harris (Texas), Maricopa (Arizona) and Orange Counties, in that order.

105. These data are taken from page 18 of *Orange County 2007 Community Indicators*, www.oc.ca.gov/ceocommunity.asp, which relies on the research of the Center for Economic and Environmental Studies at California State University, Fullerton.

106. See Jennifer Dalson, "Fear of Exile Vexes Many in Southern O.C.," *Los Angeles Times*, December 13, 2005, B3. Immigrants now make up 23 percent of the population of San Juan Capistrano, 13 percent of San Clemente and 11 percent of Laguna Miguel. See also Scott Martelle and Phil Willon, "Orange County: Latinos and Asians Continue a Transformation," *Los Angeles Times*, March 30, 2001, V, 2.

107. See Martin Wisckol, "Trung Nguyen Has Narrow Lead in Supervisor Race," *Orange County Register*, February 22, 2007.

108. For one interesting example, see Eldon Griffiths, *Walter: A German Immigrant Who Helped Make Orange County Bloom* (Orange, CA: Chapman University Press, 2001). Walter Schmid, a major figure in Orange County's transformation and growth, was an avid internationalist, according to this sympathetic portrait by the long-time president of Orange County's World Affairs Council.

109. Anthony Downs, "California's Inland Empire: The Leading Edge of Southern California Growth," *California Counts: Population Trends and Profiles*, 7, no. 2 (November 2005), 3.

110. John E. Husing, "2003 A Weak Year . . . CA's Problems to Inhibit 2004" (April 30, 2004), Powerpoint presentation, available at www.johnhusing.com/Economic_Briefing_2004.ppt. See also Johnson, "California's Population," 39 (see Chap. 1, note 2). For an interesting comment, joining the Inland Empire and the Central Valley as "The Third California," see Joel Kotkin and William Frey, "The Third California," *Los Angeles Times*, January 20, 2006.

111. Downs, "California's Inland Empire," 4.

112. As of 2003, Hispanics (Latinos) were 41 percent of the Inland Empire's population, African Americans 7 percent and Asians 4.5 percent, with strong rates of increase in all three groups. Downs, "California's Inland Empire," 8. By 2006, the percentage of Hispanics had increased to 44 percent. See the data of the 2006 American Community Survey online at http://factfinder.census.gov.

113. See "Racial/Ethnic Demographics of California Counties, 2000 to 2040," Source U.S. Census, included in *Changing Times: California Tomorrow Newsletter* (Summer 2007) G7.

114. Ibid.

115. United Parcel Service, "UPS's Expanded Ontario Hub Takes Wing: US$44 Million Project Boosts Key Link in U.S.-Asia Trade, Just in Time for the Peak Holiday Shipping Season," news release, November 20, 2002. See at www.pressroom.ups.com/pressreleases/archives/archive/0,1363,4224,00.html.

116. See California Policy Institute at Claremont, *International Trade in the San Bernardino Region: Transportation, Trends, and Employment*, prepared for the County of San Bernardino, December 2006, I-2.

117. See City of Riverside, *International Strategic Plan* (January 27, 2004).

118. This section draws on various publications from the California Research Bureau of the California State Library; the Agricultural Issues Center of the University of California, Davis; the Great Valley Center; New Valley Connections; the California Central Valley Economic Development Corporation; a report by Dr. Tappan Monroe and

Dr. William E. Jackman of Pacific Gas and Electric Company on "California's Central Valley Economy" (dated 1997); various commentaries published in the *Sacramento Bee*, the *Fresno Bee*, and the *Modesto Bee*; and the writings of Jock O'Connell, an international consultant, Peter Schrag of the *Sacramento Bee*, and Gerald Haslam, a leading academic authority on the valley. I am indebted to Andrew Tyler, a student intern from Pomona College, for assembling many of these materials. See also Mark Arax and Rick Wartzman, *The King of California: J.G. Boswell and the Making of a Secret American Empire* (New York: Public Affairs, 2004).

119. The San Joaquin Valley includes Fresno, Kern, Kings, Madera, Merced, San Joaquin, Stanislaus and Tulare counties. The Sacramento metro area includes Sacramento, Placer and Yolo counties. The North Valley is made up of Butte, Colusa, Glenn, Shasta, Sutter, Tehama and Yuba counties.

120. A deep nostalgia for the Central Valley as it was through the mid-twentieth century permeates Victor Davis Hanson's *Mexifornia*, a polemic about how California has been reshaped since the 1960s by Mexican immigration. See Victor Davis Hanson, *Mexifornia: A State of Becoming* (San Francisco: Encounter Books, 2003).

121. See "California Agriculture Commodities Exports, 2001–2003," at http://aic.ucdavis.edu/pub03.

122. See Hans P. Johnson and Joseph M. Hayes, *The Central Valley at a Crossroads: Migration and Its Implications*. (San Francisco: PPIC, 2004).

123. Jock O'Connell, "Ag Industry at Risk—Despite the Rosy Image," *Sacramento Bee*, July 29, 2001.

124. See Jock O'Connell, "Sacramento: A No Fly Zone for International Trade," *Sacramento Bee*, September 18, 2005.

125. See, for example, Robert Collier, "Uncertain Playing Field for California's Farmers," *San Francisco Chronicle*, November 25, 1999.

The lack of a California trade strategy has been forcefully pointed out by several observers, particularly Jock O'Connell and Joseph Harrison, president of the California Council on International Trade. See, for example, Jock O'Connell, "The State Strategy for Trade," *Sacramento Bee*, August 24, 2003; and Joseph W. Harrison, "The State of California's International Trade" *San Diego Union Tribune*, February 23, 2005. See also California Business, Transportation and Housing Agency, *Trade and Investment Strategy*, esp. 63–67 (see Chap. 1, note 20). This volume calls instead for an integrated overall international strategy, including trade policy but going beyond it.

Chapter 4

Some of the material on immigration policy included in this chapter was previously published in "Moving the Debate Forward: What California Can Teach Us," *Americas Quarterly*, 2, no. 3 (Summer 2008), 48–54.

1. The following paragraphs draw on a substantial literature on foreign policy and the national interest. See, for example, Hans J. Morgenthau, *In Defense of the National*

Interest (New York: Alfred Knopf, 1951); Robert Osgood, *Ideals and Self-Interest in American Foreign Relations* (Chicago: University of Chicago Press, 1953); Stephen D. Krasner, *Defending the National Interest: Raw Materials, Investments and U.S. Foreign Policy* (Princeton, NJ: Princeton University Press, 1978); David A. Lake, *Power, Protection and Free Trade: International Sources of U.S. Commercial Strategy, 1887–1939* (Ithaca, NY: Cornell University Press, 1988); Willard Clinton, *The Two Faces of National Interest* (Baton Rouge: Louisiana State University Press, 1994); and especially Peter Trubowitz, *Defining the National Interest: Conflict and Change in American Foreign Policy* (Chicago: University of Chicago Press, 1998).

My own earlier efforts to grapple with these questions include Abraham F. Lowenthal, *The Dominican Intervention* (Cambridge, MA: Harvard University Press, 1972), esp. 145–50; and Abraham F. Lowenthal, " 'Liberal,' 'Radical' and 'Bureaucratic' Perspectives on U.S. Latin American Policy: The Alliance for Progress in Retrospect," in *Latin America and the United States: The Changing Political Realities*, eds. Julio Cotler and Richard R. Fagen (Stanford, CA: Stanford University Press, 1974), 212–35, esp. 227–35.

2. The proliferation of governmental and nongovernmental actors participating in the shaping of U.S. foreign policy has been widely discussed. An important analysis of the growing role of nongovernmental actors is Jessica T. Mathews, "Power Shift," *Foreign Affairs*, January/February 1997. The literature on the involvement in foreign policy of noncentral governments includes Earl Fry, *The Expanding Role of Local Governments in U.S. Foreign Affairs* (New York: Council on Foreign Relations Press, 1998); Douglas M. Brown and Earl H. Fry, eds., *States and Provinces in the International Economy* (Berkeley: Institute of Governmental Studies Press, University of California, 1993); Brian Hocking, *Localizing Foreign Policy: Non-Central Governments and Multilayered Diplomacy* (New York: St. Martin's Press, 1993); and Michael H. Shuman, "Dateline Main Street: Local Foreign Policies," *Foreign Policy* 65 (Winter 1986–1987), 154–74. For a useful overview, see Princeton N. Lyman, "The Growing Influence of Domestic Factors," in *Multilateralism and U.S. Foreign Policy: Ambivalent Engagement*, eds. Shepard Foreman and Stewart Patrick (Boulder, CO: Lynne Rienner, 2002), 75–97.

3. Trubowitz, *Defining the National Interest*, 4. Trubowitz applies his analysis to U.S. foreign policy in the 1990s in Peter Trubowitz, "Why Consensus Is So Elusive in U.S. Foreign Policy," *The Chronicle of Higher Education*, 44, no. 37, (May 22, 1998), 64.

4. Although Trubowitz argues persuasively that "it is the realities of power inside a country, not the distribution of power in the international system, that determines the course of the nation's foreign policy," California's growing power has not had a commensurate impact on policy because the state has not focused on pursuing its international interests, or even identifying them systematically. See Trubowitz, *Defining the National Interest*, 241.

5. California's emission sources include not only passenger vehicles and electric power generation but also forest fires. On the many implications of global warming for California, see Katharine Hayhoe, Daniel Cayan, Christopher B. Field, et al., "Emissions Pathways, Climate Change, and Impacts on California," *Proceedings of the National Academy of Sciences*, 101, no. 34 (August 24, 2004), http://calclimate.berkeley.edu. On the

implications of climate change for California's wine industry, see M. A. White, et al., "Extreme Heat Reduces and Shifts U.S. Premium Wine Production in the 21st Century," *Proceedings of the National Academy of Sciences*, 103, no. 30 (June 25, 2006), available online at www.pnas.org. See also Jane Kay, "Now's the Time to Cellar Wine," *San Francisco Chronicle*, July 7, 2006, A1, A9.

6. Concern about the dangers from toxic agricultural products, toys and candies has been growing. See, for example, the series of articles in the *Orange County Register* on "Toxic Treats" published April 25–30, 2004, examining lead-containing candy imports from Mexico; and stories touching on Mattel and/or that company's imports of unsafe toys, including Nicholas Casey and Andy Pasztor, "Safety Agency, Mattel Clash Over Disclosures," *Wall Street Journal*, September 4, 2007, A1; and Nicholas Casey, "California Sues Toy Makers Over Lead Risk," *Wall Street Journal*, November 20, 2007, B8.

7. See Alan Blinder, "How Many U.S. Jobs Might Be Offshorable?" Working Paper 142 (Princeton, NJ: Princeton University Center for Economic Policy Studies, March 2007).

8. No state has more environmental organizations or more members of these. The Sierra Club has its headquarters in San Francisco, where it was originally founded in 1852, and boasts thirteen Sierra Club chapters in the state; no other state has more than one. The Natural Resources Defense Council has its headquarters in New York, and only three other offices: in Washington, D.C., San Francisco and Los Angeles. The California League of Conservation Voters is the nation's largest and oldest state's conservation political action committee, with more than 25,000 members. Global Green, the U.S. affiliate of Global Green International, is headquartered in Santa Monica, with offices in San Francisco and in Washington, D.C. Among the other California nongovernmental organizations addressing international environmental issues are Bluewater Network, the Earth Communications Office, Earth Island Institute, the Global Footprint Network, Pacific Environment, the Pacific Institute, the Nautilus Institute, the Rainforest Action Network, Redefining Progress and the Surfrider Foundation.

9. Remarkably little has been written thus far to specify California's international interests. The most extensive discussion of which I am aware, just nine pages, is Goldsborough's aforementioned essay, "California's Foreign Policy" (see Chap. 2, note 88). Philip J. Romero, then Governor Wilson's chief economist, prepared a five-page unpublished memorandum on "California's Foreign Policy Agenda" at the request of the author in February 1994.

Stipulating three core policy goals here is intended to be a contribution to promoting discussion or debate about California's foreign policy interests, not to substitute for such debate, which is essential, as emphasized in this chapter and in Chapter 5.

10. For a thoughtful discussion, see Pastor, *Widening the Winner's Circle* (see Chap. 3, note 51). See also Treverton, *Southern California's Global Engagement* (see Chap. 3, note 51); and Raúl Hinojosa-Ojeda, "The Labor Market Impacts of North American Economic Integration on Latino, Black and White Workers," in *A Latino Review of NAFTA*, ed. Antonio Gonzalez (Los Angeles: William C. Velasquez Institute, 1997).

11. An excellent discussion of what California can do to promote its exports is Koehler, *California Trade Policy* (see Chap. 3 note 93). Other useful sources are Cynthia

Kroll, *Foreign Trade and California's Economic Growth: A Summary of Findings and Directions for Policy* (Berkeley: Institute of Business and Economic Research, University of California, March 1998); and Cynthia Kroll and Josh Kirschenbaum, *The Integration of Trade into California Industry: Case Studies of the Computer Cluster and Food Processing Industry* (Berkeley: Fisher Center for Real Estate and Urban Economics, University of California, February 1998). See also Howard J. Shatz, *State International Business Programs: Organization, Evaluation, and Oversight* (San Francisco: PPIC Occasional Paper, 2004). For a full and up-to-date discussion of how California could expand the exports of goods and services, see California Business, Transportation and Housing Agency, *Trade and Investment Strategy* (see Chap. 1, note 20).

12. On the importance of targeting state trade assistance programs beneficial to "export-ready" and "export-willing" firms and sectors, see Howard T. Shatz, *Small Business and the Globalization of California's Economy* (San Francisco: PPIC, Occasional Paper, September 2003).

13. The largest percentage increases for international tourism to Los Angeles in 2004, for instance, were from China (up 56 percent), Taiwan (up 39 percent), Japan (up 29 percent), Australia (up 29 percent) and New Zealand (up 17 percent). See Debora Vrana and Ronald D. White, "Weak Dollar Has a Silver Lining for L.A. Tourism," *Los Angeles Times*, December 17, 2004, A1.

14. For a detailed and substantive treatment of the current and projected demands on California's trade infrastructure, see Haveman and Hummels, *California's Global Gateways* (see Chap. 1, note 66).

See Erie, *Globalizing L.A.* (see Chap. 2, note 31), for an excellent history of how Southern California built a world-class trade infrastructure as well as a keen analysis of the complex issues that make the region's future as a major trade and transportation center highly uncertain, absent proper policies and political support.

See also Steven P. Erie, *Enhancing Southern California's Global Gateways: Challenges and Opportunities for Trade Infrastructure Development* (Los Angeles: Pacific Council on International Policy, June 2003), www.pacificcouncil.org.

For an early and interesting essay arguing that the state of California needed to develop a state policy toward seaport management and trade infrastructure, until then left largely to local and autonomous entities, see James Fawcett, Willard Price and Kathleen West, "Seaport Management and State Policy," in *California Policy Choices*, eds. John J. Kirlin and Donald R. Winkler (Los Angeles: University of Southern California, School of Public Administration, 1991), 199–230.

15. Jerry Brown, et al., "Let Voters Decide in June," *Los Angeles Times*, March 8, 2006.

16. See Charles Burress, "Harbor Boats Ordered to Install Cleaner Engines," *San Francisco Chronicle*, November 16, 2007, A1, A9; and Jane Kay, "Petition Cites Ships as Source of Gases; Environmental Groups, State Want EPA to Control Emissions," *San Francisco Chronicle* October 3, 2007, B1, B10.

17. See Louis Sahagun, "Port Shifts Plan's Cost to Shippers," *Los Angeles Times*, March 21, 2008, B5.

18. See Jon D. Haveman and Howard J. Shatz, eds., *Protecting the Nation's Seaports: Balancing Security and Cost* (San Francisco: PPIC, 2006).

19. See also Jock O'Connell, Bert Mason and John Hager, *The Role of Air Cargo in California's Agricultural Export Trade* (Fresno: Center for Agricultural Business, California State University, May 2005).

20. See Jock O'Connell, "Goods Don't Just Move by Sea," *San Diego Union Tribune*, October 6, 2005; and O'Connell, "Sacramento: A No-Fly Zone for International Trade," *Sacramento Bee*, September 18, 2005, E1.

21. See James Flanigan, "New Thinking Is Needed to Unclog Roads and Ports," *Los Angeles Times*, December 5, 2004, C1.

22. Elizabeth Douglas, "Loss of Iraqi Oil Could Have Big Effect on State," *Los Angeles Times*, February 10, 2003.

23. On this point, I am indebted to a personal communication from Philip Verleger, an independent energy consultant.

24. See, for example, Joel Kotkin and Robert Hertzberg, "North America Needs an Energy Alliance," *The Arizona Republic*, January 21, 2007.

25. See the three-part series on Alberta's tar sands development by Mary O'Driscoll in *E & E Daily*, an energy industry publication, originally published August 16, 2005–August 18, 2005. See www.eenews.net/specialreports/tarsands. Alberta officials say that $24 billion was invested in tar sands development there from 1996 to 2002, with an additional $70 billion in investment announced through 2020 and additional investment likely as world energy prices make the tar sands development much more feasible and competitive. See also Wensan Jiang, "Can Canada Slake China's Thirst for Oil?" *University of Alberta Express News*, www.expressnews.ualberta.ca.

See also James Flanigan, "Sempra Sees LNG as Liquid Asset," *Los Angeles Times*, December 28, 2003.

26. I am indebted to an unpublished memorandum, "Reliable Oil for the U.S., Development for Mexico" by Nathan Gardels and Jose Alberro. Gardels, the editor of *New Perspectives Quarterly*, was once executive director of the Public Investment Task Force for then Governor Jerry Brown of California; Alberro was a senior Mexican participant in the NAFTA negotiations. See also Jorge G. Castañeda and Nathan Gardels, "How to Tap Mexico's Potential," *Financial Times*, March 8, 2005.

27. Federal courts upheld the California standards, to which a number of other states had already announced their adherence. See John M. Broder, "Federal Judge Upholds Law on Emissions in California," *New York Times*, December 13, 2007. But in December 2007 the administrator of the federal Environmental Protection Agency (EPA), Steven L. Johnson, broke with decades of precedent and denied California the necessary waiver to move forward on its proposed limits; California had previously received fifty-three such waivers over forty years. Mr. Johnson stated that the newly approved federal local economy mandate would be more efficient in curbing pollution than state standards, and that federal policy should prevail, rather than permit a patchwork of varying state standards. On January 2, 2008, California sued the EPA, challenging the December 2007 decision; New York, New Jersey, Connecticut, Pennsylvania and

eleven other states, as well as five environmental organizations, joined California's lawsuit.

See Felicity Barringer, "California Sues EPA Over Denial of Waiver," *New York Times*, January 3, 2008, A13; and Zachary Coile, Bob Egelko and Matthew Yi, "EPA Blocks State's Bid to Curb Car Emissions," *San Francisco Chronicle*, December 20, 2007, A1, A8.

28. Several efforts and ideas to mitigate the effects of climate change and contribute to California's energy security were under way or proposed at the state and local levels by the end of 2007, including greater use of photovoltaic technologies. See Eicke R. Weber, "The Future Is Just Overhead," *San Francisco Chronicle*, August 29, 2007, B9. Politically conservative Palm Desert is receiving tens of millions of dollars in state funds to develop a project to reduce energy consumption 30 percent by 2012, which will be a model for other communities across the state. See Noaki Schwartz, "Palm Desert, of All Places, Is Learning How to Live Green," *San Francisco Chronicle*, July 28, 2007, B3. In November 2006, liberal Berkeley approved Measure G to reduce greenhouse gas emissions by 20 percent by 2050. See *Climate Action in the City of Berkeley: A Framework Report for Community Review and Engagement*, www.berkeleyclimateaction.org/doc Manager/1000000015/FrameworkReport_June07.pdf. The city initiated a program so that homeowners could install solar panels without paying the normal upfront costs; the prospect is the first of its kind in the nation. See Carolyn Jones, "Berkeley's Radical Solar Plan: City Pays Upfront for System Installation—Recoups Through 20 Year Assessment," *San Francisco Chronicle*, October 26, 2007, A1; and Carolyn Jones, "City Council Unanimously OKs Solar Financing District; Property Owners Could Opt for Tax to Cover Setup Costs," *San Francisco Chronicle*, November 7, 2007, B12.

29. In June 2005, San Francisco was the first U.S. city to host World Environment Day. Addressing the conference, Governor Schwarzenegger announced that the state would reduce its greenhouse gas emissions and that day issued Executive Order S-3-05, mandating reducing to 1990 levels by 2020 and to 20 percent of 1990 levels by 2050. Although less ambitious than AB 1365, approved by the assembly and the Senate Committee on Environmental Policy (which would have met Kyoto Protocol standards, 5 percent below 1990 levels by 2012 for the richest countries), the governor's action went beyond the voluntary approaches that the federal government had suggested. See Mark Martin, "Governor Acts to Curb State's Gas Emissions; Goals Put Him at Odds with Many in the GOP," *San Francisco Chronicle*, June 2, 2005; Don Thompson, "Climate Experts Give Kudos to Political Efforts," *Oakland Tribune*, September 15, 2005; Terence Chea, "Governor Unveiling Global Warming Plan at UN Conference," Associated Press, June 1, 2005.

The governor's July 2006 agreement with British Prime Minister Tony Blair was a first step toward California's entry into an international trading scheme for carbon emissions and shows the state's leadership on the issue of climate change. It was followed by AB32, the California Global Warming Solutions Act and SB1365, legislation mandating greenhouse gas emissions standards for baseload electricity generation. It was also followed by a second Schwarzenegger meeting with Blair in June 2007 and talks between the governor and German Foreign Minister Frank-Walter Steinmeier to discuss California's participation with the European Union to devise a market for carbon credits to reduce greenhouse gas emissions. Steinmeier, in a speech to the Commonwealth Club and the World Affairs Council of Northern California, declared that California was "the most important testing laboratory for our global future," that Germany and California were "kindred spirits" and that he hoped for political as well as cultural and economic cooperation between California and Germany. See Patrick Wintour, "Blair Signs Climate Pact with Schwarzenegger; California Deal Paves Way to Joining EU Scheme; Agreement Represents Snub to White House," *The Guardian*, August 1, 2006; Mark Martin, "State's War on Warming: Governor Signs Measure to Cap Greenhouse Gas Emissions—Sweeping Changes Predicted in Industries and Life in Cities," *San Francisco Chronicle*, September 28, 2006, A1; Mary Jordan, "A United Call to Fight Global Warming; Blair, Schwarzenegger Push Global Leaders for Action," *Washington Post*, June 27, 2007, A14; Sabine Muscat, "State, EU Talk about Pollution," *San Francisco Chronicle*, August 30, 2007, C1; "California Greening" (editorial), *San Francisco Chronicle*, September 4, 2007; and "Getting Around the EPA" (editorial), *San Francisco Chronicle*, December 21, 2007. I have also drawn on notes prepared by my assistant, Melissa Lockhart, on a presentation made on January 18, 2008, by Mary Nichols, chairman of the California Air Resources Board.

In September 2007, Schwarzenegger addressed the UN General Assembly on the importance of measures to address climate change, noting that "California is moving the United States beyond debate and doubt to action." See Kevin Yamamura, "Governor Takes UN spotlight," *Contra Costa Times*, September 24, 2007, A1; and Tom Chorneau, "Governor Pushes on Warming," *San Francisco Chronicle*, September 25, 2007, A10.

30. A variety of state initiatives to improve international education and the usefulness of integrating international education promotion into a state's strategic planning are emphasized in Victor C. Johnson and Filmona Hailemichael, "Advancing International Education in the States," *International Educator*, November–December 2007, 6–9. See also Committee on Economic Development, *Education for Global Leadership* (New York, 2006); and Darla K. Deardorff and William Hunter, "Educating Global-Ready Graduates," *International Educator*, May–June 2006, 72–83.

31. For a wise and succinct discussion of "soft power" and its significance, see Joseph S. Nye, Jr., *Soft Power: The Means to Success in World Politics* (New York: Public Affairs, 2004).

32. See, for example, Evelyn Iritani, "Expatriates Play Key Role in India's Economic Rise," *Los Angeles Times*, August 12, 2006. Iritani emphasizes the important role of California's large Indian American community in the expansion of India's technology industry and in developing residential real estate in India.

33. See, for example, Dean Takahashi, "Flood of Fakes: Counterfeits Inundate High-Tech Market," *San José Mercury News*, February 2, 2006.

34. The TRIPS and TRIPS plus provisions in various bilateral trade agreements provide adequate and perhaps even excessive protection to the intellectual property

rights of U.S. pharmaceutical firms and have had to be overcome by developing countries to make medicines available at reasonable prices for such emergencies as the HIV/AIDS epidemics in Brazil, Haiti and Africa. See, for example, Joseph Stiglitz, *Globalization and Its Discontents* (New York: W.W. Norton, 2002), 246; and Jagdish Bagwhati, *In Defense of Globalization* (New York: Oxford University Press, 2004), 183–85.

35. See, for example, the polling data cited in Kenneth F. Scheve and Matthew J. Slaughter, "A New Deal for Globalization." *Foreign Affairs*, July/August 2007, 34–47. See also Brian Knowlton, "Global Support for Trade, Mixed with Some Doubts." *New York Times*, October 5, 2007, A10. For insights on the concerns about globalization, see Stiglitz, *Globalization and Its Discontents*; Joseph E. Stiglitz, *Making Globalization Work* (New York: Norton, 2006); Naomi Klein, *Fences and Windows: Dispatches from the Front Lines of the Globalization Debate* (New York: Picador USA, 2002); Paul Kingsnorth, *One No, Many Yeses: A Journey to the Heart of the Global Resistance Movement* (London: Simon and Schuster, 2004); Malcolm Cross and Robert Moore, eds., *Globalization and the New City: Migrants, Minorities and Urban Transformations in Comparative Analysis* (New York: Palgrave Macmillan, 2002); Peter H. Lindert and Jeffrey G. Williamson, "Does Globalization Make the World More Unequal?" NBER Working Paper 8228 (Cambridge, MA: National Bureau of Economic Research, April 2001), www.nber.org/ papers/w8228.

36. See, for example, "Perspectives on Trade and Poverty Reduction Survey," conducted by the German Marshall Fund of the United States (December 2007), www. gmfus.org.

37. The United States-Peru Trade Promotion Agreement, approved by the House of Representatives on November 5, 2007, and by the U.S. Senate on December 8, 2007, illustrated how such an approach could build support, both nationally and in California; California's support for this pact in the House was 34–16. For an insightful analysis of the changing politics of trade policy, see I. M. Destler, "American Trade Politics in 2007: Build Bipartisan Compromise," Policy Brief 1807-5 (Washington DC: Peterson Institute for International Economies, May 2007).

38. See Scheve and Slaughter, "A New Deal."

39. See Robert J. LaLonde, *The Case for Wage Insurance* (New York: Council on Foreign Relations Press Special Report, September 2007).

40. See Dowell Meyers, *Boomers and Immigrants: Forging a New Social Contract for America* (New York: Russell Sage Foundation, 2007).

41. For an excellent introduction to these complex issues, see Sandra Polaski, "U.S. Living Standards in an Era of Globalization," Policy Brief 53 (Washington DC: Carnegie Endowment for International Peace, July 2007). For a parallel discussion, proposing a redistributive change in U.S. fiscal policy to preserve the political basis for further trade and investment liberalization, see Scheve and Slaughter, "A New Deal," esp. 44–47. A different view, emphasizing how American workers have gained from globalization, is given by Daniel Griswold, *Trading Up: How Expanding Trade Has Delivered Better Jobs and Higher Living Standards for American Workers*, Trade Policy

Analysis 36 (Washington, DC: Cato Institute Center for Trade Policy Studies, October 25, 2007), 1–17.

42. For a recent discussion, see Jeromimo Cortina, et al., *The Economic Impact of the Mexico-California Relationship* (Los Angeles: Tomas Rivera Policy Institute, 2005).

43. See Wadhwa et al., *America's New Immigrant Entrepreneurs*, 4 (see Chap. 1, note 52).

44. A film, *A Day Without A Mexican*, directed by Sergio Arau and cowritten by Arau and Yareli Arizmendi, imagines what Southern California would be like if Mexican labor suddenly disappeared. See Kevin Crust, "'A Day Without a Mexican'; Satire Plays It Safe Despite Its Politically Charged Subject and Fails to Raise the Important Questions," *Los Angeles Times*, May 14, 2004.

45. See Center for Continuing Study of the California Economy, *The Impact of Immigration on the Californian Economy*, Report of the California Regional Economies Project (Palo Alto, CA, September 2005). As explained in the note on page 6 of Chapter 1, this essay uses the term "unauthorized migrant" employed by the U.S. Census Bureau, to describe those who reside in the United States without proper documentation.

46. See Miriam Jordan, "California Race Highlights Split on Immigration," *Wall Street Journal*, October 18, 2005, B1. For example, accountant Jim Gilchrist, founder of the "Minuteman Project," a volunteer force to help the U.S. Border Patrol catch "illegal" immigrants from Mexico, unexpectedly won a spot, running as a member of the American Independent Party, in the runoff election to choose a member of the House of Representatives to replace Rep. Christopher Cox.

47. There is a very extensive literature on immigration, to California and elsewhere in the United States, and the policy issues it presents. Among the main sources are the Center for Continuing Study of the California Economy, *Impact of Immigration*; Myers, *Boomers and Immigrants*; Kevin McCarthy, *Immigration and California: Issues for the 1980s* (Santa Monica, CA: RAND, 1983); McCarthy and Vernez, *Immigration in a Changing Economy* (see Chap. 2, note 68); Kevin F. McCarthy and R. Burciaga Valdez, *California's Demographic Future* (Santa Monica, CA: RAND, 1986); Kevin McCarthy and Robert Otto Burciaga Valdez, *Current & Future Effects of Mexican Immigration in California* (Santa Monica, CA: RAND, 1986); Robert F. Schoeni, Kevin F. McCarthy and Georges Vernez, *The Mixed Economic Progress of Immigrants* (Santa Monica, CA: RAND, 1996); Georges Vernez and Kevin F. McCarthy, *The Costs of Immigration to Taxpayers: Analytical and Policy Issues* (Santa Monica, CA: RAND, 1996); Roger Waldinger, "California's Immigration," in *California Policy Options, 1997*, ed. Xandra Kayden (Los Angeles: School of Public Policy and Social Research, University of California, Los Angeles, 1997); Hans P. Johnson, *California's Demographic Future* (San Francisco: PPIC, Occasional Paper, December 2003); Johnson, *State of Diversity* (see Chap. 3, note 2); Myers, *Changing Immigrants* (see Chap. 2, note 70); Myers, Pitkin and Park, *California's Immigrants Turn the Corner* (see Chap. 2, note 67); Myers, Pitkin and Park, *California Demographic Futures* (see Chap. 1, note 44); Laura E. Hill, *The Socioeconomic Well-Being of California's Immigrant Youth* (San Francisco: PPIC, 2004); Wayne A. Cornelius, "Controlling 'Unwanted' Immigration: Lessons from the United States, 1993–2004,"

Journal of Ethnic and Migration Studies, 31, no. 2 (April 2005), 775–94; Jorge Durand and Douglas S. Massey, eds., *Crossing the Border: Research from the Mexican Migration Project* (New York: Russell Sage Foundation, 2004); Agustin Escobar Latapi and Susan Martin, eds., *Mexico-U.S. Migration Management: A Binational Approach* (Washington DC: Institute for Study of International Migration, Georgetown University, 2006); Doris Meissner, et al., *Immigration and America's Future: A New Chapter*, Report of the Independent Task Force on Immigration and America's Future (Washington, DC: Migration Policy Institute, Manhattan Institute for Policy Research and Woodrow Wilson International Center for Scholars, September 2006); Ivan Light, *Deflecting Immigration: Networks, Markets, and Regulation in Los Angeles* (New York: Russell Sage Foundation, 2006); Gordon H. Hanson, *The Economic Logic of Illegal Immigration* (New York: Council on Foreign Relations, March 2007). I have also drawn on notes by Aubrey Elson, my assistant, on the annual Envisioning California conference, "Immigration in California," held at California State University, Northridge, September 19, 2007.

48. This will increasingly also be relevant in the "new growth" or "gateway" states to which larger numbers of immigrants are now going, such as North Carolina, Georgia, Nebraska, Iowa, Minnesota and Nevada. See Greg Anrig Jr. and Tova Andrea Wang, *Immigration's New Frontiers: Experiences from the Emerging Gateway States* (New York: Century Foundation Press, 2006).

49. Philip J. Romero, Andrew J. Chang and Theresa Parker, *Shifting the Costs of a Failed Federal Policy: The Net Fiscal Impact of Illegal Immigrants in California* (Sacramento, CA: Governor's Office of Planning and Research, September 1994). For a contemporary assessment of the net fiscal cost to California of migration, albeit from a different perspective, see Cortina et al., *Economic Impact*.

50. See *LULAC v. Wilson*, WL 699583 (C.D. Cal., 1995). The court ruled on November 20, 1995, that several provisions of the proposition violated federal law because they amounted to regulation of immigration, a function that is preemptively reserved to the federal government. A subsequent U.S. District Court decision on November 14, 1997, closed the matter by reaffirming the 1995 judgment and adding that several other provisions, left open in 1995, were also unconstitutional, because they had been preempted by federal legislation adopted in 1996. See the U.S. District Court's November 14, 1997, decision, reported at 997 F. Supp. 1244 (C.D. Cal. 1997), which came in a conglomeration of four cases.

51. For an interesting analysis of Proposition 187, see Stanley Mailman, "California's Proposition 187 and Its Lessons," *New York Law Journal*, January 3, 1995, www.ssbb.com (accessed November 29, 2006).

52. It is not clear how much money would have been saved, as the new notices, forms, training and labor involved in implementing the 187 mandates would have been costly, implementation would have been problematic and many of the benefits involved were already denied to undocumented immigrants, especially after the 1996 congressional approval of the Immigration Reform Act and the Welfare Reform Act. These observations were conveyed in a personal communication from Thomas Saenz, then vice president of litigation, Mexican American Legal Defense and Education Fund, August 21, 2004.

53. See Robert Collier, "Mexico Likes Texas' Governor Better," *San Francisco Chronicle*, April 29, 1998, A1.

54. Raul Hinojosa-Ojeda argues, on the basis of a California in the Global Economy computer model, that full implementation of Proposition 187 would have proved disastrous to California's economy, tax base and fiscal health. One scenario, in which undocumented immigrant labor was either deported or deterred in practice, would have caused immigrant wages to fall, and thus ironically would actually have stimulated greater demand for immigrant labor. Hinojosa concludes that Proposition 187 suffered from a "failure to understand the irreversible and transnational labor interdependence between California, Southern California and Mexico." See Raul Hinojosa-Ojeda, "Southern California in the World Economy: Current Position, Future Scenarios, and Policy-Making Challenges," draft paper (Los Angeles: North American Integration and Development Center, School of Public Policy and Social Research, University of California, Los Angeles, February 1999), 32–33, 36.

55. See Peter Andreas, *Border Games: Policing the U.S. Mexico Divide* (Ithaca: Cornell University Press, 2000).

56. See Wayne A. Cornelius, "Death at the Border: Efficacy and Unintended Consequences of U.S. Immigration Policy," *Population and Development Review*, 27, no. 4 (December 2001), 661–85. Ten times more people have died trying to cross the U.S.-Mexico border since 1995 than the number who died trying to cross the Berlin Wall from 1961 to 1989. Cf. Douglas Massey, "When Less is More: Border Enforcement and Undocumented Migrations," testimony before the Subcommittee on Immigration, Citizenship, Refugees, Border Security and International Law, Committee on the Judiciary, U.S. House of Representatives, April 20, 2007.

57. Belinda I. Reyes, Hans P. Johnson and Richard Van Swearingen, *Holding the Line? The Effect of Recent Border Build-Up on Unauthorized Immigration* (San Francisco: PPIC, 2002); and Massey, "When Less is More."

58. See the useful report, *Managing Mexican Migration to the United States* (Washington, DC: Center for Strategic and International Studies with Instituto Tecnológico Autónomo de México, April 2004).

59. See Center for Continuing Study of the California Economy, *Impact of Immigration*.

60. See, for example, Michael Hiltzik, "Border Policy is Pinching Farmers," *Los Angeles Times*, September 22, 2005.

61. See Hanson, *Economic Logic*.

62. See Center for Continuing Study of the California Economy, *Impact of Immigration*, 45–46. The center's report draws, in turn, on other sources, particularly a 1997 report of the National Academy of Sciences, National Research Council, *The New Americans: Economic, Demographic and Fiscal Effects of Immigration* (Washington, DC: National Academy Press, 1997). For an up-to-date review of the fiscal impacts of immigration, nationally and at state levels, see Daniel Griswold, "The Fiscal Impact of Immigration Reform: The Real Story," Free Trade Bulletin 30 (Washington, DC: CATO Institute, May 25, 2007).

63. The most productive and successful newcomers move to the suburbs, however, thus leaving the city of Los Angeles with the poorest and most disadvantaged. See Patrick J. McDonell, "Study Finds Immigrants' Economic Effect Mixed," *Los Angeles Times*, January 23, 1997.

64. A survey by the Field Poll in July 2006, for instance, found very strong support among California registered voters for legalizing employed, English-speaking and tax-paying undocumented immigrants who have lived in-country for some years and strong opposition to plans for sending unauthorized persons outside the United States and requiring application for readmission. See Mark DiCamello and Mervyn Field, "Illegal Immigration a Serious Problem. Strong Support for Allowing Illegal Immigrants Already Here to Stay," *The Field Poll*, Release 2205 (San Francisco: Field Research Corporation, July 27, 2006.) The September 2005 *Statewide Survey* by the Public Policy Institute of California found that a majority of adult resident Californians, 56 percent, viewed immigrants as "a benefit to California because of their hard work and job skills"; 36 percent said immigrants were a burden and 8 percent did not know. See Mark Baldassare, *PPIC Statewide Survey: Special Survey on Californians and the Initiative Process* (San Francisco: PPIC in collaboration with the James Irvine Foundation, September 2005), 24. In March 2008, PPIC's Statewide Survey reported that 59 percent of Californians believe immigrants are a benefit to California, an increase from 40 percent with this view in 1998. Sixty-six percent of those surveyed believe that unauthorized residents should be allowed to apply for work permits that would allow them to stay and work in the United States. Seventy-two percent think that unauthorized residents who have lived and worked in the United States for at least two years should be given a chance to keep their jobs and apply for legal status. See Mark Baldassare, et al., *PPIC Statewide Survey: Californians and Their Government* (San Francisco: PPIC, March 2008), available online at www.ppic.org.

65. The State Criminal Alien Assistance Program, providing federal reimbursement to the states for the costs of incarcerating unauthorized immigrants, was a modest step toward recognizing the need for federal transfers to cover some of the costs of immigration, but the program has been substantially underfunded; a May 2003 report by the Government Accountability Office indicates that California has been reimbursed less than 25 percent of its expenditure for incarcerating unauthorized migrants, and other estimates are even lower. See "Senators Feinstein and Kyl Join with 5 Western Senators to Call for Doubling of SCAAP Funding in CJS Appropriation Bill," *News from Senator Feinstein*, September 15, 2005, www.feinstein.senate.gov. See also *News from Senator Feinstein*, March 17, 2005, for additional information. A recent study on the impact of immigration on the California economy estimates that California usually gets reimbursed 10–12 percent of the costs of incarcerating undocumented prisoners. See Center for Continuing Study of the California Economy, *Impact of Immigration*, 49

66. For a review of the evidence, see Center for Continuing Study of the California Economy, *Impact of Immigration*, esp. 26–41. A study in February 2007 by Giovanni Peri argues that "there is no evidence that the inflow of immigrants over the period 1960–2004 worsened the employment opportunities of natives with similar education

and experience." See Giovanni Peri, "How Immigrants Affect California Employment and Wages," *California Counts*, 8:1

67. See Hill, *Socioeconomic Well-Being*.

68. The term "intermestic" was introduced by Bayless Manning in "The Congress, the Executive and Intermestic Affairs: Three Proposals," *Foreign Affairs*, 55, no. 2, January 1977. I have been among the popularizers of this term over many years, but it has not caught on widely, perhaps because of its stylistic infelicity. In the absence of a better one, I continue to use the word.

69. See Abraham F. Lowenthal, "United States-Latin American Relations at the Century's Turn: Managing the 'Intermestic' Agenda," in *The United States and Latin America: A Twenty-First Century View*, eds. Albert Fishlow and James Jones (New York: Norton, 1999), 109–36.

70. See Philip Martin, "Mexico-U.S. Migration," in Gary C. Hufbauer and Jeffrey J. Schott, *NAFTA Revisited: Achievements and Challenges* (Washington, DC: Institute of International Economics, 2005), 441–66, esp. 449–55.

71. Transfers might also be considered within the state to those cities, particularly Los Angeles, that spend most on the education and health care of disadvantaged immigrants. Cf. "Thinking Out Loud: Immigration—The Border and the Classroom," *Los Angeles Times*, August 8, 2005.

72. See, for example, the report of the *Field Poll* that 65 percent of Californians favor creating programs to legalize the status of unauthorized residents who have been in the state for a number of years, 67 percent favor temporary worker programs and 59 percent oppose building a wall along the U.S.-Mexico border. See *The Field Poll*, Release 2229 (San Francisco: Field Research Corporation, April 10, 2007). For a thoughtful discussion of steps to speed the integration of immigrants, see Vernez, *New Melting Pot* (see Chap. 3, note 7).

73. Serious consideration should also be given to measures that would provide voting rights to immigrant noncitizens for local school board elections and perhaps for municipal government more generally. A number of jurisdictions in the United States, including New York; Chicago; Cambridge, Massachusetts; and Takoma Park, Maryland, have innovated in this respect, going back to practices that were common in the United States until the 1920s in order to facilitate the more rapid integration of immigrants and provide adequate representation of the interests of all residents. See Ronald Hayduk, "Democracy for All: Restoring Immigrant Voting Rights in the U.S.," *New Political Science*, 26, no. 4 (December, 2004), 499–523; and Tara Kini, "Sharing the Vote: Noncitizen Voting Rights in Local School Board Elections," *California Law Review*, January 2005, 271–321. See also Abraham McLaughlin, "A Move to Extend Vote to Immigrants," *The Christian Science Monitor*, October 26, 1998.

74. HR 4437 is widely referred to as the Sensenbrenner bill, because it was introduced by Representative James Sensenbrenner of Wisconsin. His six cosponsors of the bill included four from California, Representatives Foxx, Lungren, Issa and Miller.

75. Doris Meissner, senior associate of the Migration Policy Institute and one of the country's foremost authorities on immigration policy, believes that the 110th Congress will

defer further consideration of this controversial issue and that a newly elected administration may also prefer to sidestep the issue, at least at first (personal communication).

76. See Julia Preston, "Surge in Immigration Laws Around U.S.," *New York Times*, August 6, 2007.

77. A discerning analysis of how civic leaders can act as intermediaries between citizens and the political process, rebuilding the trust necessary to confront difficult public policy challenges, is Daniel Yankelovich and Isabella Furth, "Public Engagement in California: Escaping the Vicious Cycle," *National Civic Review*, Fall 2006, 3–11.

78. For early explorations of these flows and their implications, see Lowenthal and Burgess, *California-Mexico Connection* (see Chap. 2, note 87); and Katrina Burgess and Abraham F. Lowenthal, "Managing California-Mexico Relations," in *California Policy Choices* (Sacramento: School of Public Administration, University of Southern California, 1990). The following pages draw in part on these earlier works and on the points made in a policy workshop I organized and chaired in April 2000 on "Mexico Transforming: Implications for California." See "Mexico Transforming: Implications for California," draft rapporteurial report of policy workshop (April 17, 2000) at the PPIC, San Francisco; manuscript in author's possession. They also reflect much more recent conversations with both California and Mexican officials.

A very different approach to the California-Mexico connection, grounded in nostalgia for California of the 1950s, is Hanson, *Mexifornia* (see Chap. 3, note 120). Yet another vision, rooted in concern for the preservation of American national identity, is Samuel P. Huntington, *Who Are We? The Challenge to America's National Identity* (New York: Simon & Schuster, 2004). For my critique of the Huntington volume, see Abraham F. Lowenthal, "The Enemy Within?" *Commonweal*, December 14, 2004, 21–23. Cf. Gary M. Segura et al., "Symposium on Immigration and National Identity," *Perspectives on Politics*, 4, no. 2 (June 2006), 277–313.

79. For an extended discussion of transnational connections with Mexico and their implications, see Denise Dresser and Veronica Wilson, *Envisioning North American Futures: Transnational Challenges and Opportunities* (Los Angeles: Pacific Council on International Policy, 2005). A pioneering early study of cross-border coalitions and transnational networks in U.S.-Mexico relations was Cathryn L. Thorup, "The Politics of Free Trade and the Dynamics of Cross-Border Coalitions in U.S. Mexican Relations," *Columbia Journal of World Business*, 26, no. 2 (Summer 1991), 13–26. See also Robert S. Leiken, *The Melting Border: Mexico and Mexican Communities in the United States* (Washington, DC: Center for Equal Opportunity, 2000); Lester D. Langley, *Mex-America: Two Countries, One Future* (New York: Crown Publishers, 1988); and Gaspar Rivera-Salgado, "Cross-Border Grassroots Organizations and the Indigenous Migrant Experience," in *Crossborder Dialogues: U.S.-Mexico Social Movement Networking*, eds. David Brooks and Jonathan Fox (La Jolla: Center for U.S.-Mexican Studies, University of California, San Diego, 2002), 259–74.

80. For obvious reasons, it is difficult to establish authoritative and reliable estimates on the numbers of unauthorized immigrants, and high and low estimates often reflect political and policy biases. Some of the most careful works are Frank D. Bean,

Jennifer Van Hook and Karen Woodrow-Linfield, *Estimates of Unauthorized Migrants Residing in the United States: The Total Mexican, Non-Mexican, and Central American Unauthorized Populations in Mid-2001* (Washington, DC: Pew Hispanic Center, Special Report, November 2001); B. Lindsay Lowell and Roberto Suro, *How Many Undocumented: The Numbers Behind the U.S.-Mexico Immigration Talks* (Washington, DC: Pew Hispanic Center, March 21, 2002); Philip Martin, *Guest Workers: New Solution, New Problem?* (Washington, DC: Pew Hispanic Center, March 21, 2002); and Office of Policy and Planning, U.S. Immigration and Naturalization Service, *Estimates of Unauthorized Immigrant Population Residing in the United States, 1990 to 2000* (Washington, DC, January 2003), www.dhs.gov/xlibrary/assets/statistics/publications/Ill_Report_1211.pdf.

The estimate of 2.8 million unauthorized immigrants in California in January 2005 comes from the Office of Immigration Statistics in the U.S. Department of Homeland Security. See Suzanne Gombon, "Fall Estimates 10.5 Million Illegal Immigrants," *Washington Post*, August 18, 2006.

For a discussion of the mischievous use of bad data, see Michael Hiltzik, "Golden State: Clearing Out Bad Data on Illegal Immigrants," *Los Angeles Times*, December 22, 2003, C1.

81. The estimate of $6 billion in annual remittances from Mexicans in California is from Manuel Orozco, probably the leading authority on remittances, in a personal communication. See also *All in the Family: Latin America's Most Important International Financial Flow*, Report of the Inter-American Dialogue Task Force on Remittances, January 2004, www.thedialogue.org/PublicationFiles/all_family.pdf.

82. Chris Karl, "Tapping Generosity of Immigrants," *Los Angeles Times*, June 8, 2000, A1.

83. Much of the data in this and subsequent paragraphs comes from Howard J. Shatz and Luis Felipe López-Calva, *The Emerging Integration of the California-Mexico Economies* (San Francisco: PPIC, 2004).

84. See California Chamber of Commerce's "All About Trade and Investment," compiled from U.S. Department of Commerce May 2008 data, available at www.calchamber.com (accessed June 23, 2008).

85. See U.S. Customs statistics posted by Otay Mesa Chamber of Commerce at www.otaymesa.org.

86. See Evelyn Iritani, "Mexican Resorts Show No Sign of Catching U.S. Housing Cold," *Los Angeles Times*, August 26, 2006.

87. These mutual visits are attracting increasing attention in the print and electronic media in both countries. See, for example, Annabelle Saray, "Mexican Officials Seek Votes in U.S.," Associated Press, *Antelope Valley Daily News* (CA), December 15, 2004; Sam Enriquez, "Mexican Hopefuls Eye Votes in L.A.," *Los Angeles Times*, August 22, 2005; and Sam Enriquez, "Nuñez Trip Hits Heavy Resistance: On Mexican Goodwill Trip, Assembly Chief Has to Defend Bid for State of Emergency on Border," *Los Angeles Times*, August 27, 2005.

88. See Gaspar Rivera-Salgado, "Transnational Political Strategies: The Case of Mexican Indigenous Migrants" in *Immigration Research for a New Century: Multidisciplinary*

Perspectives, eds. Nancy Funer, Ruban Rumbault and Steven Gold (New York: Russell Sage Foundation, 2000), 134–56; Zabin and Rabadan, *Mexican Hometown Associations* (see Chap. 1, note 47); and Felipe Lopez, Luis Escala Rabadan and Raul Hinojosa-Ojeda, *Migrant Associations, Remittances and Regional Development between Los Angeles and Oaxaca, Mexico*, Research Report 10 (Los Angeles: North American Integration and Development Center, University of California).

89. See Dresser and Wilson, *Envisioning North American Futures*. See also Brooks and Fox, *Crossborder Dialogues*; and Chappell Lawson, "Voting Preference and Political Socialization Among Mexican-Americans and Mexicans Living in the United States," *Mexican Studies/Estudios Mexicanos*, 19, no. 1 (Winter 2003), 65–80.

90. For full elaborations of this argument, see David E. Hayes-Bautista, Werner O. Schink and Jorge Chapa, *The Burden of Support: Young Latinos in an Aging Society* (Stanford, CA: Stanford University Press, 1988), and Dowell Myers, *Boomers and Immigrants*.

91. See the analysis by Hill, *Socioeconomic Well-Being*.

92. See Marielena Lara, et al., "Acculturation and Latino Health in the United States: A Review of the Literature and its Sociopolitical Context," *Annual Review of Public Health*, 26 (April 2005): 367–97.

93. These ideas are more fully presented in *A Call to Action: Immigration and Integration in California*, Report of the Immigration Policy Student Task Force (Los Angeles: School of International Relations, University of Southern California, May 2007).

I am indebted to the task force, and especially to Chelsea Cooper, for these points. Cf. Maria Teresa Taningu, *Revisiting the Latin Health Paradox*, Policy Brief (Los Angeles: Tomas Rivera Policy Institute, August 2007).

94. New York had adopted a similar policy under Governor Pataki in 2003, but in 2007 Governor Eliot Spitzer announced a change in policy, making it possible for unauthorized residents to obtain driver's licenses upon establishing proof of identity without also requiring evidence of legal immigration. Spitzer called this a "common sense change" that would improve traffic safety, lower insurance costs and enhance law enforcement. Other states with similar policies in 2007 were Hawaii, Maine, Maryland, Michigan, New Mexico, Oregon, Utah and Washington. See Nina Bernstein "Going Against National Trend, State Gives Illegal Immigrants Easier Path to Driver's Licenses," *New York Times*, September 22, 2007, B12.

95. See Little Hoover Commission (Michael E. Alpert, chairman), *We the People: Helping Newcomers Become Californians* (Sacramento, June 2002). This study was spurned in the post-9/11 environment. See Peter Skerry, "Give Illegal Immigrants Licenses—Obligations," *Los Angeles Times*, August 21, 2006.

96. Comparable steps have been adopted in recent years in Texas, New York and Utah. See Kim Cobb, "States Taking Initiative as Immigration Swells," *Houston Chronicle*, August 31, 2003. By 2006, ten states had similar provisions, according to the National Conference of State Legislatures, but more recently, a number of states have barred unauthorized migrants from access to in-state tuition privileges. See National Conference of State Legislatures, "2007 Enacted State Legislation Related to

Immigrants and Immigration," August 6, 2007, www.ncsl.org/programs/immig/2007immigrationupdate.htm.

97. The foregoing discussion draws upon Vernez, *The New Melting Pot*; and Roberto Suro, *Strangers Among Us: How Latino Immigration Is Transforming America* (New York: Knopf, 1998), esp. chapter 18, 302–23. Cf. Chicago Council on Foreign Relations, *Keeping the Promise: Immigration Proposals from the Heartland: Report of an Independent Task Force* (Chicago: Chicago Council on Foreign Relations, 2004). See also Chicago Council on Global Affairs, *A Shared Future: The Economic Engagement of Greater Chicago and Its Mexican Community* (Chicago: Chicago Council on Global Affairs, 2006).

98. Important work on these issues is being done by the California-Mexico Health Initiative of the California Policy Research Center, but it requires much more funding to have a substantial impact.

99. See Stephen E. Flynn, "Rethinking the Role of U.S.-Mexican Border in the Post 9/11 World," testimony before the Committee on Foreign Relations, U.S. Senate, March 27, 2004.

100. Examples of the kind of work that could be encouraged in this regard include the research on governance in Mexico that has been undertaken over the past few years at the Center for U.S.-Mexican Studies at the University of California, San Diego; the research on the external role in promoting and reinforcing effective democratic governance that has been conducted at Stanford University's Center on Democracy, Development and the Rule of Law; and the work at San Diego State University's Trans-Border Institute, especially in its Justice in Mexico project.

101. See Pacific Council on International Policy, *Mexico Transforming* (Los Angeles, 2000), www.pacificcouncil.org. See also Julia Preston and Samuel Dillon, *Opening Mexico: The Making of a Democracy* (New York: Farrar, Straus and Giroux, 2004).

102. A proposal to establish such a California-Mexico Fellows program was advanced by the author of this book in 1999 in testimony before the California Assembly, endorsed and announced by then California Lieutenant Governor Cruz Bustamante, and discussed in a series of subsequent meetings, but was never actually implemented. See Ralph Frammolino, "California and the West: Exchange of State, Mexican Students Urged," *Los Angeles Times*, August 5, 1999, A3.

103. For early explorations of Mexico's need to focus on California, see Carlos Rico, "From State to 'state': Managing Mexico's California Connection," and Carlos Gonzalez Gutierrez, "The Mexican Diaspora in California: Limits and Possibilities for the Mexican Government" in Burgess and Lowenthal, *California-Mexico Connection*, 239–53 and 221–35, respectively.

An interesting report on Mexico's intense efforts to cultivate mutually beneficial relations with California is José Angel Pescador Osuna, "La Conexion California-Mexico: Competencia Global Cara a Cara," presentation made at the ninth PROFMEX/ADVIES International Conference, Morelia, Michoacan, December 13, 1997, and published in *Mexico and the World*, University of Guadalajara, vol. 3, no. 2 (Spring 1998). Sr. Pescador was Mexico's Consul General in Los Angeles at the time.

Canada, too, has stressed California's unique importance, opening up new offices in San Jose and San Diego to complement those in Los Angeles and San Francisco and developing a robust program of trade and investment missions to California; arranging visits by the prime minister, the foreign minister and other cabinet officials, as well as provincial premiers; and lobbying the California legislature and public to avoid protectionism on such products as fish, lumber and filmmaking. Personal communication and interview with Colin Robertson, then consul general of Canada in Los Angeles, in 2004.

104. Bay Area Economic Forum, *Ties That Bind* (see Chap. 2, note 77) illustrates the kind of analysis that could be done on a statewide basis regarding China, paralleling this chapter's emphasis on relations with Mexico. Former California State Senator John Vasconcellos has proposed a comparable study on the potential for constructing a California-Brazil partnership. See http://sinet2.sen.ca.gov/soir/Brazil/reports.htp. The U.S. Embassy in Santiago, Chile and the Department of State worked with California officials in 2008 to develop a partnership arrangement with Chile, initiated by that country's Foreign Ministry and jointly announced by Chile's President Michelle Bachelet and Governor Schwarzenegger in Sacramento in June 2008.

Chapter 5

1. The literature on the involvement in foreign policy of noncentral governments includes Fry, *Expanding Role of Local Governments* (see Chap. 4, note 2); Brown and Fry, *States and Provinces* (see Chap. 4, note 2); Hocking, *Localizing Foreign Policy* (see Chap. 4, note 2); and Shuman, "Dateline Main Street," 154–74 (see Chap. 4, note 2). Recent studies include Samuel Lucas McMillan, "Subnational Foreign Policy Actors: How and Why Governors Participate in U.S. Foreign Policy," *Foreign Policy Analysis*, 4 (2008), 227–53; Timothy J. Conlan and Michelle A. Sager, "The Growing International Activities of the American States," *Policy Studies Review* 18, no. 3 (Autumn 2001), 12–28; Peter Howard, "The Growing Role of States in U.S. Foreign Policy: The Case of the State Partnership Program," *International Studies Perspectives* 5 (2004), 179–96; Timothy J. Conlan, Robert L. Dudley and Joel F. Clark, "Taking on the World: The International Activities of American State Legislatures," *Publius: The Journal of Federalism* 34, no. 3 (Summer 2004), 183–99; and Julie Blase, "State-Level Foreign Mechanisms Along the U.S.-Mexico Border: Criminal Justice Cooperation Between Texas and Mexico," paper prepared for the Southwest Social Science Association meeting in New Orleans, LA, March 28, 2002, www.la.utexas.edu.

2. The proliferation of governmental and nongovernmental actors participating in the shaping of U.S. foreign policy has been widely discussed. An important analysis of the growing role of nongovernmental actors is Mathews, "Power Shift," (see Chap. 4, note 2). For a useful overview, see Lyman, "Influence of Domestic Factors," 75–97 (see Chap. 4, note 2).

3. Bills to restrict offshoring of jobs have been introduced in at least thirty-seven state legislatures, for example, with a dozen anti-offshoring bills in California alone.

Some bar state services from using foreign call centers and other offshore resources, others restrict offshoring when sensitive information is involved, and others require detailed disclosure of foreign sources. See Bay Area Economic Forum, *Future of Bay Area Jobs* (see Chap. 3, note 80).

4. See Kelly Rayburn, "Council Opposes War Against Iran," *Oakland Tribune*, November 8, 2007, 13.

5. I have drawn for this paragraph on a memorandum from Mark Frame (June 16, 2008), who draws in turn on the records of the Berkeley City Council and various articles in the *San Francisco Chronicle*.

6. For an illuminating discussion of this phenomenon, arguing that the rights of immigrants and refugees are often affirmed at the local level even as they are being constricted at the national level, see Miriam J. Wells, "The Grassroots Reconfiguration of U.S. Immigration Policy," *International Migration Review*, 38, no. 4 (2004), 1308–47.

7. Madison, Wisconsin, was the first U.S. municipality to approve, in 1976, a purchasing ordinance aimed at pressuring the apartheid regime in South Africa; nearly 150 other local governments as well as 30 state governments would join Madison in the 1970s and 1980s. At the turn of the twenty-first century, similar laws directed toward conditions in Tibet, Indonesia and Nigeria were in place in California, Massachusetts and New York. See Jeanne J. Grimmett, "State and Local Economic Sanctions: Constitutional Issues," Congressional Research Service Report for Congress (April 2, 2007), http://opencrs.com, among other sources.

8. See Jesse McKinley, "California: State to Divest Iran Holdings," *New York Times*, September 25, 2007, A20.

9. See, for example, Carla Fried, "How States Are Aiming to Keep Dollars Out of Sudan," *New York Times*, February 19, 2006; Carla Mrinucci, "Schwarzenegger Upstaging Angelides on Sudan Genocide Fight," *San Francisco Chronicle*, September 26, 2006.

10. In the first quarter of 2008, at least 1,106 bills related to immigrants and immigration were considered in forty-four states; twenty-six states enacted forty-four laws and adopted thirty-eight resolutions or memorials. See the various reports of the National Conference of State Legislatures on immigration legislation by states, updated as of March 31, 2008, www.ncsl.org/programs/immig/.

11. Various statutes imposing fines on landlords who rented to unauthorized residents or barring unauthorized residents from working or renting homes in Farmers Branch, Texas; Valley Park, Missouri; and Hazelton, Pennsylvania, were struck down by state or federal judges. See Ralph Blumenthal, "Texas Lawmakers Put New Focus on Illegal Immigration," *New York Times*, November 16, 2006; and Julia Preston, "Judge Voids Ordinance on Illegal Immigrants," *New York Times*, July 27, 2007. In May 2008, a federal judge in Texas found that a revised local ordinance in Farmers Branch, Texas—redrafted to take into account an earlier court ruling—was still unconstitutional and could not be enforced. See *New York Times*, May 29, 2008, A15.

12. See "Judge's Ruling Against Pennsylvania Town's Anti-Illegal Immigrant Law Could Have Broader Impact," Associated Press, July 28, 2007. See also Ken Belson and

Jill P. Capuzzo, "Towns Rethink Laws Against Illegal Immigrants," *New York Times*, September 26, 2007, A1. Cf. "Backlash Backfires," an editorial criticizing Colorado's anti-immigrant laws in the *Los Angeles Times*, February 3, 2007.

13. "Apreuben Presupuesto con Texas para Vigilar la Frontera," *El Financiero*, May 28, 2007.

14. Randall C. Archibald, "Arizona Is Split over Hard Line on Immigrants," *New York Times*, December 14, 2007, A1.

15. See Julia Preston, "U.S. Sues Illinois to Let Employers Use Immigration Databases," *New York Times*, September 25, 2007, A18. Cf. Molly Hennessy-Fiske and Jim Puzzanghera, "Immigration Screening Could Snag Too Many Workers," *Los Angeles Times*, May 29, 2007.

16. See, for example, "New York's Immigrant Drivers" (editorial), *New York Times*, September 22, 2007, and "Lou Dobbs Crusades Against Spitzer's Driver's License Plan for Illegal Immigrants," *New York Times*, October 17, 2007.

17. Governor Spitzer withdrew his original proposal, substituting a three-tiered driver's license scheme that, as the *New York Times* editorialized, "looks like bad government policy and a bureaucratic nightmare in the making." See "Governor Spitzer Retreats," *New York Times*, October 20, 2007, A26, and Danny Hakim, "Spitzer Dropping His Driver's License Plan," *New York Times*, November 14, 2007.

18. For some time, San Francisco has operated under a sanctuary ordinance that prohibits use of local government resources to aid federal authorities in apprehending unauthorized immigrants. See Wyatt Buchanan, "S.F. Supervisors Approve ID Cards for Residents," *San Francisco Chronicle*, November 14, 2007; and "Mayor Signs Law Creating City ID Cards for Undocumented Residents," Associated Press, *San Francisco Examiner*, November 28, 2007. For a critical view of the ID card measure, see Cinnamon Stillwell, "San Francisco ID Program: Legitimizing Illegal Immigration," *San Francisco Chronicle*, November 28, 2007.

19. A study of the international activities of American state legislatures singled out California as by far the most active state in receiving foreign delegations, having hosted 637 international dignitaries from 67 countries in one recent year. See Timothy J. Conlan, Robert L. Dudley and Joel F. Clark, "Taking on the World: The International Activities of American State Legislatures," *Publius: The Journal of Federalism* 34, no. 3 (Summer 2004), 191.

20. Veteran business consultant Jock O'Connell points out that many of those who join such trips are more interested in other business with the governor than in developing real business opportunities abroad. See Jock O'Connell, "And Good Peking Duck Is All Arnold Can Hope For," *Los Angeles Times*, November 13, 2005.

21. Gustav Koehler, *California Trade Policy* (Sacramento, CA: California Research Bureau, 1999).

22. Mayor Villaraigosa traveled to Asia on a trade and investment promotion mission early in his first year and went to El Salvador and Mexico a few months later, though he had to cut the visit short, ironically, because of violence between Los Angeles police officers and participants in the Mexican Cinco de Mayo celebration in Los Ange-

les. See Louis Sahagun, "Mayor Promises Action Against Abusive Officers," *Los Angeles Times*, May 6, 2007.

23. San Francisco has fourteen sister city relationships, San Diego has fifteen, Oakland has nine, San Jose has seven and Los Angeles has twenty-five. See www.sistercities.com (accessed June 12, 2008).

24. This paragraph draws primarily from Howard J. Shatz, "Statement on State Foreign Offices," prepared for an informational hearing before the Committee on Banking, Commerce and International Trade, California Senate, Sacramento, July 2, 2003, available on the Web site of PPIC, www.ppic.org.

25. For an insider but balanced account and analysis of the denouement of the California offices, see Smurr, "California Adrift" (chap. 1, n. 80).

26. Danny Hakim, "On Wall Street, More Investors Push Social Goals," *New York Times*, February 11, 2001. See also California State Treasurer, "State Treasurer Phil Angelides Launches 'Green Wave' Environmental Investment Initiative," news release, February 3, 2004.

27. See Robert Collier, "State Employees' Pension Fund Flexes Its Muscle Around the World," *San Francisco Chronicle*, July 21, 2002. Interestingly, CalPERS investment consultants reported in 2007 that the fund had lost more than $200 million in potential profits because of rigid investment limits on emerging-market countries, especially China and Russia, and CalPERS was reportedly currently reviewing its policies. See Gilbert Chen, "CalPERS to Ease Up on Social Activist Role," *Sacramento Bee*, June 19, 2007.

28. Robert Collier, "Newsom Backs Sweatshop Plan," *San Francisco Chronicle*, June 28, 2005. Critics complained that San Francisco's measures against sweatshop labor in China failed to deal with similar conditions in the city's own garment industry, south of Market and in pockets of the Mission District. See "Sweatshop Crackdown," *San Francisco Chronicle*, June 30, 2005.

29. See Matthew Yi, "Six Western States and Parts of Canada Join to Cut Greenhouse Gases," *San Francisco Chronicle*, August 22, 2007.

30. The first court test of state efforts, spawned by California's efforts to regulate auto emissions of greenhouse gases, upheld the provisions. See Felicity Barringer, "U.S. Court Backs States' Measures to Cut Emissions," *New York Times*, September 13 2007. In December 2007, the administrator of the federal Environmental Protection Agency denied California's request for the necessary waiver to permit this resolution, but California has sued the agency for the right to proceed. See Felicity Barringer, "California Sues EPA over Denial of Waiver," *New York Times*, January 3, 2008, A12.

31. See Robert Collier, "State Bypasses Kyoto, Fights Global Warming," *San Francisco Chronicle*, February 17, 2005.

32. See Mayor's Office of Economic and Work Force Development, Clean Technology, on the City of San Francisco's Web site, www.sfgov.org.

33. See Arnold Schwarzenegger, "Muscular Environmentalism: Green Without Guilt," *New Perspectives Quarterly*, 24, no. 2 (Summer 2007). Schwarzenegger calls for California to take the lead, "to shake the federal government enough to wake them up." For more on Governor Schwarzenegger's role, see Chapter 4, note 29.

34. See Regan Morris, "Schwarzenegger Vetoes California Ballot Question on U.S. Policy in Iraq," *New York Times*, September 13, 2007. See also Jennifer Steinhauer, "California Primary Ballot May Include Iraq Question," *New York Times*, June 2, 2007.

35. See Randall C. Archibold, "State Steps Gingerly on Immigration," *New York Times*, October 14, 2007, A14.

36. See Andrew Blankstein and Richard Winton, "Ask and Deport, Family Urges," *Los Angeles Times*, April 9, 2008.

37. Until his death in February 2008, Representative Tom Lantos chaired that committee, on which also served, in the 110th Congress, California Representatives Howard Berman, Jim Costa, Elton Gallegy, Dana Rohrabacher, Edward Royce, Linda Sanchez, Brad Sherman, Diane Watson and Lynn Woolsey. Representative Henry Waxman chaired the House Committee on Oversight and Government Reform; George Miller, the Education and Labor Committee; and Bob Filner, the Committee on Veterans' Affairs. Berman was vice chairman of the Judiciary Committee and chaired its Subcommittee on Courts, Internet and Intellectual Property. Jane Harman, for four years the ranking member of the House Permanent Select Committees on Intelligence, served on the Committee on Homeland Security and chaired its Subcommittee on Intelligence. Brad Sherman chaired the Foreign Affairs Subcommittee on Terrorism, Nonproliferation and Trade. Loretta Sanchez chaired the Border, Maritime and Global Counterterrorism Subcommittee of the House Homeland Security Committee. Zoe Lofgren chaired the Immigration, Citizenship, Refugees, Border Security and International Law Subcommittee of the House Judiciary Committee, the members of which included California Democrats Berman, Linda Sanchez and Maxine Waters as well as Republicans Gallegly and Daniel E. Lungren. Mike Thompson chaired the Terrorism, Human Intelligence, Analysis and Counterintelligence Subcommittee of the House Permanent Select Committee on Intelligence. Barbara Lee served on the Foreign Operations Subcommittee of the House Appropriations Committee and was senior Democratic whip and first vice-chair of the Congressional Black Caucus. Xavier Becerra played a leadership role in the Congressional Hispanic Caucus, which included more representatives from California than from any other state.

California Republicans also play leadership roles in the House. Ranking minority members in the 110th Congress included Jerry Lewis on the House Appropriations Committee; Duncan Hunter on the House Armed Services Committee; Howard McKeon on the Committee on Education and Labor; and David Dreier on the Rules Committee. Wally Herger was the ranking Republican on the Trade Subcommittee of the House Ways and Means Committee, and Lungren served also as the ranking Republican on the Transportation Security and Infrastructure Protection Subcommittee of the Homeland Security Committee.

38. Congressman Lantos was succeeded in his district by Representative Jackie Speier, who won a special election on April 8, 2008, to finish Lantos's term, was sworn in on April 10, and promptly delivered a fiery speech attacking the Iraq policies of President George W. Bush. See Zachary Coile, "Speier Blasts Iraq War in First House Speech," *San Francisco Chronicle*, April 11, 2008.

39. See "California Institute and Related Organization Events," available on the California Institute's Web site, www.calinst.org/events (accessed September 27, 2007).

40. See Greyson Bryan, "Should California Have a Foreign Policy" (unpublished memorandum, 2001, consulted and cited with the author's permission).

41. Information on the Pacific Council's binational projects can be found at www.pacificcouncil.org. The announcement of the Chile-California agreement is at http://gov.ca.gov/press-release/9889/ (accessed June 17, 2008).

Index